Epworth Commentaries

General Editor
Ivor H. Jones

The First Epistle of St Paul to the Corinthians
(2nd revised edition)

2005.

The First Epistle
to the Corinthians

2nd revised edition

NIGEL WATSON

 EPWORTH

Copyright © Nigel Watson 2005

British Library Cataloguing-in-Publication data

A catalogue record for this book is available
from the British Library

ISBN 0-7162-0593-9

First published in 2005
by Epworth
4 John Wesley Road
Werrington
Peterborough PE4 6ZP

Printed and bound in Great Britain by
William Clowes Ltd, Beccles, Suffolk

CONTENTS

GENERAL INTRODUCTION

The *Epworth Preacher's Commentaries* that Greville P. Lewis edited so successfully in the 1950s and 1960s having now served their turn, the Epworth Press has commissioned a team of distinguished academics who are also preachers and teachers to create a new series of commentaries that will serve readers into the twenty-first century. We have taken the opportunity offered by the publication in 1989 of the Revised English Bible to use this very readable and scholarly version as the basis of our commentaries, and we are grateful to the Oxford and Cambridge University Presses for the requisite licence and for granting our authors generous access. They will nevertheless be free to cite and discuss other translations wherever they think that these will illuminate the original text.

Just as the books that make up the Bible differ in their provenance and purpose, so our authors will necessarily differ in the structure and bearing of their commentaries. But they will all strive to get as close as possible to the intention of the original writers, expounding their texts in the light of the place, time, circumstances and culture that gave them birth, and showing why each work was received by Jews and Christians into their respective Canons of Holy Scripture. They will seek to make full use of the dramatic advance in biblical scholarship world-wide but at the same time to explain technical terms in the language of the common reader, and to suggest ways in which Scripture can help towards the living of a Christian life today. They will endeavour to produce commentaries that can be used with confidence in ecumenical, multiracial and multifaith situations, and not by scholars only but by preachers, teachers, students, church members and anyone who wants to improve his or her understanding of the Bible.

Ivor H. Jones

PREFACE

In the first edition of this commentary, I acknowledged my indebtedness to two earlier commentaries in particular, namely, those by C. K. Barrett and Gordon Fee. Since 1992, the flow of commentaries, monographs and articles has quickened in pace. I now wish to record my indebtedness to the commentaries by Ben Witherington III (Eerdmans/Paternoster, 1995); Richard B. Hays (Interpretation Series, 1997); Raymond F. Collins (Sacra Pagina, 1999); Anthony C. Thiselton (NIGTC, 2000); and J. Paul Sampley (NIB, 2002). Two German commentaries have also proved of great value: those by H.-J. Klauck (Die Neue Echter Bibel, 1987) and Wolfgang Schrage (EKK, 1991–2001).

Having acknowledged that debt, however, I wish to reiterate what I said in the preface to the first edition about the need for any interpreter of a biblical passage to begin by engaging directly with the text. It is only too easy to begin the study of any passage of the Bible by turning to the best available commentaries, but I am firmly convinced that this is a mistaken procedure for anyone who wants to produce something that bears the stamp of their own individuality. In the writing of this commentary I set my face against it from the beginning. From the moment I began to work on 1.1–9 till the moment, two years later, when I turned to 16.19–24, I followed the same method. First of all, I engaged with the text, working through a set of ten questions which I have evolved over the years and which I have found helpful for sensitizing me to the text's structure and emphases and nuances. After a break I then attempted a complete exegesis of the passage, in which I developed whatever perceptions I had gained from the preliminary exercise. Only after doing that did I turn to the commentaries and other secondary literature. The final stage consisted of a rewriting of the original exegesis in the light of my reading.

Paul's letters to the Corinthians have a great deal to teach us about the need for the message of the gospel to be embodied in the persons of its bearers. In completing the revised edition of this commentary, I wish to renew the original dedication to four good friends who, in their own ministries, have not flinched from the cost of that embodiment: Joe and Barbara Fraser and Gail and Alastair Pritchard.

Nigel Watson
January 2005

ABBREVIATIONS

AV	Authorized Version
CBQ	*Catholic Biblical Quarterly*
LXX	Septuagint Greek Translation of the Hebrew Bible
NEB	New English Bible
NIV	New International Version
NRSV	New Revised Standard Version
NTS	*New Testament Studies*
REB	Revised English Bible
RV	Revised Version

INTRODUCTION

Corinth and Paul

There is an account of Paul's first visit to Corinth in Acts 18.1–18. He must have reached the city around AD 50, on his so-called Second Missionary Journey. According to Acts, he stayed there 18 months.

Corinth had been for centuries one of the most important cities of Greece and indeed of the Roman Empire.[1] Situated on an isthmus, it was ideally located for commercial enterprise, at the junction of sea routes to west and east. Since 27 BC it had been the seat of administration of the Roman province of Achaea, which covered most of modern Greece. It has been estimated that, out of a total population of 100,000, about one third will have been slaves.

Sherman Johnson has described it as 'a cosmopolitan port city like Rotterdam, Hong Kong and New York'.[2] It boasted a theatre seating 14,000, an odeon or concert hall seating 3,000, the Isthmian athletic games, which were second only to the Olympics, and, no doubt, hundreds of itinerant musicians, dancers and mountebanks.[3]

It is often said Corinth enjoyed a reputation for sexual vice which was outstanding even by the fairly lax standards of Graeco-Roman paganism. However, it seems doubtful whether vice was any more widespread there than in other ports of the same size.[4]

A city like Corinth might well have been thought to provide unpromising soil for planting the Christian gospel, but Paul made many converts in Corinth, and by the time he left the city a flourishing church had come into being. The extent of his success is shown by the opening verses of 2 Cor. 3.

Shortly after Paul left Corinth, he settled in Ephesus, on the eastern shore of the Aegean, and spent the greater part of three years, from c. 52/53 to 55/56, in the evangelization of the Roman province of Asia.

But Paul's Ephesian ministry was punctuated from time to time by disquieting reports about his converts in Corinth, particularly about their moral behaviour. In response, he sent the Corinthians a letter warning them to have nothing to do with loose-living people. He refers to this letter in 1 Cor. 5.9.

That reference makes it quite clear that our 1 Corinthians was not the first letter Paul wrote to the Corinthian church. It was rather preceded by this earlier letter, usually known as the 'Previous Letter'.

It has been held by many scholars that a fragment of the Previous Letter survives embedded in 2 Cor. 6.14—7.1, but this theory is not without its difficulties and is no longer as popular as it once was.[5]

Not long afterwards, news was brought to Paul by members of the household of a Corinthian lady of substance named Chloe, who is mentioned in 1.11. These people told Paul that the church was beginning to split up into factions centering around various Christian leaders – Paul himself, Peter and Apollos, a learned and eloquent preacher from Alexandria.

At about the same time, three visitors had arrived from Corinth – Stephanas, Fortunatus and Achaicus. These men would have filled in any gaps in Paul's information. He mentions them in 16.17.

Around the same time, a letter arrived from the Corinthian church, asking for guidance on some thorny problems of conduct. It is indeed quite possible that this letter was brought by the three visitors. It also seems quite likely that this letter from Corinth was itself a reply to Paul's Previous Letter. Paul begins to reply to the letter from Corinth in 7.1. There is therefore a lively exchange taking place, an ongoing to-and-fro, between Paul and the community in Corinth, through a variety of oral and written channels.

A deteriorating relationship

There is, however, another factor that needs to be taken into account, if we are to give an adequate account of the circumstances that occasioned 1 Corinthians, and that is a developing conflict between the church in Corinth and Paul himself.

Gordon Fee has aptly observed that 'the language and style of 1 Corinthians are especially rhetorical and combative. Paul is taking them on at every turn . . . he is attacking and challenging with all the weapons in his literary arsenal.' Two pages later, referring to 1.10— 4.21, he speaks of 'its mixture of irony, rhetoric and sarcasm'.[6]

To be sure, the situation is not as bad as the one reflected in the last four chapters of 2 Corinthians, where we discover that intruders have infiltrated the Corinthian community and created turmoil. While Paul needs to defend his apostolate, the fact that the Corinthians had written to him, asking for his advice, shows that, in their eyes, he must still be a figure with some authority. Nowhere in 1 Corinthians is there any hint that he is confronting agitators from outside. Rather, the opposition is led by 'some of you' (15.12).

It is also probable that the situation had been exacerbated by the Previous Letter. As we have seen, it makes good sense to assume that the letter from Corinth was a response to that earlier letter of Paul's. Given the combative nature of so much of Paul's response in 1 Corinthians, it seems highly likely that in their own letter the Corinthians had not only asked questions but also taken exception to some of his pronouncements and prohibitions. This would explain not only the combative tone of much of Paul's letter, including its sarcasm and irony, but also his extensive use of rhetorical devices, including expressions like 'Do you not know that . . .' (used ten times)[7] and 'If anyone thinks that he/she is . . .' (used three times).

In response to the letter from Corinth, as well as the oral reports that he had received, Paul addresses at least eleven different, and somewhat disparate, concerns. Of these, ten are, in the first instance, behavioural. Only chapter 15 addresses a strictly theological error, and even here Paul concludes both major sections with ethical warnings and imperatives (vv. 33f., 58). Yet in every case his greater concern is the theological stance behind the behaviour.

Paul – letter writer with a difference

There is evidence from the Hellenistic world of a considerable amount of theoretical reflection on letter writing as a means of overcoming the pain of physical separation. There was also considerable reflection on the variety of purposes that letters might serve.[8] The writer known nowadays as Pseudo-Demetrius distinguishes no fewer than 21 different types of letter. Paul's First Letter to the Corinthians exhibits the characteristics of several of these types, including the friendly letter, the letter of recommendation, the letter of admonition, the letter of response and the letter of apology (in the sense of self-defence).[9]

At the same time, Paul's letters exhibit a theological weight that sets them apart. They are written in the service of the gospel and seek to explicate and apply the gospel to the various communities to which they are addressed. They are also invested with the authority of an 'apostle of Jesus Christ by God's call and by his will' (1 Cor. 1.1). Paul can thus be said to have created a new genre of letter, the letter that is at once evangelical and apostolic.[10]

An outline

After a brief introduction, Paul takes the Corinthians to task for their divisions and parties, reported to him by the members of Chloe's household (1.10—4.21).

Between 5.1 and 6.20 Paul deals with the other matters that are of concern to him about which he has also been informed by word of mouth: the case of incest; the question of Christians and the law courts; and the question of liberty and licence.

Between 7.1 and 16.18 Paul deals one by one with the matters raised in the letter from Corinth. The opening words of 7.1 make it quite clear that he is now responding to their letter, and each time that he uses the same formula (in a shortened form) in the chapters that follow we can be reasonably confident that he is now turning to another of the questions that they had raised.

Chapter 15, which deals with the resurrection of the dead, lacks the introductory formula, 'Concerning . . .' However, Paul has good reasons for introducing this subject; he has heard that there are people in Corinth who are asserting that 'there is no resurrection of the dead' (v. 12).

An occasional writing

It should already be apparent that 1 Corinthians is a good example of what is sometimes called an occasional writing, that is, a writing that is occasioned by a particular situation. The full force of what Paul has to say on any of the issues he takes up can only be perceived when we can discern where the Corinthians themselves stood. Fortunately the letter provides us with sufficient data to enable us to reconstruct their position with some confidence, *at least, as it was perceived by Paul.*

Mirror-reading?

The last phrase is italicized, because 'mirror-reading', that is to say, using Paul's letter as a mirror of Corinthian Christianity, is a procedure that has occasioned quite a lot of critical discussion during the last two decades. Would the Corinthians have recognized Paul's perception of their beliefs as true and fair? How can we be sure that Paul did not oversimplify or even misunderstand their position on this or that point?

The Introduction to Schrage's commentary includes a judicious discussion of this question. To be sure, he concedes, Paul may have exaggerated some of the Corinthians' views to the point of caricature. We also have to reckon with the normal obstacles to the process of communication being operative in Corinth too, such as misunderstanding, accommodation to one's own expectations, forgetfulness, linguistic barriers, overemphasis and so on. Nevertheless, the picture of the Corinthians that emerges from the letter is not to be dismissed as a pure construction of Paul's. It must continually be remembered that Paul worked for one-and-a-half years in Corinth, which makes it difficult to assume that serious misunderstanding occurred.[11]

It is also significant that some scholars, like Richard Hays, who refrain from attempting to give an account of Corinthian beliefs have no difficulty in accepting that, at certain points, like 7.1 or 8.1a, Paul is quoting statements by the Corinthians themselves. But to concede that is surely to accept that some reconstruction of the Corinthian standpoint is possible.

At the same time, there is force in Hays's observation that 'in many cases, the practices of the Corinthians were motivated by social and cultural factors . . . that were not consciously theological at all. It is Paul who frames the issues in theological terms.'[12]

A corrective

At point after point Paul takes up a critical stance over against what he perceives to be the Corinthian position. In spite of its appearance of being loosely organized, his letter is a sustained attempt to correct Corinthian misapprehensions of the gospel and its implications for belief and conduct. The problem that confronts him is not on all fours with the one he faced in writing 1 Thessalonians (see 1 Thess. 3.10), that is, of filling in gaps, of making good whatever is lacking in the faith of the Corinthian Christians, but of highlighting, arresting and correcting false developments.

In the opening paragraph of the letter Paul pays the Corinthians some striking compliments. He thanks God for all the enrichment that has come to them in Christ. 'You possess full knowledge', he goes on, 'and you can give full expression to it . . . There is indeed no single gift you lack' (vv. 5, 7).

These complimentary remarks become all the more remarkable, when read in the light of the letter that follows. With every topic that Paul takes up, it becomes apparent that the Corinthian level of understanding falls far short of what Paul would wish. Moreover, the problem is not simply one of ignorance but of misapprehension. They have accepted the teaching they have been given not only by Paul himself but also by other teachers, Apollos in particular, and have developed it in wrong directions.

What makes it all the more urgent for Paul to correct these misconceptions is the fact that they have affected adversely the relationship between himself and his converts. In the process of developing what they no doubt saw as a more sophisticated theology than what they had been offered, they have come to hold a low opinion both of Paul and of his gospel.

The extent of the remedial instruction that Paul sees to be necessary becomes apparent when we set out side by side the Corinthian position on the various issues discussed in the letter, as this can be reconstructed each time from Paul's allusions to it, and what Paul himself offers as a truer perception of the meaning of the gospel for belief and conduct.

Wisdom

The first misconception that Paul addresses has to do with wisdom. It is clear from chapters 1—4 that the Corinthians understood salvation pre-eminently in terms of the acquisition of wisdom, while chapter 8 implies that they also prided themselves on all having knowledge (8.1). However, they had failed to appreciate the radical difference between the wisdom of the world and the wisdom of God.

When he speaks of 'the wisdom of the world', Paul sometimes has in mind primarily a technique of persuasion, oratorical skill (see e.g. 1 Cor. 1.17; 2.1, 4), sometimes a means by which people aspire to the knowledge of God, that is, a philosophy (see 1.20f.). In the eyes of his 'cultured despisers' in Corinth, Paul lacked wisdom, both in respect of the content of his message and in respect of his oratorical skill. Indeed, in respect of its content, his message was, in their eyes, comparable to milk for babes, whereas they themselves had moved on to the solid food fit for the mature (2.6; 3.1–4). As for having wisdom in the sense of rhetorical skill, here too Paul fell short.

Paul's response is not to deny that the gospel has anything to do with wisdom (2.6–16) but rather to affirm that it turns human ideas of wisdom upside down. Considered as a quality of God, wisdom is revealed in an event that the natural man, the natural woman, accounts sheer absurdity, the cross. Moreover, there is only one way in which believers may attain to true wisdom, and that is by receiving it as a gift from God in Christ, as what one might call *sapientia aliena*, a wisdom not of one's own (1.30).

In his treatment of wisdom in chapters 1—4 Paul asserts as forcefully as he ever does in Romans that 'salvation is of the Lord'. In both letters he begins by demolishing a false self-reliance. Believers may not boast before God of their wisdom any more than of their works (1.29, 31: cf. Rom. 3.27). In the same way as the cross is the condemnation of the righteousness of humanity, so it is the condemnation of the wisdom of the world. As it is through the renunciation of righteousness that humanity attains righteousness, so it is through the surrender of its own wisdom that it receives wisdom. Whoever wishes to be wise in this world must become a fool and thus find wisdom (3.18).

As for his alleged lack of wisdom in the sense of rhetorical skill, Paul does not deny this for a moment but claims that, far from being a weakness, it is a positive advantage. If he is to direct his hearers' attention to God's act and God's act alone, there can be no room for pyrotechnic displays of rhetorical virtuosity such as were offered by the travelling sophists who could be heard in the marketplaces of any Mediterranean city. Such rhetorical skill would leave his hearers gaping at his cleverness and rob the cross of its force. All his effort must be directed towards allowing the message of the cross of Christ to speak with unimpeded power.

Knowledge

As for knowledge, once again Paul does not deny that that too is part of the enrichment that comes to believers in Christ (1.5; 8.1). What he does maintain is that true knowledge stems from finding oneself known by God (8.2f.). Such a knowledge will have an effect that is the very opposite of puffing a person up. It will rather be accompanied by the awed humility of one who knows that whatever he has he owes to the gracious initiative of God in Christ (1.25–31; 2.9–16; 3.18–23; 8.3).

Nor will such knowledge lead believers to despise a fellow-believer, whatever the limitations of the other's insight. Just as believers find themselves known by God and in that discovery find true knowledge, so do they find themselves loved by God and in that discovery acquire the power to love (8.3), and to love not only God but the fellow-believer, the brother or sister for whom Christ died (8.11).

Everything God has to give

Perhaps the most fateful misconception of the Corinthians, however, was their assumption that God had already given them all God had to give.

This component of Corinthian spirituality is often described as an over-realized eschatology, but, while this is in some ways a convenient expression, it is misleading if it suggests that the Corinthians were thinking within a Jewish framework. In fact, one of the main roots of this assumption of theirs would appear to be their unfamiliarity with Jewish patterns of thinking, in particular, their lack of a sense of 'a progressive and purposeful history'.[13]

Indeed, one aspect after another of their own habitual patterns of thought seems to have predisposed the Corinthians in this direction. The characteristic Jewish belief in a progressive and purposeful history goes along with a sense of the human person being bound up with other persons and indeed with creation. Hence no person can be fully saved until the universe is redeemed. Paul's own sense of the interdependence of different parts of the universe is expressed most vividly in Rom. 8.15–23. For many people in the Hellenistic world, however, each person is primarily an individual and therefore has no need to wait for the redemption of the universe before he or she attains their own personal redemption.

Again we have seen what store the Corinthians set by wisdom and knowledge. These they appear to have conceived of not primarily in ethical terms, namely, as a progressively deeper understanding of the divine will, but as some sort of instantaneous enlightenment about the way of salvation. Plato in the *Symposium* represents the way of the truly enlightened person as a lifelong ascent of the soul from the love of beautiful things to the love of beauty itself, but the richness and depth of Plato's conception seem to have been largely lost in the popular philosophy of the time.

Whatever the roots of their form of eschatology, there is no doubt that, as perceived by Paul, the Corinthians had grossly exaggerated the fullness of the blessings with which they had been endowed. The contrast between their understanding of the Christian life at this point and Paul's is seen most clearly in 4.8–13, where, with cutting sarcasm, he sets side by side, on the one hand, the way the Corinthians see themselves – already blessed with everything God has to give, spiritual millionaires, kings – and, on the other, Paul's own experience of what it means to be an apostle.

With this passage we may associate all those in which Paul implies that the Corinthians are 'puffed up' (see 4.6, 18, 19; 5.2; 8.1; 13.4) or guilty of boasting or false confidence (4.7, 18–21; 5.6).

Moreover, this assumption that they have arrived can be seen to underlie one after another of the problems Paul has to deal with. It is in fact the most pervasive fault that he identifies.

Allied to a dualistic understanding of human personality, it had promoted the asceticism that Paul addresses in chapter 7. There were people in Corinth who were advocating the renunciation of marriage, or at least the physical expression of sexuality, on the grounds that these things belonged to the present age, which is passing away, and therefore ill became those who were living already the life of heaven.

The inappropriate behaviour in worship for which Paul takes them to task in 11.2–16 was probably largely due to the conviction of the women concerned that sexual differentiation no longer had any meaning.

The misuse of the Lord's Supper is readily accounted for, if the Corinthians had supposed that in celebrating the supper they were already enjoying the messianic banquet in its fullness (11.17–22).

Their overvaluation of speaking in tongues, evidenced in chapter 14 (cf. 13.1), most likely reflects their belief that in tongue-speaking they were already speaking the language of heaven.

Moreover, it is abundantly clear from the frequency and vigour with which Paul holds before them the prospect of judgement that they supposed themselves to be living already beyond any judgement there might be.[14]

What was so fateful about this misconception of the Corinthians was that it had affected adversely their attitude to Paul. Clearly one whose life was so conspicuously one of struggle and hardship had not arrived. Therefore, if their understanding of the Christian life was correct, there must be something defective about him.

Paul's response to the over-realized eschatology of the Corinthians is to qualify constantly their 'now already' by 'not yet'. They may see themselves as kings already, enjoying the kingdom of God in its full-ness, heaven on earth, but the life that Paul is living as an apostle is a pattern for Christian existence in general, it is Christian existence writ large (4.16), and the reality of apostolic ministry, as Paul knows it, is something far removed from heaven on earth. It is a life of ignominy, weakness, dishonour, hardship and persecution (4.8).

They may suppose themselves to be living already beyond what-ever judgement there may be, but Paul continually pricks the bubble of their presumption. The quality of workmanship of each person's contribution to the life of the church will be inexorably exposed for what it is (3.12f.; cf. 4.1–5; 5.1–5; 6.9–11; 9.24–27; 10.1–12; 11.27–34).

For the church is still on the way. Mere participation in the sacra-ments therefore affords no guarantee of salvation (10.1–13; cf. 9.24–27). The Lord's Supper is iron rations for people who are still on the way (11.23–26). Believers live in the shadow of an imminent end (7.29–31). What they have experienced is an anticipation of the end, a proleptic, not a fully realized eschatology (13.8–13).

(Cross) and resurrection?

The over-realized eschatology of the Corinthians is associated, in Paul's eyes, with another distortion, an overemphasis on the resurrec-tion; more precisely, an emphasis on the resurrection at the expense of the cross. The evidence for this distortion is largely inferential. We may assume that the Corinthians were guilty of it from the way Paul insists in the opening chapter that the wisdom of God is the wisdom of the cross and the power of God the power of the cross and then goes on to remind them in the following chapter that he had resolved that while he was among them he would not claim to know anything but Jesus Christ – Christ nailed to the cross (2.2). The vigour of Paul's tone suggests that these were truths of which the Corinthians badly needed to be reminded. For them, it seems, the central moment in the gospel story was the resurrection, the cross being no more than the occasion of Christ's glorious triumph.

Cross and resurrection

Paul's response to what he sees as an unbalanced emphasis on the resurrection is in no way to belittle its importance. On the contrary, in chapter 15 he declares it to be of the heart of the matter. However, as already seen, he goes out of his way to emphasize the absolute centrality of the cross.[15]

Body versus soul

A further misconception that Paul appears to have faced in Corinth was a dualistic understanding of personality, according to which the human person is compounded of a material and an immaterial component, the body and the soul, which confront each other as opponents. By postulating this understanding of personality in the background, we are enabled to account not only for the denial by some in Corinth of the general resurrection but also for the presence of tendencies to both libertinism and asceticism.

Within a dualistic world-view, the soul, and the soul alone, is seen as being capable of redemption, since the body, which belongs to the material world, passes away at death. The soul's hope lies in gaining freedom from the body. For the dualist, therefore, the message of the resurrection of the body is not good news but bad news, for it appears to imply that the soul is to be condemned to its prison for ever.

In the area of sexuality it is clear from the history of the early church that dualism could lead to either of two attitudes, depending on the rigour with which the dualistic view is held. On the one hand, if the body is seen as simply being of no account, it follows that what I do with my body is also of no account. Hence libertinism. On the other hand, if the body is seen as actually evil, it follows that the only 'spiritual' course of action is to abstain from all expression of sexuality. Hence asceticism. Both of these attitudes are attested in Corinth, the first in 5.1f. and 6.12–20, the second in 7.1–7.

A unitary anthropology

Paul's response is, in effect, to affirm the integrity of the human person.

His reaction to Corinthian misconceptions of the resurrection of the dead is first to reaffirm the resurrection of Christ (15.1–11) and then to insist that Christ's resurrection must be seen as the guarantee of our own. The two beliefs stand or fall together (15.12–19).

Indeed, God's act in raising Christ from the dead must be seen as his promise not only of our own resurrection but of the restoration of the whole creation (15.20–28). Yet this does not mean condemnation to perpetual existence in our present bodies but rather resurrection to a new form of bodily existence appropriate to the age to come (15.35–37).

In response to Corinthian libertinism, Paul affirms that sex has to do not just with the sexual organs but with the whole person as *sōma*, that is, the person as capable of relationship with others, above all, with God. As *sōma*, I am called to be united to Christ, to become a limb or organ of Christ's body. Shall I then take a part of Christ's body and make it over to a prostitute (6.15)? On the contrary, recognizing that my body is a temple of the indwelling Holy Spirit, I will place myself wholly at Christ's disposal and thus glorify God in my body (6.19f.).

As for asceticism, Paul concedes that there are advantages in remaining single, especially in these critical times (7.8, 25–34), but far be it for him to forbid, or even discourage, marriage. Marriage should not be regarded as a second best, it is rather the way that some are both called and empowered to follow. Married people therefore should not allow anyone to bully them into thinking that sex is evil or that marriage is wrong in and of itself (7.1–7, 36, 38).

Salvation and ethics

A further shortcoming that Paul perceives in the Corinthian community is a failure to discern any vital connection between salvation and ethics. This blind spot is probably related not only to their over-realized eschatology and their dualism, about which we have already spoken, but also to their understanding of the Spirit and what it meant to be a spiritual person.

As for their eschatology, since the Corinthians supposed that they had already arrived, they saw no compelling reason to live out their new existence in ethical ways. If the sacraments are a guarantee of salvation, why bother about ethics?

As for their dualism, the implication of such a view is, as we have seen, that only the top storey of the personality, so to speak, is of any spiritual significance. It follows that all activities that are conspicuously bodily in nature, such as sexual relations or eating and drinking, become matters of indifference, if not actually inimical to true spirituality.

As for the gift of the Spirit, the Corinthians appear to have understood this gift as a boosting and enrichment of the ego to the nth degree. It had to do with *me*, not with my relationship to my neighbour. Only on such a hypothesis can one account for the Corinthian community being so conspicuously lacking in any sense of mutual responsibility. They were torn apart by competing factions (chs. 1—4). They were taking one another to court (ch. 6). They were taking delight in parading their Christian freedom, reckless of the effect on weaker brethren (ch. 8). They were failing to wait for underprivileged brothers and sisters who came late to the eucharistic meal (11.17–34). And yet they prided themselves on being spiritual people, possessed of the Spirit. Clearly, for them, the Spirit had little to do with love.

Linked with all this is a concept of freedom that Paul also finds defective, a concept succinctly expressed in what appears to be a Corinthian slogan that Paul quotes in 6.12, 'I am free to do anything.'

The vital link

Paul systematically demolishes each one of these anti-ethical misconceptions. Christians have not arrived, they are still on the way and may yet forfeit the salvation of which they have already had a foretaste (6.9f.; 9.24–27). The end of the ages has indeed come upon us, but 'if you think you are standing firm, take care, or you may fall' (9.12).

The sacraments are no guarantee of salvation, no medicine of immortality. Rather do they bring about an encounter with one who is Lord and Judge, as well as Saviour (10.1–12; 11.27–32).[16]

As for those activities which the Corinthians judged merely bodily, such as sexual relations or eating and drinking, these too are areas of life where one must constantly seek the mind of Christ. I am called to glorify God in my body (6.20), whether as a married person or a single person, depending upon the nature of the *charisma* I have received from God (7.7b). Whatever is set before me at a pagan banquet, I must always consider the effects of my actions on my Christian brethren (8.1–13; 10.23–33). Whatever I eat or drink, I must do it to the glory of God (10.31). And if the eucharistic meal results in underprivileged embers being deprived and shamed, it ceases to be the Lord's Supper (11.20).

As for the Spirit, it is given to the believer in the form of empowerment for service. To receive a spiritual gift or, as Paul prefers to put it, a gift of grace, *charisma*, means to be energized and thereby called to ministry (ch. 12).

Thinking rightly about the Spirit

By his teaching about *charismata*, Paul is seeking to redress, at one and the same time, their defective understanding of ethics and their defective understanding of the Spirit. He seeks to correct their understanding of the Spirit in other ways as well. We may infer that the Corinthians thought of the gifts of the Spirit primarily in terms of things that were abnormal, spectacular, 'out of this world'; and, further, that they saw the Spirit as the especial possession of a privileged few, a spiritual élite. For Paul, on the other hand, extraordinariness is irrelevant as a criterion of the Spirit's presence. The gifts of the Spirit may be spectacular but may also be quite unspectacular (12.28).

Furthermore, Paul insists that the Spirit leaves no believer ungifted. There is a stereotyped repetition of the fact that God gives to everyone (12.4–11).

In view of the deficiencies in the understanding of the Spirit that the Corinthians held, it is not surprising that Paul, no doubt contradicting their own assessment of themselves, declares them to be 'unspiritual, living on the purely human level' (3.1–4). That is what they deserve to be called, so long as their common life is marked by jealousy and strife. The truly Spirit-filled person, on the other hand, 'envies no one, is never boastful, never conceited, never rude' (13.4).

As for being free, the kind of freedom Christians enjoy is not one which allows them to say of any proposed course of action, 'I don't mind if I do,' and leave it at that. For Paul, Christian freedom is not simply freedom from, although a freedom of that kind is involved, but also freedom for – freedom for the other, freedom for God (6.12f., 19f.; 10.23–33; cf. 3.21f.).

Glory for me?

A further blind spot that Paul discerns in Corinthian Christianity is an inability to conceive of salvation in other than essentially individualistic terms. That is evident from the want of any real sense of mutual responsibility which we discussed in the previous section. Here is a community torn apart by competing factions which apparently has no sense of any incongruity between its divisions and its claim to have experienced salvation in its fullness. But, as Paul sees it, the process of salvation includes, as of first importance, endowment with *charismata*, which are actualized in mutual service, thus creating true community (ch. 12). One point that Paul particularly stresses in that twelfth chapter is that no one person is gifted with all the *charismata* (12.29–30; cf. 8–11). God gives everyone a specific competence but gives omni-competence to no one. It follows that other Christians need the service that I, as a charismatic person, can render to them, just as I need the various services that they can render to me. All are dependent on one another, all need one another. Every believer needs the enlightenment, challenge and encouragement of fellow-believers (14.1–6).

We noted at the outset the remarkable passage in the opening thanksgiving in which Paul describes the church in Corinth as being richly endowed with *charismata* and lacking in none. It is a generous assessment of the Corinthian church. Paul could well have added the comment that it was overgenerous, unless and until they could show that they were a true community sustained by mutual service and mutual consideration, in short, a community that could appropriately be compared to a living body (12.12–31).

Enough has been said to show that 1 Corinthians can fairly be described as we suggested at the outset, namely, as a sustained attempt to correct Corinthian misapprehensions of the gospel and its implications for belief and conduct. The Corinthian problem is not simply one of ignorance but of misapprehension. The task that Paul is attempting is not simply one of filling in gaps but of highlighting, arresting and correcting false developments.

Root causes

If so, the question naturally arises, What are the causes of these false developments?

It is sometimes said that they are due to the Corinthians having assimilated the gospel to Hellenism.[17] To be sure, several features of Corinthian Christianity spring to mind as being readily susceptible of explanation in this way, for example, their interpretation of the gospel in terms of wisdom and knowledge, their dualistic understanding of human nature, their individualism. Again, as we have seen, their over-realized eschatology appears to stem largely from their unfamiliarity with Jewish patterns of thought.

However, although the hypothesis of Hellenization goes a long way towards accounting for the distinctive features of Corinthian Christianity, it does not appear to be a completely adequate explanation. Two features, in particular, the overemphasis on the resurrection at the expense of the cross and the failure to see any vital connection between salvation and ethics, are surely due, at least in part, to the inveterate tendency of the human heart to play down the challenge of the gospel and overemphasize its comfort, in other words, to reshape God in our own image.

It is because this is so that the study of 1 Corinthians is of such perennial importance and fascination. If all that the Corinthians had done had been to assimilate the Christian message to a philosophy with which they were familiar, it is hard to see how Paul's efforts to correct their misconceptions could have held such continuing interest for later generations of readers. It is, I suggest, because he is dealing with something deeper, namely, the tendency of the natural man, the natural woman, to reshape the gospel into something less austere, disturbing and challenging, that his letter has continued to speak to generation after generation with renewed pertinence and power.

FURTHER READING

Adams, Edwards and Horrell, David (eds), *Christianity at Corinth: The Quest for the Pauline Church*, Louisville and London: WJK Press, 2004.

Allo, E.-B., *Premiere Épître aux Corinthiens*, Paris: Gabalda, 1956.

Anderson Scott, C. A., *Christianity according to St. Paul*, Cambridge: Cambridge University Press, 1927.

Arndt, W. F. and Gingrich, F. W., *A Greek-English Lexicon of the New Testament*, Chicago/Cambridge: University of Chicago Press/ Cambridge University Press, 1957.

Barclay, John, 'Mirror-Reading a Polemical Letter: Galatians as a Test Case', *Journal for the Study of the New Testament*, 31, 1987, pp. 73–93.

——, *Obeying the Truth*, Edinburgh: T. & T. Clark, 1988.

Barrett, C. K., 'Christianity at Corinth', *Bulletin of the John Rylands Library*, 46, 1964, pp. 269–97.

——, *The First Epistle to the Corinthians* (Black's New Testament Commentaries), London: A. & C. Black, 1968.

——, *The Acts of the Apostles* (International Critical Commentary), Edinburgh: T. & T. Clark, 2 vols, 1994 and 1998.

Barrow, R. H., 'Slaves', in M. Cary et al. (eds), *The Oxford Classical Dictionary*, Oxford: Oxford University Press, 1949, pp. 843–5.

Bonhoeffer, Dietrich, *The Cost of Discipleship*, London: SCM Press, 1948.

Buechner, Frederick, *The Life of Jesus*, New York: Weathervane, 1974.

Burghardt, Walter J., *Grace on Crutches*, New York: Paulist Press, 1986.

Byrne, Brendan, S.J., 'Sinning against One's Own Body; Paul's Understanding of the Sexual Relationship in 1 Cor. 6:18', *Catholic Biblical Quarterly*, 45, 1983, pp. 608–16.

——, *Paul and the Christian Woman*, Homebush, NSW, Australia: St. Paul Publications, 1988.

Cave, Terence, *The Cornucopian Text: Problems of Writing in the French Renaissance*, Oxford: Clarendon Press, 1979.

Cervin, Richard S., 'Does *kephale* mean "Source" or "Authority Over" in Greek Literature?' *Trinity Journal*, 10, 1989, pp. 85–112.

Chesterton, G. K., *St. Francis of Assisi*, London: Hodder & Stoughton, 1923.

Chow, John K., *Patronage and Power: A Study of Social Networks in Corinth*, Sheffield: JSOT Press 1992.

Collins, Raymond F., *First Corinthians* (Sacra Pagina), Collegeville, Minnesota: Michael Glazier, 1999.

Conzelmann, Hans, *1 Corinthians* (Hermeneia), Philadelphia: Fortress Press, 1975.

Dodd, C. H., *The Interpretation of the Fourth Gospel*, Cambridge: Cambridge University Press, 1953.

Dunn, James D. G., *Romans* (Word Biblical Commentary), Dallas: Word Books, 1988.

——, *The Acts of the Apostles*, London: Epworth Press, 1996.

——, *The Theology of Paul the Apostle*, Grand Rapids: Eerdmans, 1998.

——, *Jesus Remembered*, Grand Rapids: Eerdmans, 2003.

Eichrodt, W., *Theology of the Old Testament*, London: SCM Press, 2 vols, 1961 and 1967.

Farmer, H. H., 'Christ and the Sickness of Humanity', in *Best Sermons of 1925*, London: Nisbet, 1926.

——, *The Servant of the Word*, London: Nisbet, 1941.

Fee, Gordon D., *The First Epistle to the Corinthians* (New International Commentary on the New Testament), Grand Rapids: Eerdmans, 1987.

Fishburne, C. W., '1 Cor III. 10–15 and the Testament of Abraham', *New Testament Studies*, 17, 1970, pp. 109–15.

Fisk, Bruce N., 'Eating Meat Offered to Idols: Corinthian Behavior and Pauline Response in 1 Corinthians 8–10', *Trinity Journal*, 10, 1989, pp. 49–70.

Fitzgerald, J. T., *Cracks in an Earthen Vessel: An Examination of the Catalogues of Hardships in the Corinthian Correspondence*, Atlanta: Scholars Press, 1988.

Fitzmyer, Joseph A., *The Acts of the Apostles* (Anchor Bible), New York: Doubleday, 1998.

Fotopoulos, John, *Food Offered to Idols in Roman Corinth*, Tübingen: Mohr Siebeck, 2003.

Froer, Hans, *You Wretched Corinthians!* London: SCM Press, 1995.

Furnish, Victor Paul, *II Corinthians* (Anchor Bible), New York: Doubleday, 1984.

——, 'Corinth in Paul's Time: What can Archaeology tell us?' *Biblical Archaeology Review*, 15(3), 1988, pp. 14–27.

Harrison, James, *Paul's Language of Grace in its Graeco-Roman Context*, Tübingen: Mohr Siebeck, 2003.

Hay, David M., *Glory at the Right Hand: Psalm 110 in Early Christianity*, New York: Abingdon, 1973.

Hays, Richard B., *First Corinthians* (Interpretation), Louisville: John Knox Press, 1997.

Hooker, Morna, 'Authority on Her Head', *New Testament Studies*, 10, 1963–4, pp. 410–16.

Horrell, David G., *The Social Ethos of the Corinthian Correspondence*, Edinburgh: T. & T. Clark, 1996.

——, 'Domestic Space and Christian Meetings at Corinth: Imagining New Contexts and the Buildings East of the Theatre', *New Testament Studies*, 50, 2004, pp. 349–69.

Jeremias, Joachim, *The Parables of Jesus*, London: SCM Press, 1954.

——, *Jerusalem in the Time of Jesus*, London: SCM Press, 1969.

Johnson, Sherman E., *Paul the Apostle and His Cities*, Wilmington: Glazier 1983.

Judge, E. A., *The Social Pattern of Christian Groups in the First Century*, London: Tyndale, 1960.

Käsemann, Ernst, *Jesus Means Freedom*, London: SCM Press, 1969.

——, 'Ministry and Community in the New Testament,' *Essays on New Testament Themes*, London: SCM Press, 1964, pp. 63–94.

——, 'The Pauline Doctrine of the Lord's Supper', *Essays on New Testament Themes*, pp. 108–35.

——, 'Sentences of Holy Law in the New Testament,' *New Testament Questions for Today*, London: SCM Press, 1969, pp. 66–81.

Kasper, Walter and others (eds), *Mit der Bibel durch das Jahr 1993*, Stuttgart: Kreuz Verlag, 1992.

Klauck, H.-J., *1. Korintherbrief*, Würzburg: Echter Verlag, 1987.

Knox, John, *Chapters in a Life of Paul*, London: A. & C. Black, 1954.

Leon, Philip, 'M.R.A., a Contemporary Crux in the Philosophy and Application of Religion', *The Hibbert Journal*, 54, 1956, pp. 139–53.

Lewis, C. S., *The Screwtape Letters*, London: Collins, 1942.

McDonald, J. I. H., *The Resurrection: Narrative and Belief*, London: SPCK, 1989.

McFague, Sallie, *Speaking in Parables*, London: SCM Press, 1976.

——, *Metaphorical Theology*, Philadelphia: Fortress Press, 1982.

Majercik, Ruth, 'Rhetoric and Oratory in the Greco-Roman World', in David Noel Freedman and others (eds), *The Anchor Bible Dictionary*, New York: Doubleday, 1992, vol. 5, pp. 710–12.

Malherbe, Abraham J., *Ancient Epistolary Theorists*, Atlanta: Scholars Press, 1988.

Marshall, I. H., *Last Supper and Lord's Supper*, Exeter: Paternoster Press, 1980.

Marshall, Peter, *Enmity in Corinth: Social Conventions in Paul's Relations with the Corinthians*, Tübingen: J. C. B. Mohr, 1987.

Martin, D. B., *The Corinthian Body*, New Haven/London: Yale University Press, 1995.

Meeks, Wayne A., *The First Urban Christians: The Social World of the Apostle Paul*, New Haven/London: Yale University Press, 1983.

Mitchell, Alan C., 'Rich and Poor in the Courts of Corinth', *New Testament Studies*, 39, 1993, pp. 562–86.

Mitchell, Margaret, *Paul and the Rhetoric of Reconciliation*, Tübingen/Louisville: J.C.B. Mohr/Westminster Knox, 1992.

Moffatt, James, *The First Epistle to the Corinthians* (Moffatt New Testament Commentary), London: Hodder & Stoughton, 1938.

Moule, C. F. D., *The Birth of the New Testament*, London: A. & C. Black, 1962.

Murdoch, Iris, *The Good Apprentice*, London: Chatto and Windus, 1985.

Murphy-O'Connor, Jerome, O.P., *St. Paul's Corinth*, Wilmington: Glazier, 1983.

Perkins, Pheme, *Resurrection: New Testament Witness and Contemporary Reflection*, New York/London: Doubleday/Geoffrey Chapman, 1984.

Ramsey, A. M., *The Gospel and the Catholic Church*, London: Longmans Green, 1936.

——, *Introducing the Christian Faith*, London: SCM Press, 1961.

Roetzel, Calvin, *Paul: The Man and the Myth*, Edinburgh: T. & T. Clark, 1999.

Sagovsky, Nicholas, *Ecumenism, Christian Origins and the Practice of Communion*, Cambridge: Cambridge University Press, 2000.

Savage, Timothy B., *Power through Weakness: Paul's Understanding of Christian Ministry in 2 Corinthians*, Cambridge: Cambridge University Press, 1996.

Schaefer, Ruth, *Paulus bis zum Apostelkonzil*, Tübingen: Mohr Siebeck, 2004.

Schillebeeckx, Edward, *Jesus*, London: Collins, 1978.

Shanor, Jay, 'Paul as Master Builder: Construction Terms in First Corinthians', *New Testament Studies*, 34, 1988, pp. 461–71.

Schlatter, Adolf, *Paulus, der Bote Jesu*, Stuttgart: Calwer, 1934.

Schrage, Wolfgang, *Der erste Brief an die Korinther* (Evangelisch Katholischer Kommentar zum Neuen Testament), Zurich and Braunschweig/Neukirchen-Vluyn: Benziger Verlag/Neukirchener Verlag, 4 vols, 1991–2001.

Schüssler Fiorenza, Elisabeth, *In Memory of Her*, London: SCM Press, 1983.

Schweizer, Eduard, *Spirit of God*, London: A. & C. Black, 1960.

——, *Church Order in the New Testament*, London: SCM Press, 1961.

——, *The Church as the Body of Christ*, London: SPCK, 1965.

——, *The Lord's Supper according to the New Testament*, Philadelphia: Fortress Press, 1967.

Suurmond, J.-J., 'A Fresh Look at Spirit-Baptism and the Charisms', *Expository Times*, 109, 1998, pp. 103–6.

Taylor, John V., *The Primal Vision*, London: SCM Press, 1963.

Theissen, Gerd, *The Social Setting of Pauline Christianity: Essays on Corinth*, Edinburgh: T. & T. Clark, 1982.

——, *Psychological Aspects of Pauline Theology*, Edinburgh: T. & T. Clark, 1987.

Thiselton, Anthony C., *The First Epistle to the Corinthians* (New International Greek Testament Commentary), Carlisle/Grand Rapids: Paternoster/Eerdmans, 2000.

Thompson, Cynthia L., 'Hairstyles, Head-coverings, and St. Paul: Portraits from Roman Corinth', *Biblical Archaeologist*, 51, 1988, pp. 99–115.

Watson, Nigel, 'Justified by Faith; Judged by Works – an Antinomy?' *New Testament Studies*, 29, 1983, pp. 209–21.

——, *Striking Home: Interpreting and Proclaiming the New Testament*, London: Epworth Press, 1987.

——, *Easter Faith and Witness*, Melbourne: Desbooks, 1990.

——, 'Review Article on A. C. Wire, *The Corinthian Women Prophets*', *Australian Biblical Review*, 40, 1992, pp. 58–63.

——, *The Second Epistle to the Corinthians*, London: Epworth Press, 1993.

——, '"The Philosopher Should Bathe and Brush His Teeth," – Congruence between Word and Deed in Graeco-Roman Philosophy and Paul's Letters to the Corinthians', *Australian Biblical Review*, 42, 1994, pp. 1–16.

Wedderburn, A. J. M., *The Reasons for Romans*, Edinburgh: T. & T. Clark, 1988.

Wheeler Robinson, H., *The Christian Experience of the Holy Spirit*, London: Nisbet, 1928.

Winter, B. W., 'Secular and Christian Responses to Corinthian Famines', *Tyndale Bulletin*, 40, 1989, pp. 86–106.

Witherington III, Ben, *Conflict & Community in Corinth: A Socio-Rhetorical Commentary on 1 and 2 Corinthians*, Carlisle/Grand Rapids: Paternoster/Eerdmans, 1995.

Wright, N. T., *The Climax of the Covenant*, Edinburgh: T. & T. Clark, 1991.

——, *Paul for Everyone: 1 Corinthians*, London: SPCK, 2003.

——, *The Resurrection of the Son of God*, London: SPCK, 2003.

Ziesler, John, *The Epistle to the Galatians*, London: Epworth Press, 1992.

COMMENTARY

Greeting and Thanksgiving
1.1–9

Paul begins his letter with:
(i) an epistolary greeting (vv. 1–3), followed by
(ii) an expression of thanksgiving for the grace of God that has been given to the Corinthians, along with an expression of confidence that Christ will complete the work that has been begun in them (vv. 4–9).

The greeting
1.1–3

These verses expand what in ordinary letters was said in a line or two. The essential elements of such an address were the name of the sender, the addressee and a word of greeting. Acts 15.23 and 23.26 and James 1.1 all exemplify this convention. It has now become clear that the combination of the concepts of grace and peace in an epistolary greeting was not, as was once thought, a Christian innovation, but was already quite a common custom,[18] but it can still be said that in the openings to his letters Paul has given deep religious significance to what had become a conventional form – a striking illustration of how faith in Christ can penetrate to the details of everyday life.

1.1 As sender, Paul designates himself as one who has been called to be an apostle of Christ Jesus through the will of God. The question of the marks of a true apostle becomes central later in this letter, especially in chapter 9, and remains central throughout 2 Corinthians.

Etymologically, the word 'apostle' means one who has been sent, an emissary or messenger. The word is not common in extra-biblical Greek but is already being used in the New Testament with a distinctively Christian meaning. Sometimes, as in 2 Cor. 8.23; Phil. 2.25, it implies no more than that someone has been sent by a particular church. Usually, however, it denotes someone who is a special representative of Christ and has been called to play a unique foundational role in the church as a whole. As so used, it can denote a narrower group, the original 'inner circle', the Twelve (Luke's preferred usage) or a larger group, as in the letters of Paul. At the same time, Paul is adamant that this is not a title that individuals can claim for themselves. It is clear from 1 Cor. 9.1 that he considers it to be an essential qualification that one should have seen the risen Lord. But a direct divine commission is also necessary; hence his insistence, not only here but in other letters as well, that he has been called to be an apostle or that he is an apostle by the will of God or some such phrase (see Rom. 1.1; 2 Cor. 1.1; Gal. 1.1).

In describing himself as an *apostle of Christ Jesus by God's call and by his will,* Paul is making it clear from the very beginning that he is an apostle by virtue of an authentic call. He does not yet have to contend with as strong a challenge to his apostolic authority as he will face when he writes 2 Corinthians or Galatians, yet he is already aware of groups in Corinth who consider that they owe him no particular obedience, even though he is the founder of their church.

In greeting his readers, Paul courteously associates with himself a fellow-Christian, Sosthenes. Paul refers to him simply as 'our brother' – a title that would be appropriate to any Christian. In Luke's account of Paul's first visit to Corinth in Acts 18.1–17, we also read of a Sosthenes who was the ruler of the synagogue that accused Paul before Gallio, the local proconsul, and who was later beaten up by the pagan crowd. It is conceivable, but not provable, that this Sosthenes was converted and followed Paul to Ephesus.

1.2   As recipients of his letter Paul names first of all *God's church at Corinth.* 'Church' here refers to the local gathering of believers, yet it is at the same time the local embodiment of the people of God.

The church is brought into being through God's act, and so Paul's readers are now further addressed as *dedicated to him in Christ Jesus, called to be his people.* The Greek words here translated 'dedicated' and 'his people' are related.

Further, the Corinthians *have been* 'sanctified' or 'made holy' in Christ Jesus and are *called to be* his 'saints' or 'holy ones'. In this dual description there is a tension between the concept of holiness as a state that has been consummated and as a goal that has yet to be achieved. Holiness is both something they have already and something to which they are called.

In the Old Testament holiness properly belongs to God alone. Other things, however, also become holy in a derivative and dependent sense through being set apart by God for God's purposes and drawn into God's life. God sets apart things, places, times, persons and, above all, a people. By so doing, God draws them into God's own life and imparts holiness to them or sanctifies them. Yet this holiness remains an exacting holiness. To the people whom God has set apart God says, 'You shall be holy, for I am holy' (Exod. 22.31). In the same way, Christians have already been sanctified, they belong already by baptism to God's people, they have been claimed by God and drawn into God's life. Yet they are equally called to be holy, called to become that which in a sense they already are. And the way in which they are to become holy is not by making heroic efforts of their own but by allowing God's Holy Spirit to have its way with them.

The phrase 'God's church' has already served to remind the Corinthians that they are part of a wider fellowship. Now Paul widens their vision still further by associating with them *all who invoke the name of our Lord Jesus Christ wherever they may be – their Lord as well as ours.*

1.3   Paul concludes his greeting by invoking upon his readers *grace and peace from God our Father and the Lord Jesus Christ.* These are the two essential blessings that he wishes for all his readers (cf. Rom. 1.7; 2 Cor. 1.2; Gal. 1.3; Phil. 1.2; 1 Thess. 1.1). Grace denotes both God's undeserved and unconditioned goodwill and the expression of that goodwill in God's saving acts. Peace is the effect of this activity, salvation as a present and future reality. This grace and peace flow from God our Father but have been made effective in human experience through our Lord Jesus Christ.

Thanksgiving and hope
1.4–9

Paul has already signalled that the life in Christ is marked by both having and hoping. In this second paragraph he confirms that impression.

1.4f.   Thus he thanks God for his grace given to them in Christ Jesus. He thanks God *for all the enrichment that has come* to them *in Christ* so that they *possess full knowledge* and *can give full expression to it.* The reference here is evidently to spiritual knowledge, regarded as the gift of God. There is, in these opening verses, an accumulation of verbs in the passive voice, which emphasize the dependence of the Corinthians on the action of God. It is God who sanctifies (v. 2), who gives (v. 4), who makes rich (v. 5), who confirms (v. 6) and who calls (v. 9). It is clear from the rest of the Corinthian correspondence that the gifts of knowledge and utterance were those by which the Corinthians set most store, and that is, no doubt, the reason why Paul singles them out for special mention here.

1.6   This enrichment has served to confirm the apostolic witness to Christ, into whose fellowship they have been called (v. 9).

1.7   Paul can even write that *there is indeed no single gift you lack.* In the light of all the shortcomings in faith and hope and love that the following chapters are about to disclose, it is remarkable that he should go so far in affirming the Corinthian church as a genuinely Christian community that has been abundantly blessed by God. In a moment he will be taking them to task for all sorts of sins against the fellowship, but in these opening paragraphs there is no hint of all that. Rather does he want them to be left in no doubt that he acknowledges the reality of their calling and of their endowment by God with every kind of gift of grace. Every time he remembers them in his prayers, he can only thank God (v. 4).

1.8   Nor does he doubt that they will be affirmed by God on the day of judgement. He is confident that God will keep them *firm to the end, without reproach on the day of our Lord Jesus.* One can only marvel at Paul's ability to see all the warts of these Corinthian Christians and yet not waver in his faith that in Christ their salvation is, and will remain, secure.

At the same time we can already see signs of Paul's intention to make up what is lacking in their faith. We have already spoken in the Introduction of the prevalence at Corinth of an over-realized eschatology, that is, of the belief that God had already given them all God had to give. We can picture Paul's hearers nodding in agreement as they heard him acknowledging the richness of their spiritual endowment, so that there was no gift of grace in which they were deficient. Verses 7b and 8, however, would have brought them the salutary reminder that the drama of salvation was not yet complete. Usually Paul adapts an Old Testament phrase and speaks of the 'day of the Lord'. For him, however, as is already clear from v. 8, 'the day of the Lord' is 'the day of our Lord Jesus'. Then they will know themselves even as they are already known by God (cf. 1 Cor. 13.12). Equally timely, in view of the proneness of the Corinthians to spiritual complacency, is Paul's reminder that their hope lies in God alone. Whatever spiritual gifts they have come from God (v. 5). And Christ will finish the work that has been begun in them, so that on the day of our Lord Jesus Christ they will be 'without reproach' in God's sight (v. 8).

That Paul should entertain such a hope for the bickering Christians of Corinth may strike us as utterly extraordinary, but the essential idea behind these words is probably not one of absolute flawlessness but rather that of total commitment. In the AV we read in the Old Testament of kings whose hearts were 'perfect with the Lord' all their days. Modern versions usually substitute for the Hebrew words used in such passages some other rendering. In 1 Kings 15.14, for example, the REB translates the Hebrew word *shalem* by 'faithful', and in Deut. 18.13 the synonymous word, *tamim,* is rendered by 'undivided'.

In v. 3 God the Father and the Lord Jesus Christ are considered as one indivisible source of grace and peace. In the same way in vv. 8 and 9 both Christ and God are presented to Paul's readers as the sole grounds of their hope to be found without reproach on the day of the Lord. It is Christ who will strengthen them, so that they are found blameless at the end.

1.9   Equally, Paul's hope for his converts may be said to rest on the faithfulness of God, through whom they have been called *to share in the life of his Son Jesus Christ our Lord.* Thus already in these opening paragraphs we see Paul's concern to win his readers away from a false self-confidence and ground their faith and hope afresh on the God and Father of our Lord Jesus Christ, who has yet to complete the saving work but who can be trusted to keep faith with those who have been called.

Divisions in the Church
1.10—4.21

The contradiction of a divided church
1.10–17

The next paragraph is marked by an abrupt change of tone. Indeed, a whole gamut of emotions comes to the surface in the course of one paragraph: pastoral concern, dismay, astonishment, relief, zeal for the gospel.

1.10   Paul comes straight to the point with an appeal for a common mind and the repudiation of cliques. The intensity of his feelings is made immediately apparent by his solemn appeal to 'the name of Christ'. This is in fact the tenth time that Christ has been named in the first ten verses. So deep is Paul's concern for his readers that he reiterates his plea for unity three times over in v. 10: *agree among yourselves, and avoid divisions; let there be complete unity of mind and thought.*

1.11   In vv. 11 and 12 Paul states the reason why he considers this plea so urgently necessary: he has heard from Chloe's people that there are divisions in the church at Corinth. Parties have formed around the names of various evangelists, thus reproducing within the church the rivalries that existed between different philosophical schools. There are amusing satirical comments on the competition among the various philosophical schools of the day in the dialogue by the second-century author, Lucian, entitled *The Sale of Creeds*. Lucian presents the Greek gods, Zeus and Hermes, auctioning off a varied assortment of live creeds, including tenets of every description.

1.12   Here Paul dramatizes the allegiances of the different parties in the church in Corinth. Each is saying, *'I am for Paul,'* or *'I am for Apollos,' 'I am for Cephas,'* possibly even *'I am for Christ.'* With admirable diplomacy Paul names first of all those who were his own partisans.

8

Apollos had consolidated Paul's ministry in Corinth (see 1 Cor. 3.5–9). A native of Alexandria, he is described in Acts 18.24f. as being 'an eloquent man, powerful in his use of the scriptures', and also well instructed in the facts about Jesus, yet knowing only the baptism of John, until enlightened by Priscilla and Aquila, colleagues of Paul's.

For a fuller discussion of the origin and nature of these parties see the excursus, *Parties in Corinth*, at the end of this section.

1.13 To underline the absurdity of the state of affairs that he has just sketched, Paul asks a string of rhetorical questions that are almost brutally direct.

Surely Christ has not been divided! Implicit in this statement (a question in the original) is the notion of the church as the body of Christ, which will be developed in chapters 10—12. By their partisanship the Corinthians are in effect severing the limbs of the one Christ to whom they all belong.

Was it Paul who was crucified for you? That is to say, they are in danger of giving to mere human leaders that ultimate allegiance that belongs to Christ alone, as their only sufficient Saviour. As Paul will put it in 4.1, they should think of Paul and his fellow-apostles simply as servants of Christ, entrusted by him with the mysteries of God and answerable solely to him.

Was it in Paul's name that you were baptized? Some Christians may have been claiming to possess a greater share of the Spirit, and therefore greater power and wisdom, because they had been baptized by this or that evangelist. Once again Paul uses his own name, not the names of Apollos or Cephas, to show up the error of the Corinthian partisanship. The phrase 'in (lit. into) the name of . . .' occurs quite frequently in the business language of papyri and inscriptions, where it means 'to the account of . . .' The use of the same phrase with reference to baptism implies that the person baptized becomes the exclusive property of Christ.

1.14f. With gratitude Paul recalls that he had not baptized any of them, except Crispus and Gaius, to that extent diminishing the danger that anyone might be tempted to think that they had been baptized into Paul's own name. The Crispus named here is likely to be the same Crispus who is mentioned in Acts 18.8 as the ruler of the synagogue who was won to the faith through Paul's preaching. Since his conversion represented a great triumph for the evangelists, it is understandable that Paul chose to baptize him with his own hands. The Gaius named here must also have been an important personage, probably the same person who is mentioned in Rom. 16.23 as being host to Paul himself and to the whole church.

1.16 Almost immediately Paul corrects himself, noting that he did also baptize the household of Stephanas. This correction is an illuminating disclosure of Paul's method of composition. Once the letter was dictated, it was left unrevised.

1.17 If baptism is not Paul's primary task, what is? His short answer is *to proclaim the gospel*. But Paul says more. In a few words he sums up not only the nature of his task but his authority for performing it, the manner in which it is to be carried out and, by implication, its goal. His authority lies in his being Christ's apostle, Christ's 'sent one'. As for the manner in which his task is to be carried out, it is imperative that this be consistent with the content of his message. The content of his message is the good news of God's saving work in Christ. That being so, Paul finds himself under the strongest compulsion to direct his hearers' attention to God's act and God's act alone, to proclaim the gospel *without recourse to the skills of rhetoric, lest the cross of Christ be robbed of its effect*. There can be no room for pyrotechnic displays of rhetorical virtuosity such as were offered by the travelling sophists who could be heard in the marketplaces of any Mediterranean city. Such oratorical skill would leave his hearers gaping at his cleverness and rob the cross of its force. All his effort must be directed towards allowing the message of the cross of Christ to speak with unimpeded power. That is the goal of his apostleship.

In this memorable programmatic sentence Paul introduces two themes of the utmost importance for the letter as a whole: wisdom and the cross of Christ. The phrase translated by the REB 'without recourse to the skills of rhetoric' literally runs 'not with wisdom of word'. Wisdom is to be the dominant theme from this point through to the end of chapter 2. In the present context the word refers not so much to the content of the message as to the manner of its presentation, the sort of oratorical brilliance that would distract the hearers from the content and thus rob his message of its power. As for the cross of Christ, that represents nothing less than the heart of Paul's gospel, to which he will be recalling his readers again and again.

PARTIES IN CORINTH

Much has been written on the question of how the various parties referred to in v. 12 may have arisen and what they stood for.

Since Paul and Apollos had both evangelized in Corinth, Paul first and Apollos later, it is understandable that each should have attracted over-zealous partisans.

What about the party of Cephas? There is no direct evidence that Peter (to give him his usual name) had ever preached in Corinth, but it is very likely that the church there included among its members people who had come to the city from some other centre where they had been converted, directly or indirectly, by Peter's preaching.

So much for the parties represented by the first three rallying cries. The real difficulty arises with the fourth. How, one may well ask, could there emerge *within* the church a party that chose as its rallying cry, 'We are for Christ'? Did not all who had been baptized belong equally to Christ?

At least five different explanations of v. 12 have been put forward by scholars over the past 200 years. Many scholars have interpreted the words, 'I am for Christ,' as the slogan of an identifiable group in the church at Corinth. This text was crucial to Baur's construal of early Christian history. The 'Christ party', according to Baur, held that true apostles had been disciples of Jesus of Nazareth and upheld the continuing validity of the Law. On the basis of this and other texts, Baur developed his thesis of a major antithesis between Pauline Christianity and Petrine Christianity in the early church. Other scholars, like Lütgert, Moffatt and Allo, have taken the view that there was indeed a 'Christ party' in Corinth, but a party made up of ultra-spiritual Gnostics.

In the first edition of this commentary, I adopted a view similar to that of Lütgert and others. I argued that we can discern, in the background of 1 Corinthians, the presence of people holding a coherent set of beliefs, such as I have sought to outline in the Introduction. At the same time, I added that the case that could be made for linking that set of beliefs with the slogan, 'I am for Christ,' was not nearly so strong.

Other scholars interpret the words, 'I am for Christ,' as an interjection by an indignant scribal copyist, originally written in the margin. This marginal gloss was then taken by the next scribe to be an unintended omission, which he then incorporated into the text.

Others believe that the words in question represent an ironic touch added by Paul himself. Paul has 'gone one better', in order to expose the absurdity of the Corinthian partisanship. This view goes back to Tertullian and Chrysostom. Chrysostom remarks, in his homily on 1 Corinthians (3.5), 'Paul added these words, to sharpen the reprimand'. In modern times, this view has been held by Lake, Hurd, Schrage and Mitchell.

There is also further evidence from the Patristic period in 1 Clement 47.3, where Clement alludes to the three groups of followers of Peter, Apollos and Paul but makes no allusion to a group claiming to be the followers of Christ.

One argument against this view is that the four declarations are parallel in form. If Paul had really been intending 'to go one better', would he not have used the more strongly adversative 'but', namely *alla*, instead of repeating the same word, *de?* We must remember, however, that the Corinthians were familiar with the situation, as we are not. It is therefore unlikely that they would have seen in Paul's words an allusion to a party that claimed to be exclusively the party of Christ, if such a party did not exist.

I myself now incline to the view that the words in question represent an ironic touch added by Paul himself. The evidence from the Patristic age should surely carry considerable weight. Tertullian and Chrysostom, Chrysostom particularly, were Greek speakers as we are not, and were also familiar with the conventions of Hellenistic rhetoric. That, in my view, tips the balance.

Something that becomes more and more apparent as one reads this epistle is just how wide is the gap between Paul's understanding of the gospel and that of his readers. The misconceptions of the nature of leadership in the Christian community that have already become apparent in this opening section will become even more prominent as we proceed. They all reflect a failure to appreciate the implications of faith in a Lord who 'emptied himself, taking the form of a servant' (Phil. 2.7).

The folly of divine wisdom – the weakness of divine power
1.18–25

The phrase 'wisdom of word' and the mention of the cross now launch Paul into an exposition of the word of the cross as the wisdom as well as the power of God. In the eyes of the unbelieving world it appears the very opposite, but in the cross God has turned all our human values upside down. It is a striking fact that Paul can describe the gospel simply as 'the word of the cross'.

1.18 Here Paul stresses the division which 'the word of the cross' inevitably produces among its hearers. Some see it as *sheer folly,* while others find in it *the power of God.*

To the question, 'How is one to account for this difference in the impact that the message of the cross makes on different hearers?' Paul gives more than one answer. In v. 21 he speaks of those who are being saved as 'those who have faith'; in v. 24 he speaks of them as 'those who are called'. Both designations are important. Salvation is available to those who have faith, but faith is a response to God's call.

As the response differs, so does the outcome. Paul clearly envisages here a parting of the ways. A decision for the gospel leads to salvation, a decision against it to destruction. Yet he does also entertain the hope that the entire created universe will ultimately be wholly subject to God's rule (see 1 Cor. 15.28; Phil. 2.10f.).

By using the words 'folly' and 'power', Paul is already preparing for vv. 22f., where he will set the gospel in sharp contrast both with the expectations of the Jews, who await a conclusive demonstration of divine power, and with the mind-set of the Greeks, who regard the quest for wisdom as the highest human pursuit. Of these two contrasts, however, it is the contrast with wisdom which dominates the thought of the paragraph. Words of the wisdom/folly cluster occur 19 times in this paragraph, whereas words of the power/weakness cluster occur 5 times. Clearly, wisdom rather than signs represents the characteristic preoccupation of the Corinthian community.

Contemporary Hellenistic writers conceive of wisdom in terms of an understanding of science, philosophy and art. In Paul, 'wisdom' has quite a range of meanings. Sometimes, as in 1 Cor. 1.17; 2.1; and 2.4, it denotes a technique of persuasion, oratorical skill. In 1.20 and 21, however, 'wisdom' appears to denote a means by which people aspire to the knowledge of God. Here Paul insists that the way to the true knowledge of God is by revelation alone.[19]

1.19 Accepting the gospel entails a radical revision of one's understanding of wisdom, the acknowledgement that God's ways are not our ways. Paul sees this overturning of human concepts predicted in Isa. 29.14: '*I will destroy the wisdom of the wise, and bring to nothing the cleverness of the clever.*'

In its context, the quotation is a forceful affirmation that 'salvation is of the Lord'. Yahweh declares through the mouth of the prophet that he will himself save Jerusalem from the Assyrians, apart from all political calculations and alliances. He will therefore dumbfound those who have a reputation for wisdom, that is, for political sagacity, by again doing 'marvellous things with this people, wonderful and marvellous'. Paul applies the verse to the so-called wise men of his own day. In the cross God has acted in a way that transcends all human calculation and insight; God has demonstrated a wisdom of a new order altogether.

1.20   It follows therefore that, in order to appropriate the wisdom of God revealed in the cross, one must first acknowledge that what one once thought to be wisdom has been shown up as folly. This is the thought which Paul develops in v. 20, by a series of rhetorical questions of increasing length. God has made foolish the wisdom of the world, so that the man whom the world counts wise, the *man of learning* (though Paul may have in mind specifically the Jewish scribe), the *subtle debater of this present age*, is left, as we might put it, without a leg to stand on.

1.21   The world, for all its wisdom, has not known God. Rom. 1.19–25 implies that it was theoretically possible for the world to attain to a limited knowledge of God, namely, of God's everlasting power and deity. But this theoretical possibility has not been used. As a result, God has been compelled to take a new initiative. The locus of God's self-disclosure is a series of events, culminating in the crucifixion of Jesus of Nazareth. Such is the content of the church's proclamation, its *kerygma*. Its primary calling is to tell this story to all who will hear and to invite them to believe that here is to be found the final revelation of God, of God's power and wisdom. Through that story God in God's wisdom has seen fit to bring men and women to salvation.

   Yet, on the face of it, this is an extraordinary claim. For the event that is the climax of the Christian story appears to be precisely the sort of happening that, far from awakening faith in men and women, rather confirms their worst fears that God, if there is a God, is powerless and that human existence is ultimately absurd. Paul himself knows full well how extraordinary the Christian claim is. Hence his characterization of the gospel as 'folly', that is, as a kind of madness. He now develops this thought in vv. 22 and 23, by showing how the gospel calls in question the expectations and preoccupations of Jews and Gentiles alike.

1.22f.   Characteristically, *Jews demand signs.* As used here, the word 'sign' combines the notions of power and proof. When God brought God's people out of Egypt, it was 'with a strong hand and outstretched arm, with terrifying deeds, and with signs and portents' (Deut. 26.8). When at last the Messiah came forth in God's name, he would be authenticated by the signs that he performed.

But what does this Jesus do? He refuses to perform the signs for which the people, his people, are clamouring. He calls down no fire from heaven. He does not come down from his cross but hangs there as a helpless victim, absorbing the worst that his enemies can do to him. Could God show forth God's power like this? To the Jew who is longing to see God's enemies given their just deserts such a claim can only be a stumbling block.

And what of the Greek? Characteristically, Greeks *look for wisdom*, and by that Paul appears to mean not a practical sagacity in the conduct of one's daily life but rather a particular kind of religious knowledge. There is ample evidence from the first two or three centuries of people all over the Hellenistic world searching for such a knowledge (*gnōsis*). The presuppositions of this movement were broadly Platonic. The object of people's search was the kind of knowledge that would enable the soul to rise above the things of sense and commune with ultimate reality.

What could such a seeker be expected to find in the cross? He might well find in it confirmation of Plato's cynical prediction, 400 years earlier, that such is bound to be the fate of a perfectly just man in a society like ours. But the way to the knowledge of God? Hardly. How could this raw piece of human living help him to commune with a God who was above all change and pain? Christ crucified the revelation of the wisdom of God? How could such a message be seen as anything other than sheer folly, unmitigated absurdity?

That the message of the cross continued to be an offence to many a hearer cannot be doubted. Echoes of derisive rejections of the Christian message can be heard in Justin's *Apology* and *Dialogue with Trypho*, in Origen's *Contra Celsum* and Lucian's account of the death of Peregrinus. There is also the mute witness of a crude drawing, found among the ruins of the Palatine Hill in Rome, of a slave bowing down to a crucified figure with an ass's head. Underneath are the words, 'Alexander worships his god.'

1.24f.   Yet, for those who hear in the gospel the call of God, the cross does indeed prove to be God's power, God's wisdom, power that, for all its seeming weakness, is stronger than men and women and what they count as power, wisdom that, for all its seeming folly, is wiser than men and women and what they count as wisdom. For in this life, this dying, they see being enacted unlimited forgiving love, love that is battered, bruised, spat upon, crucified – and still remains love. Such love will in the end have its way. It is true power, the power of God.

Those who are seeking saving wisdom may also, to their surprise, find in the cross the answer to their quest, in so far as the cross offers them a picture of God that makes the problem of suffering bearable. To sensitive minds, the problem of the suffering of the innocent has always represented one of the greatest obstacles to belief in a wise and loving God. As Philip Toynbee has remarked, 'The problem for many of us is not whether God will forgive us but how we are ever to forgive him.'[20]

A message that contains at its heart the story of Gethsemane and Golgotha may well seem to epitomize the offence of innocent suffering in its most concentrated form. That problem is not theoretically resolved but loses something of its sting, if one can believe that God shares our human anguish, shares what a character in one of Iris Murdoch's novels calls 'the deep and awful and irremediable things that happen to people'.[21]

In a meditation on what is left of a mediaeval wooden crucifix Frederick Buechner has given a hint of how he, a one-time agnostic, came to find in Christ crucified the way to the knowledge of God.

Our age is full of people for whom the language of religious faith is a dead language and its symbols empty, for whom the figure of Jesus is vague and remote as a figure in a dream. But for all this it is hard to imagine anyone's looking at this battered relic of the faith of an earlier age without being moved. . . . Legless and armless, except for those who over the centuries have tried to be his legs and arms; wrecked, powerless, except for the power to stir the deepest intuitions and longings of the human heart – if ever there was a man worth dying with and dying for, this is how he should have looked. If ever there should turn out unbelievably to be a God of love willing to search for men even in the depths of evil and pain, this is the face we would know him by.[22]

Rhetoric

To locate Paul in his cultural setting, we need to grasp the central place of rhetoric, the art of persuasion, in the education and public life of the time. Nowadays the word 'rhetoric' is often qualified by the adjective 'mere' and contrasted with utterances of substance, but it is difficult to overemphasize its importance and popularity in Graeco-Roman society. Ever since Socrates in the fifth century BC, there had been an antagonistic relationship between rhetoric, the art of persuasion, and philosophy, the search for the knowledge of the truth and of the nature of the good life. By this time, however, rhetoric had become the central discipline in Roman higher education.

With the snuffing out of democratic institutions under the empire, opportunities for serious rhetoric were drastically curtailed, and rhetoric of display and ornament came more and more to the fore. Stress came to be placed on style and the use of a multiplicity of figures of speech. Schoolboys would be asked to compose speeches on fictitious and fantastic themes, like the praiseworthiness of a flea or the shamefulness of being bald. More and more value came to be placed on the ability to argue for any point of view, irrespective of its truth.

Furthermore, rhetoric was elevated to a form of public entertainment. Corinth was the venue for the Isthmian Games, which included oratory contests. A theatre seating 14,000 was also located there, so that the city was a natural mecca for orators.

The influence of ancient ideas of rhetoric can be seen in later centuries, particularly in sixteenth-century Europe. Erasmus, in one of his many writings, takes the conventional response to a letter, 'Your letter gave me great pleasure,' and reformulates it over and over again. As he proceeds, his language becomes more and more exuberant, resulting in expressions like these: 'Sugar is not sugar, if it placed beside your letter. What wine is to a thirsty man, so is your letter to me.'[23] Though the product of a much later century, this writing probably conveys a correct impression of the flavour of some of the rhetoric of Paul's day.[24]

Is Paul a rhetorician?

Looking back over this paragraph of Paul's letter, the reader may well sense a contradiction with the sentiments Paul expressed in the previous paragraph. In v. 17 Paul professed his calling to preach the gospel 'not with an orator's cleverness' (Knox's version), yet now he has demonstrated no mean rhetorical skill. There is a whole series of contrasts, highlighted at times by balanced antithetical parallelisms (vv. 18, 22–25). There is a telling use of rhetorical questions (v. 20), a skilful exploitation of different nuances of the word 'wisdom' (v. 21), and an effective use of paradox (vv. 21, 25). How can this skilful deployment of rhetoric be reconciled with Paul's disclaimer in v. 17?

It can at least be said in Paul's defence that all of these rhetorical devices are germane to his subject matter. Underlying the various contrasts running through the passage is a fundamental contrast between God and humankind. The antithetical parallelisms together with the rhetorical questions serve simply to highlight this fundamental contrast. A further conviction that is fundamental to the passage is that the God revealed in the gospel confounds all human expectations. Such a conviction cries out for expression through paradox and the juxtaposition of different senses of the one word. The various rhetorical devices Paul has chosen to use are not being used in order to display Paul's skill as an orator but to throw the gospel into the sharpest relief. James Denney used to say that no man can convince men and women at one and the same time that he himself is clever and that God is great. The rhetorical devices Paul is using here are all intended to convince his readers that God is great.

All of grace, all of God
1.26–31

Paul now continues to develop the theme of the astonishing grace of God, which was introduced in 1.18. He has just said that in the eyes of the world the power of God seems sheer weakness, the wisdom of God sheer folly. He now makes the point that God's reversal of human expectations is to be seen in the make-up of the church. God has chosen what the world counts foolish, weak, ignoble, despicable, mere nothings, as the first fruits of the new humanity.

1.26   That the church has such a character is clear from the composition of the Corinthian community itself. Few of them, Paul reminds them, are wise by any human standard, few powerful or of noble birth. A more literal rendering would be: 'Few of you are wise according to the flesh.' This is the first occurrence in this epistle of the word 'flesh', which conveys a wide range of meanings. Most often it refers to humanity in its creatureliness and therefore its fallenness. Here it refers to conditions which are essentially outward and temporal. For a fuller discussion of the social status of the early Christians see the excursus, *The Church and Social Groupings*, at the end of this section.

1.27f. Paul's statements in vv. 27f. are more general, implying that the composition of the church in Corinth is an accurate reflection of the church's essential nature. Indeed, the fact that the church in Corinth or anywhere else is not made up of the cream of society is no mere historical accident but a pointer to the fundamental truth that salvation is in no way a reward or recognition of achievement; it is, on the contrary, a matter of grace from start to finish. The point is made in a series of statements that rises to an impressive climax. In saving men and women through the cross, God has chosen what the world counts folly, in order to shame the wise, that is, in order to show that wisdom counts for nothing. In the same way, God has chosen what the world counts weakness, in order to show that power counts for nothing. God has chosen things without rank or standing in the world, mere nothings, in order to overthrow the existing order, that is, in order to show that nothing that men and women are or have or have achieved accounts in any way for the miracle of salvation. In the presence of God, the astonishing God revealed in the cross, all the things on which men and women rely for status dwindle to nothing. J. B. Phillips aptly renders v. 27d: 'to explode the pretensions of the things that are'.

The word translated by the REB 'overthrow' (*katargeō*) is used eight times in 1 Corinthians, in clearly eschatological contexts, to express Paul's conviction that the effect of the coming of Christ is to make the old order ineffective, powerless.

In vv. 27f. there is an echo of the contemptuous opinion of the lower classes held by many members of the upper classes in Graeco-Roman society. The anti-Christian philosopher, Celsus, writing around AD 180, expresses this contempt, when he asserts that the church attracted only 'the foolish, dishonourable and stupid, and only slaves, women and little children' (quoted by Origen, *Cels.* 3.44).

Throughout vv. 27 and 28, Paul uses neuter forms of the adjective to describe the objects of God's surprising choice. This seems to be deliberate. In a legal sense, slaves were not persons but things.

1.29 It is not that God, in choosing the uneducated, the powerless and the ignoble, has rejected outright those with education, power and nobility. On the other hand, it is an essential condition of receiving the grace of God that one flings away all attempts to qualify and accepts what God offers as a free gift. *So no place is left for any human pride in the presence of God.* In this sense the wise man has to become a fool.

We have already noted that between v. 26 and v. 27 there is a progression from the thought of the actual composition of the church in Corinth to that of the church's essential nature. In fact, the thought of vv. 26–29 focuses more and more sharply on God, who in God's sovereign freedom brings to nothing that which is and chooses that which does not exist. The passage is reminiscent of an equally forceful passage in Romans where, once again in order to rule out all merit, all deserving, Paul picks up a phrase used in the Old Testament to describe an unjust judge and by a daring reapplication transfers it to God. God, he declares, is the one who 'justifies the ungodly' (Rom. 4.5). Such a God is not one who recognizes and rewards righteousness but rather one who creates it out of nothing, one who 'gives life to the dead and calls into existence the things that do not exist' (Rom. 4.17). No one who has glimpsed this God in the face of Jesus Christ would ever want to boast or imagine that anything of their own, anything that they possessed, could ever qualify them to enter the presence.

1.30 In v. 30 Paul addresses his readers directly once again. *It is by God's act*, he reminds them, that *you are in Christ Jesus*. The Williams translation reads: 'So you owe it all to him.'

The phrase 'in Christ' is found more than 50 times in the New Testament, nearly always in Paul's letters. Sometimes it virtually means no more than 'as a Christian', but here Paul is clearly thinking of incorporation into Christ considered as the source of all new life.

In the second part of v. 30 Paul spells out what this new life in Christ means and declares that *God has made him our wisdom . . . our righteousness, our holiness, our liberation.* Knox translates: 'whom God gave us to be all our wisdom, our justification, our sanctification, and our atonement'. Paul has already described Christ as the wisdom of God in v. 24. No doubt he places wisdom first here because it was to wisdom above all that the Corinthians aspired.[25] Whereas in 1.21 and 2.7 'wisdom' denotes God's wise plan of salvation, in 1.30 it denotes rather the actual substance of salvation.

Righteousness represents the primary object of Jewish aspiration.

A central theme of Romans is that the glory of God's saving righteousness consists in making righteous, that is, in bringing into right relationship with God, those who have no righteousness, no goodness, of their own. To be made holy, or sanctified, means to be claimed by God as God's own and drawn into God's life (see the comment on v. 2). Verbs related to the term 'liberation' are frequently used in the Old Testament to refer to the Exodus. In the present context the thought is of Christ as the one who liberates human persons from sin and makes them holy. Christ is indeed the wisdom of God, as the Corinthians doubtless affirm. What they have not yet fully grasped is that the glory of the divine wisdom consists precisely in saving them from sin.

1.31 And all this is to be found in Christ. All that is required on the human side is the stretching out of one's empty hands to receive what God is waiting to bestow. Those who have done that know that there is no room left for boasting. They have come to see that *If anyone must boast, let him boast of the Lord* (Jer. 9.24). It is already becoming apparent that this is another truth of which the Corinthians themselves urgently need to be reminded.

The word 'boast' has already occurred in v. 29. The word group is overwhelmingly Pauline, and most of the occurrences are found in 1 and 2 Corinthians.[26]

THE CHURCH AND SOCIAL GROUPINGS

1 Corinthians is often quoted as evidence that at this stage few Christians were drawn from the more educated or more wealthy and influential levels of society. Various references in Paul's letters to slaves as members of the church are often taken as confirming this conclusion. However, it calls for some qualification. For one thing, it is unlikely that Paul would have written what he has in this chapter had there not been educated and privileged Christians in Corinth who were contemptuous of the social status of others. As for slaves, while some undoubtedly worked in conditions of squalor, others held responsible positions in households, in business and industry and in the public service of the State or township.[27]

Furthermore, Gerd Theissen has compiled a list of all the people in Corinth who are named as leaders, home-owners, providers of hospitality or travellers. In this way he identifies 9 people of some means, who will have provided space, food and leadership for the factions.[28]

There is also a reference in Rom. 16.23 to 'Erastus, treasurer of this city' (which is clearly Corinth). To this literary evidence for Erastus's social position archaeological evidence can probably be added. A pavement slab from Corinth probably dating from the first century AD carries the inscription, 'Erastus in return for aedileship laid [the pavement] at his own expense.' While it cannot be proved that this is the same Erastus as is referred to in Rom. 16.23, it seems highly likely. In any case, the reference in Rom. 16.23 is sufficient to show that the Corinthian community included a person of high social status.[29] On the other hand, as C. F. D. Moule points out, there is no evidence at this stage of Christianity having reached the lowest of the low, namely, the land-slaves and condemned criminals who worked in forced labour gangs on great estates or in mines and factories.[30] It would seem therefore that the social level of most Christian communities was towards the lower end of the social scale without touching rock bottom. However, within any local group, as well as between different local groups, there must have been considerable variation.

A messenger that matched the message
2.1–5

Paul addresses his readers directly once more, reminding them that the style and content of his preaching among them, as well as the spirit in which he had undertaken it, had been fully consistent with the exposition of the gospel that he has just given. The dominant theme of the previous paragraph has been that of wisdom – both human and divine. Human wisdom has been referred to under two main aspects. Thus in 1.17 Paul declares that his mission is to preach the gospel 'not with wisdom of word', that is, *without recourse to the skills of rhetoric.* Here 'wisdom' refers to a style of teaching. In 1.22, however, where 'wisdom' is the object of human search, the word denotes a liberating knowledge. Over against human wisdom there stands the wisdom of God, which confounds all human expectations and is revealed in its fullness in the cross. Not only does this wisdom stand in the sharpest contrast to human wisdom in the second of the two senses noted above, it also calls for a quite different style of presentation from 'wisdom' in the sense of rhetorical skill.

2.1   Paul's purpose in vv. 1 and 2 is to affirm not only that the content of his preaching had been purely and simply the wisdom of God but that the manner of his presentation had also been entirely congruent with his theme. He begins with the manner. He had come to them *without any pretensions to eloquence or wisdom in declaring the truth about God*. He had not dazzled his listeners by his rhetorical or philosophical prowess, he had simply proclaimed the truth about God.

2.2   Not only had Paul renounced all human wisdom in his presentation of his message, he had resolved to make the content of his message nothing less than the wisdom of God, nothing but *Jesus Christ – Christ nailed to the cross*. As we might put it, he didn't want to know about anything else. And he had preached Christ as one who had been crucified and remained the crucified one – such is the force of the perfect passive participle used by Paul.

We can hardly fail to be struck at this point by a significant omission, the omission of any explicit reference to the resurrection. Paul's original readers would no doubt have found this omission even more striking. Even though the Corinthians had failed to grasp all the implications of the resurrection for themselves, there is ample evidence that they saw Christ's resurrection as the central moment in the gospel story and thought of the cross as being no more than the occasion of his glorious triumph. For them, Christ was a heavenly being who had left the cross far behind him. For them, being a Christian meant sharing his risen life and enjoying all the blessings God had to give. Therefore in declaring that his theme among them had been nothing but Christ and him crucified, Paul is already engaging in a critique of Corinthian theology.

At the same time, for Paul the death of Jesus is not to be understood apart from the resurrection and only becomes the object of proclamation through it.

2.3f.   It was not as an accomplished orator, supremely confident in his persuasive powers, that Paul had come to them. On the contrary, he had come before them *in weakness, in fear, in great trepidation*. No preacher, Paul implies, with an ounce of insight into the gospel or even a glimmer of perception of the world of difference between God's wisdom and human wisdom could approach the task of proclamation in any other spirit. Not that Paul was tormented by the fear of punishment by God or rejection by his hearers. The fear of which he speaks here is rather, like the 'fear and trembling' of which he speaks

in Phil. 2.12, the awe of one who knows himself called into partnership with God, the shaken humility of one who finds himself standing
on holy ground. In the world of the Bible, fear and trembling
represent the appropriate response to epiphany and revelation.

2.5 As the bearer of such a gospel, Paul knows that he must do
nothing to draw the attention and admiration of his hearers to himself and his own cleverness. All his efforts must be directed towards
uplifting Christ and him crucified, so that the faith of his hearers *might
be built not on human wisdom but on the power of God.*

The previous verse points to a further reason why the preacher must
not draw attention to himself. The Spirit must be allowed to bear its
own witness to the truth of the message. And this had happened. His
preaching had *carried conviction by spiritual power.* More literally, it had
been attended by proof and power given by the Spirit. Paul uses here
a technical rhetorical term, *apodeixis,* proof, demonstration.

Wherein exactly this proof had consisted Paul does not say. It is not
likely that he is referring to miracles that he himself had performed
in Corinth. In that case, he could hardly have opposed his preaching
to Jewish demands for miracles, a few lines earlier. It is more likely that he is thinking of the internal testimony by which the Spirit
had convinced his hearers of the truth of his message. He could also
be thinking of the Spirit's further work in liberating and transforming their lives and endowing them with spiritual gifts. For Paul, the
power of God is not confined to the past. The message of the gospel
is not simply a report of a powerful act of God in the past. It is itself
the vehicle of God's power. It is, as Paul puts it in Rom. 1.16, *the saving
power of God for everyone who has faith.*

To sum up this section, the previous chapter revolves around a fundamental contrast: between reliance upon oneself and reliance upon
God. That is the fundamental decision with which the gospel confronts men and women. What Paul is insisting upon in this section is
that the proclamation of the gospel must also be undertaken in a spirit
not of self-reliance but rather of reliance upon God alone to convict
and convince. Had Paul himself set about his task in any other way,
there would have been a glaring contradiction between the message
and the messenger.

This is the first hint of a theme that comes more and more to the
forefront in the course of Paul's correspondence with Corinth. If there
is one theme that more than anything else dominates the passionate
argumentation of the second epistle, it is the inescapable necessity for

a congruence between the messenger and the message that he or she proclaims.[31]

God's open secret
2.6–10a

Paul has just declared that the manner of his proclamation has not been marked in any way by eloquence or wisdom. Nevertheless, the content of his proclamation is indeed wisdom, but a wisdom not of this age. In this new paragraph he continues a process of redefining the favourite terms of the Corinthians, which began at 1.18. Wisdom, as we have seen, represents the primary goal of Corinthian aspiration. It appears that, as aspirants towards wisdom, the Corinthians also chose to describe themselves as 'mature' or 'perfect' and as 'spiritual people' or 'people who have the Spirit' (3.1).

2.6   'I too am concerned with wisdom,' Paul now tells them. 'It is the substance of my message for the mature, but it is *not a wisdom belonging to this present age or to its governing powers, already in decline.*' He could have added: 'The maturity that makes people fit to receive this wisdom is not of this present age either. There is a distinction between those who are mature and those who are not, just as there is a distinction between those who are spiritual and those who are not, but the marks of true maturity and spirituality are quite different from what you imagine.' Throughout the passage Paul is picking up Corinthian terminology but filling it with his own content.

The word translated 'governing powers' can be used to refer to earthly rulers, as in Rom. 13.3, but here seems to refer, more widely, to all powers and forces hostile to God, which can, however, use earthly rulers as their tools. At the end of history, they will yield, inevitably, to God (15.24, 26). The word that is translated 'in decline' in 2.6 is also used, in the active voice, in 15.24, 26, where it is translated by 'depose'.

What the marks of true maturity and spirituality are will be expounded in chapter 3. For the present, Paul concentrates on the nature of the wisdom that is the content of his proclamation.

2.7   This wisdom is the wisdom of God, which (to translate literally) 'God foreordained before the ages with a view to our glory'. 'Wisdom' here therefore must mean God's plan of salvation, God's wise way of bringing humanity to fulfilment. It is not something apart from the gospel, it is rather that same gospel seen in greater depth.

This plan of salvation is God's secret. To translate literally once more, 'It is the hidden wisdom of God, contained in a mystery.' It is, however, precisely this wisdom, this mystery, that the preachers of the gospel proclaim (the main verbs in vv. 6 and 7 are in the plural). The secret has become an open secret.

Paul has probably borrowed the word 'mystery' from Jewish apocalyptic literature. Some modern authors make a useful distinction between mysteries and problems. A problem is, in principle, capable of solution, whereas a mystery is not. The only appropriate response to a mystery is one of fear and wonder.

2.8 God's secret remains inaccessible until it is revealed. *None of the powers that rule the world has known that wisdom.* Here, as in v. 6, Paul seems to be thinking of 'the powers that rule the world' as tools of demonic powers. More specifically, he seems to be thinking of those, like Pilate or Herod, who were responsible for the death of Jesus. By crucifying Jesus, these rulers demonstrated their blindness to the wisdom of God. To heighten the depth of their blindness, Paul describes Jesus as *the Lord of glory* – a striking phrase, which implies that glory, an attribute of God's inmost being, belongs to Jesus Christ as of right.

Though the crucifixion was, at one level, the work of blind unbelief, it also made it possible for God's wise plan to come to fruition. By doing their worst, the rulers of this age gave God the opportunity, if we may put it thus, to do God's best.

2.9 The truth is that we are dealing here with blessings that are inconceivable for the natural man, the natural woman. In support of this proposition, Paul appeals to Scripture. The words he quotes are not found in this precise form in the Old Testament as we know it, although there are various echoes of its component parts. The closest parallel is Isa. 64.4, which speaks of the God of Israel as an incomparable God. Origen, in the third century, gives the source of the quotation as the (now lost) Apocalypse of Elijah.

2.10a Christians, however, are no longer in the situation of the natural man or woman. To them God has revealed what is in store for those who love God. It is significant that Paul describes the recipients of God's revelation as those who love God, not, as the Corinthians would surely have said, those who know God. The agent of this revelation is the Spirit, the Holy Spirit, without whom no one can confess that Jesus is Lord (cf. 1 Cor. 12.1). We thus return to the central theme of the paragraph, namely, God's open secret, God's purpose of salvation, which, in the words of Jesus, is hidden from the learned and wise but revealed to the simple (Matt. 11.25).

'None but thy word can speak thy name'[32]
2.10b–16

2.10b   The focus of Paul's attention now moves from God's open secret to the Spirit as the revealer of the secret things of God. He has just described the Spirit as the agent of revelation of *God's hidden wisdom, his secret purpose framed from the very beginning to bring us to our destined glory.* The Spirit is uniquely qualified to reveal God's secret purpose, *for the Spirit explores everything, even the depths of God's own nature.*

In speaking of *the depths of God's own nature* as the object of the Spirit's exploration, Paul is using language that became popular in later Gnostic groups. It is likely, however, that Paul is drawing on apocalyptic and wisdom traditions that speak of the unfathomable mystery of God, accessible to human beings only through revelation. See Job 11.7f.; Dan. 2.22. Such language would have been of especial interest to the Corinthians, with their aspirations towards wisdom and knowledge. In v. 12 Paul directs them to God's self-disclosure in the gifts of God's grace.

The whole section from 10b to 16 is of particular interest, because of the light it throws on Paul's understanding of the Spirit. What is especially striking is the way Paul describes the Spirit as exercising fully personal functions and at the same time existing in a certain detachment from the fount of deity, the inmost being of God. For this there is clear precedent in the literature of post-exilic Judaism, especially Haggai, Zechariah, Trito-Isaiah and some of the Psalms. There is in this literature a deepening of the understanding of the Spirit, a development from the thought of the Spirit as a power proceeding from God to something more like the presence of God in person.[33] It is as mediator and revealer that the Spirit is depicted in v. 10b.

2.11   Here Paul proceeds to draw an analogy. He has been speaking of the Spirit's knowledge of the secret things of God. That knowledge is analogous to the knowledge that the human spirit has of the inner life of the human person. Here 'spirit', whether used of the human person or of God, is equivalent to *nous*, mind.

2.12   But the Spirit of God is also God's gift to us. After v. 10 we might expect Paul to say that the Spirit has been given to us to enable us to know the depths of God's own nature, but instead he speaks of it having been given *so that we may know all that God has lavished on us*. The actual word he uses, *(ta) charisthenta*, literally (the) 'things graciously given', is connected with the word *charismata*, which has already been used in 1.7 and is to form the central theme of chapter 12, but it is probably being used here not in a technical sense but rather to refer to all that God has given us in Christ.

The movement from *the depths of God's own nature* to *all that God has lavished on us* is surely significant and probably represents a further critique of Corinthian preoccupations, on Paul's part. If, as we have suggested, the Corinthians thought of themselves as mature, as spiritual Christians, they probably also prided themselves on their insight into *the depths of God's own nature*. That is precisely what we find the Gnostics of the second century doing, and incipient forms of Gnosticism can be detected in the background of Corinthian Christianity. Paul may already have sensed that his readers were in danger of engaging in fruitless speculation. Here he goes out of his way to direct their attention to the blessings that God has graciously given us, that is, to God as made known in the gospel. It is this, above all, that the Spirit communicates. As Luther always insisted, to know Christ is to know his benefits. And therefore the test of whether the Corinthians truly have the Spirit, as they claim, is precisely whether they have insight into the message of the crucified Saviour.

But at the same time Paul would have been equally emphatic that the converse of Luther's dictum is also true: to know Christ's benefits is to know Christ; in other words: to know *all that God has lavished on us* is to know *the depths of God's own nature*, for what God proves to be through the gospel is what God is in God's inmost being. Paul's gospel is not mere milk, as the Corinthians suppose.

2.13   Not only does the Spirit enable us to know the gracious gifts of God, the Spirit also makes possible the communication of that know-ledge to others. Paul can say of himself and other Christian teachers that *we speak of these gifts of God in words taught us not by our human wisdom but by the Spirit*. Furthermore, the truths they seek to impart can only be received by *those who have the Spirit*, that is, by spiritual people.

The last phrase of v. 13 in the Greek, which corresponds to the first clause of the verse in the REB, is capable of interpretation in several different ways. The REB speaks of *interpreting spiritual truths to those who have the Spirit*, but a good case can be made for the view that the phrase means, 'interpreting the things of the Spirit by means of words taught by the Spirit'. As Schrage points out, it is a weakness to take the Greek word, *pneumatikois* as masculine, when it is immediately followed by the neuter form, *pneumatika*, without Paul giving any indication of a change of gender.[34] Either way, however, the Spirit is the key to everything.

2.14   Here Paul speaks, by contrast, of those who reject the truths that the Spirit is seeking to impart, those who cannot grasp them but rather find them folly. The actual word Paul uses to describe such a person is *psychikos*. The noun *psychē* in Paul means essentially life, vitality. Paul seems to use the adjective, *psychikos*, to mean the person who admits no other knowledge than that which is accessible to their natural reason. Since such a person is implicitly contrasted with the *spiritual person* in v. 15, the translation *unspiritual* is appropriate.

In Gnostic texts from the second century AD we find these terms being used to denote classes of human beings that are fixed and unalterable. Such a division, however, would be alien to Paul's thought. He is thinking rather of the person who lives on the purely material plane, without being touched by the Spirit of God. Such a person is 'unspiritual' by virtue of a deliberate choice.

To know what belongs to the Spirit we must let the Spirit teach us, *because it needs to be judged in the light of the Spirit*. The word translated 'judged' could equally well be translated 'discerned'.

2.15   To receive the Spirit is to be gifted with discernment. In v. 15 Paul actually says that *a spiritual person can judge the worth of everything*, but he is no doubt thinking of the evaluation of spiritual phenomena. At the same time such a person *is not himself subject to judgement by others*. For those who do not have the Spirit, to sit in judgement on those who do is presumptuous. Verse 15 can readily be read as a protest on the part of Paul, who unquestionably believes himself to be a spiritual person, against incompetent critics in the Corinthian community who are calling this claim of his in question. If so, his thought is already running ahead to 4.1–5.

2.16 The central thought of this section has been that it is only through God's Spirit that we are able to know God or the truths of God. The point of the quotation in v. 16 appears to be that God must remain unknown until God takes the initiative and makes Godself known. But God has made Godself known. God has given us of Godself, in order that we may know God. Through most of the paragraph Paul has used the term 'Spirit' to describe this self-giving activity of God, but here he speaks of *the mind of Christ*. The shift in terminology was probably suggested by the quotation from Isaiah with its reference to 'the mind of the Lord'. Paul regularly takes a reference to 'the Lord' in the Old Testament as a reference to Christ. The way in which he switches from 'the Spirit' to 'the mind of the Lord' illustrates the intimate connection between these two concepts in his thinking.

Immature Christians
3.1–4

In the previous paragraph Paul has expounded the indispensable role of the Spirit. The Spirit reveals the depths of God's own nature and the Spirit teaches the church's teachers, instructing them what words to use in order to interpret spiritual truths to those who have the Spirit. Perceptive hearers in the Corinthian community would have recognized by now that Paul was expounding a somewhat different understanding of wisdom from that which they had taken for granted, but it is not likely that they would have detected so far any suggestion that their own understanding of spiritual truths was seriously deficient. Indeed, we can readily imagine them nodding agreement as they listened to the last paragraph. 'Of course,' we can picture them saying, 'spiritual truths are only for spiritual people, for people like us.' The idea that they themselves might not belong to the company of truly spiritual people would never have occurred to them.

3.1 But now Paul jolts them out of their complacency. *But I could not talk to you, my friends*, he declares with brutal directness, *as people who have the Spirit*. On the contrary, he had had to deal with them on another plane, *the natural plane, as infants in Christ*.

The actual Greek word that REB has rendered by the phrase, *on the natural plane* is *sarkinos*, which is derived from *sarx*, flesh, and means, literally, fleshy or fleshly. In v. 3 Paul uses another adjective derived from the same noun, namely, *sarkikos*.

'Flesh' is one of the key words of Paul's vocabulary. As used by him and indeed by biblical authors in general, it refers not so much to a part of human nature as to the whole person regarded from a particular point of view, namely, as creature. However, the precise shade of meaning varies considerably in different contexts.

First, it can be used in a wholly neutral sense to denote that which is outward and visible, as, for example, in 1 Cor. 1.26, where the words which literally mean 'wise according to the flesh' are aptly translated by REB 'wise by any human standard' (cf. Rom. 4.1).

Second, the term 'flesh' can be used to refer to humanity in its distance and difference from God and therefore as mortal, frail and vulnerable. The associations of 'flesh' with weakness are particularly clear in Rom. 6.19; 8.3; 2 Cor. 4.11.

But since human beings in their frailty are in fact sinners, 'flesh' can also be used in a third main sense to refer to humanity in its opposition to God (see e.g. Rom. 7.5, 18; 8.3–12).

The range of meanings conveyed by the word *sarx* is therefore a very wide one. In some contexts, such as Gal. 2.20, life 'in the flesh' can refer to the ordinary circumstances of human existence. In others, such as Rom. 8.4–9, it denotes a sphere to which the Christian no longer belongs.

The range of meanings conveyed by the adjectives derived from *sarx*, namely, *sarkinos* and *sarkikos*, is also wide. *Sarkikos* regularly conveys a pejorative sense, corresponding to the third sense of *sarx* noted above. *Sarkinos* can also convey the same meaning, as for example in Rom. 7.14. Where a distinction is made, *sarkinos* has connotations of finitude and frailty (corresponding to the second sense of *sarx* noted above).

It seems to be in the latter sense that Paul is using *sarkinos* in the present passage, since in order to substantiate the charge that the Corinthians are 'fleshly' he points simply to their immaturity not, as in later verses, to their lovelessness. His point is that they are acting as if they had not received the Spirit at all.[35]

3.2　However this may be, it is clear that Paul has had to treat the Corinthians, and still has to treat them, as *infants in Christ*, feeding them on *milk instead of solid food* (cf. Heb. 5.12, where the same metaphor is used). After all this time and all the pains he and others have taken over them, they ought to be immature no longer.

Once again we see Paul overturning their own estimate of themselves. They clearly thought of themselves as spiritual, as having been lifted above the merely human level by their possession of the Spirit, whereas their behaviour shows that they are in fact 'fleshly'. In the same way they no doubt thought of themselves as mature, whereas they are in reality mere infants. At the same time they had probably dismissed Paul's gospel as mere milk for babes. Paul readily agrees that he has not been able to feed them strong meat, but that is not due to the rudimentary nature of what he had to offer but to their inability fully to understand what he had to say. In fact, the gospel of the crucified offers all the meat one could wish for, the only true meat, whereas the kind of wisdom they have been pursuing is no more than ersatz meat.

3.3f.   But the Corinthians are guilty of something worse than mere immaturity. As has already become apparent in the opening chapter, their common life is marred by jealousy and strife, with one declaring, *'I am for Paul,' and another, 'I am for Apollos.'*

As Paul moves from the charge of immaturity to that of contentiousness, he uses the adjective that more often implies active sinfulness, namely, *sarkikos*. He adds that the behaviour of the Corinthians shows that they are *all too human* – an expression that throws further light on the connotations of the derivatives from the word 'flesh', used in the previous verses.[36]

Not us but God
3.5–9a

Verse 4 has brought us back to the actual state of the Corinthian Christians, with their passionate and divisive preferences for individual apostles. Paul now seeks to show up the absurdity of such partisanship, by setting forth the true role played by himself and other leaders of the church.

3.5   *After all*, he asks, *what is Apollos? What is Paul?* It is interesting that he does not at this point name Cephas (cf. 1.12; for Apollos see Acts 18.24–28; 1 Cor. 1.12; 4.6; 16.12). Each one is no more than a servant who, through performing *the task which the Lord assigned to him*, that is, through exercising his own charisma from Christ, has been used by God to bring the Corinthians to faith.

3.6   Paul had planted the seed of the gospel and Apollos had watered it, but neither can claim the credit for the crop that followed. Neither here nor in the following verses is there any hint that Paul and Apollos saw themselves as opponents or rivals.

3.7   No farmer would claim to have *manufactured* the harvest of his fields. All that he can claim to have done is to have enabled the potential fruitfulness of the soil to come to fruition. So it is with the Christian mission field. Paul and Apollos have been *simply God's agents* in bringing the Corinthians to faith. Therefore *it is not the gardeners with their planting and watering who count* but only God who makes the seed grow.

These verses express a true modesty but not a false modesty. Paul does not belittle the work done by himself or Apollos but he recognizes that the creation and nurture of faith is the work neither of apostle nor of teacher but of God. As Barrett puts it, 'Apostles are not to be idolized, but they are not insignificant.'[37] It is also striking how strongly Paul affirms the legitimacy of Apollos's ministry as one complementary to his own. He himself could have claimed to have done more than simply sow the seed, since on his first departure from Corinth he had left behind him a numerous community, but here he modestly gives himself the role only of initiator and graciously gives full recognition to Apollos, who had followed him.

3.8   Paul now goes on to make a twofold emphasis. On the one hand, he and Apollos, though exercising different roles, are both engaged in the one mission, so that *they work as a team* – a timely reminder for the partisan Corinthians, who have been playing one off against the other. On the other hand, each is responsible for the work he performs and therefore *each will get his own pay for his own labour*. Exactly wherein that pay will consist will be spelt out in more detail in the next paragraph.

3.9a   For the moment Paul insists once more that he and Apollos are simply *fellow-workers in God's service*. Then, picking up once more the dominant image of the paragraph, Paul declares the Corinthians to be *God's garden*.

In the space of the last four verses the word 'God' has occurred four times – the sign of a theocentric concern that works up to a climax at the end of the chapter. It is God's work in which Paul and Apollos are engaged. It is God who gives the increase. 'For from him and through him and to him are all things' (Rom. 11.36).

'The day in whose clear shining light . . .'
3.9b–17

3.9b   In elaborating the point that he and Apollos have been simply God's agents in bringing the Corinthians to faith, Paul has likened the church to a garden, and himself and Apollos to gardeners. Now he chooses a different image. *Or again*, he continues, *you are God's building.* Some editors make this statement the ending of the previous paragraph.

With the introduction of a new image Paul's thought begins to move in a new direction. The main aim of the previous paragraph was to lead the Corinthians to a proper appreciation of the true place of himself and Apollos in the divine economy. 'We', he has said in effect, 'are simply gardeners in the garden of the Lord.' Now he represents the church as a building, and himself and Apollos and others like them as builders.

3.10   We might expect Paul to develop this image in a similar way, by stressing that they are merely builders and that it is the building which matters. To some extent he does do this. At least, he now makes it clear that the building that is the church is not the work of any one evangelist, even an apostle. *God gave me the privilege of laying the foundation like a skilled master builder; others put up the building.* The REB rendering, 'skilled', is appropriate in the context, but there are also overtones of the usual sense of the word, namely, 'wise'.

3.11   Paul now goes on to stress that the one irreplaceable foundation of the church is Jesus Christ, who is, in a sense, already given. In laying that foundation in Corinth, Paul has shown true wisdom.

It is possible that Paul's solemn declaration in v. 11 has a particular relevance to the Corinthian situation. Whether or not Peter had been at work in Corinth, it is clear that there were people in the church there who were pushing his claims. These people may well have made use of the tradition, preserved in Matt. 16.13–20, that Jesus had renamed him Peter and declared that on this rock he would build his church. If so, Paul's statement would have served as a salutary reminder that no church leader has anything but a strictly subordinate role.

From v. 10b Paul begins to give the new image a new application, thereby developing a hint already given in v. 8b. His main aim in the present paragraph is not to show up the absurdity of any idolizing of the various evangelists who have visited Corinth but rather to warn all would-be builders of the church that the quality of their contribution to the church's fabric will inevitably be exposed for what it is in the final judgement. The kind of judgement he envisages at this point is an exposure of the worth of the work they have done for God. In his elaboration of this picture Paul diverges significantly from some currents in the Judaism of his time.

3.12f.   The demolition of a building exposes to the light of day the various materials that have been used in its construction. In the same way, the day of judgement will expose the quality of each person's contribution to the life of the church in Corinth (the word 'each' is in an emphatic position in the Greek), whether they have built *with gold, silver and precious stones, or with wood, hay and straw* (v. 12). All of these materials were of some use for building, including the last three – wood for roof beams and doors, hay and straw for the roof itself. The last three types of material, however, in contrast to the first three, are all flammable.

The picture of a fire sweeping through a town and destroying everything combustible will resonate very strongly with readers from regions like the southern states of Australia or the western states of the USA, where bushfires are a constant threat during the summer months.

3.14f.   The fire of the divine judgement will destroy everything shoddy. The work of the faithful builder will survive the fiery trial and 'he will have his pay', to quote Goodspeed's version. The jerry-builder, on the other hand, will see his work burn down and suffer some sort of loss or penalty.

The Greek word underlying 'rewarded' in the REB rendering of this verse most commonly refers to wages and should probably be understood in that sense here. Jay Shanor has argued convincingly that, in his development of the building metaphor, Paul has been influenced by the conditions commonly imposed on contractors and workmen engaged in the building or repair of a temple or other public building.[38] It was common practice for final payment to be withheld pending final inspection. Conversely, a builder whose work did not measure up would be fined.

But, even if Paul is drawing on the language of building contracts, the question still remains, What is the nature of the pay/reward that he envisages for the faithful builder, or of the fine/penalty that he envisages for the jerry-builder? Perhaps the reward will simply be the satisfaction of seeing one's work survive, the penalty the mortification of seeing it dissolve in the flames. What is clear is that the reward and the penalty that Paul envisages will not be identical with salvation and damnation, for he states explicitly that even the Christian jerry-builder *will escape with his life, though only by passing through the fire* (v. 15).

It is highly instructive to compare this judgement scene with a similar scene in the Testament of Abraham (chapters 12 and 13), whether or not that work is to be dated earlier than Paul's letter. The Testament of Abraham presents a consistent doctrine of salvation by preponderance of merits. The sins and righteous deeds of each soul are weighed by an angel, and his works are tested by fire. If his righteous deeds outweigh his sins and his works survive the fire, he enters heaven; if they do not, he is sent to hell. Thus the fiery trial determines the soul's eternal destiny.

In Paul's judgement scene, however, there are no scales, and the trial by fire is given a quite different function. It does not now determine the issue of salvation but rather whether Christian workmen will receive some sort of reward or the reverse. Their salvation stands, for that is a matter not of merit but of grace and remains sure, so long as they abide in faith.[39]

3.16f.   After reminding his readers that they are *God's temple, where the Spirit of God dwells,* Paul then issues a further warning: *Anyone who destroys God's temple will himself be destroyed by God.* Here Paul seems to envisage the possibility of a judgement with an outcome more severe than that envisaged in v. 15, namely, the destruction of the wrongdoer. It is understandable that he should envisage a more serious fate for the person who sets out deliberately to destroy the church than for the person who is simply a shoddy builder, but Paul may not have envisaged the total annihilation of such people, so that a better translation might be something like: 'Disaster awaits the person who brings disaster upon the church.'

What is clear is that the punishment will fit the crime. This is a common feature of judgement pronouncements throughout the Bible (see e.g. Mark 8.38; Luke 12.9; Rom. 1.21–32; 1 Cor. 14.38).[40]

This is the first of a number of passages in this epistle in which the theme of judgement comes to the fore. The judgement theme in fact figures more prominently in this epistle than in any other (see 4.1–5; 5.1–5; 6.9–11; 9.24–27; 10.1–12; 11.27–34).

The prominence of this theme is surely directly related to the condition of Paul's Corinthian readers. Again and again we shall find that his warnings are directed at a state of presumption, the illusion that one is free to do whatever one wishes, the state Paul so often describes as that of being 'puffed up'. This word or a cognate is found seven times in the Corinthian epistles (1 Cor. 4.6, 18, 19; 5.2; 8.1; 13.4; 2 Cor. 12.20); elsewhere in the New Testament only in Col. 2.18.[41]

The Christians of Corinth must have found these warnings of Paul's profoundly uncomfortable and disconcerting. Yet they are not his last word. His aim is always to make possible a renewed encounter with the gospel, so that a sounder faith may come to birth.

'All things are yours and you are Christ's'
3.18–23

In the final paragraph of the chapter Paul returns to the dominant theme of chapters 1 and 2, the attainment of wisdom through the renunciation of wisdom. Even more starkly than in the opening chapters he sets out the alternative: either the wisdom of the world or the wisdom that counts in the sight of God.

3.18–19a *Make no mistake about this: if there is anyone among you who fancies himself wise – wise, I mean, by the standards of this age – he must become a fool if he is to be truly wise.* The problem with the Corinthians is that they do fancy themselves wise, just as they think of themselves as having attained to knowledge (8.2) and as being spiritual (14.37). *But the wisdom of this world is folly in God's sight.*

3.19b–21a To reinforce the point that the wisdom of the world is folly in the sight of God, Paul then quotes Job 5.13 and Ps. 94.11: *'He traps the wise in their own cunning,'* and again, *'The Lord knows that the arguments of the wise are futile,'* and then adds: *So never make any human being a cause for boasting.*

3.21b–22 This terse exhortation links the theme of wisdom human and divine with the earlier theme of Corinthian partisanship. Those who recognize that true wisdom is a gift from God know they cannot boast of anything of their own, anything they possess, anything human; their only boast can be the Lord. But those who recognize the characteristic Corinthian partisanship for the folly that it is will

37

also acknowledge the folly of boasting in any human leader. The Corinthians have been saying, 'I belong to Paul,' 'I belong to Apollos,' 'I belong to Cephas.' The truth is, Paul declares, that each one of these leaders belongs to you. All of them are God's gift to you. Indeed, they represent but a fraction of the good things God has in store for you. With a breathtaking comprehensiveness reminiscent of Rom. 8.31–39, Paul then sweeps together *the world, life and death, the present and the future* and reiterates that *all are yours*.

Can death belong to the Christian? Perhaps we could paraphrase Paul's words like this: Anywhere in the world, in life or death, in the present or the future, the inexhaustible grace of God is there for the asking. God will be with us, even in our dying.

3.23 But Paul does not stop there. Had he done so, he would have encouraged the Corinthians to think of the grace of God as overflowing bounty and nothing more. But grace is inseparable from vocation. The truth that *all are yours* must be held in tension with the complementary truth that *you belong to Christ*. Christ is not only Saviour but also Lord. God, the God of the Bible, the God and Father of Jesus Christ, meets us (to use a favourite expression of H. H. Farmer's) not only as final succour but as absolute demand. What is more, it is only through the recognition of God's demand that we are saved from distorted ideas of God's succour.[42]

Furthermore, Christ himself belongs to God. He to whom we belong is himself the obedient Son. As in John, whose Christology is no less exalted than Paul's, Christ remains the one who is sent by the Father and who is utterly devoted to the Father's will.

Thus Paul brings to a climax the theme of belonging initiated in 1.12. The partisanship so prevalent in Corinth is a travesty of Christian belonging. The truth is that at one and the same time *all are yours, and you belong to Christ, and Christ to God.*

Answerable to the Lord alone
4.1–5

Throughout the earlier chapters, but particularly in the last three verses of the previous chapter, Paul has been rebutting an exaggerated estimate of himself and his fellow-evangelists. Now he anticipates the question, 'How then are we to think of you? What exactly is your role in the purpose of God?'

4.1–2   His answer is that *we are to be regarded as Christ's subordinates and as stewards of the secrets of God*. He thus reiterates the christocentric and theocentric emphasis that we have noted at various points, particularly in 3.1–9 and 3.23.

The phrase, *stewards of the secrets of God*, gives some precision to the more general phrase, *Christ's subordinates*, and generates the thought of the rest of the paragraph. The Greek word rendered 'steward' denotes a person (often a slave) entrusted with the management of a household, a business or an estate, and then, by extension, anyone entrusted with responsibility and therefore accountable to others. The essential thing about stewards is that they are not the owners of the property or enterprise which they are managing. They have rather been entrusted with it by another, to whom they remain responsible and to whom they will eventually have to give account. Yet it is the perpetual temptation of any steward, particularly if his master is absent for a long time, to act as if the property he is managing were in fact his own.[43]

Every Christian minister is a steward not of property but of *the secrets of God*. The word that REB translates as 'secrets' is literally 'mysteries' and has already been used at 2.1 and 2.7 to refer to truths too profound for human ingenuity, which God has revealed. In the present context, however, it is not the content of the message with which Christian ministers have been entrusted that is Paul's primary concern but rather the implications of their being stewards of it. If a steward is by definition a person who has been *entrusted* with something, it follows that there is one quality above all that he or she must possess. Stewards are required to show themselves trustworthy (cf. Luke 12.42).

4.3   Furthermore, they must expect to be called to give an account of their stewardship, but to one person and one person alone, their master. Since Christian ministers are 'stewards of the secrets of God', they are accountable to God alone. Let not the Corinthians, with their predilection for weighing up one evangelist against another, be in any doubt about that.

Before the final episode in Paul's dealings with the Corinthian community is complete he will have been deeply hurt more than once by their paying heed to scurrilous attacks upon his person and his apostleship, but at this point he is able to say that all the criticisms or praises that the Corinthians may heap upon him are of negligible moment. *To me*, he writes, *it matters not at all if I am called to account by you or by any human court.* The word here translated 'court' is literally 'day'; the phrase, 'the day of judgement', has evidently suggested to Paul this extension of the word's normal meaning.

4.4 Nor is it Paul's role to pass judgement upon himself. He is indeed confident enough to be able to say, *I have nothing on my conscience*, but the fact that he is not aware of any failures in his ministry does not mean that its worth is thereby established. His judge remains the Lord alone – an expression that could signify God the Father but, in view of the reference in the next verse to the Lord's coming, probably means Christ. Paul's declaration of a clear conscience is surely not to be taken as implying that he has no awareness of sin whatever. His point must be that he is not aware of anything in his dealings with the Corinthians which he now wishes undone.

4.5 If Paul exercises such restraint in evaluating his own work, how much more ought the Corinthians to abstain from rash judgements! *So pass no premature judgement*, Paul writes, *wait until the Lord comes.* Judgement is his prerogative, and he will surely exercise it. *He will bring to light what darkness hides and disclose our inward motives.*

We have already noted in connection with 3.9b–17 how frequently Paul has recourse in this epistle to the thought of judgement. This passage shows something of the liberating effect that this belief had on Paul in that it freed him from dependence on the approval of others. As Barrett observes, 'If Paul had attended to all the criticisms of himself and of his work made within his own churches (to go no further), he would have given up his apostolate.'[44]

The thought of one's whole life being subject to the judgement of God might well appear to be profoundly unsettling. Paul himself acknowledges in this passage that the divine judgement will bring to light hidden intentions of his heart of which he himself is unconscious. And yet he is at peace. As Theissen puts it in an illuminating discussion, 'Paul is "reconciled" with the unconscious which is unknown to him.'[45] The Holy One, who is not mocked (Gal. 6.7), will affirm all that has been praiseworthy.

Given not achieved
4.6–13

Paul now begins to address the spiritual state of the Corinthians more directly and more sharply than he has done hitherto.

4.6 In the previous section he has developed the motif of the coming judgement, applying it directly to the Corinthian situation. The point of v. 6a appears to be that he has applied the preceding argument to himself and Apollos only, omitting other names.

Paul's teaching will have proved disturbing to the Corinthians, but everything he has said has been said for their benefit, with a view to their spiritual welfare, more precisely, that they might *learn the true meaning of 'nothing beyond what stands written'*. Paul's words here are tantalizingly elusive. Written where? In the Scriptures? In the previous part of the letter? Each of these views has its advocates. Some commentators declare the phrase to be incomprehensible or resort to the hypothesis of a gloss by a scribe. Others again find in the phrase an allusion to contemporary methods of teaching young children to form letters by providing them with a model script. The child has to learn how to copy the teacher's letters exactly, making them neither too small nor too large. On this view, the phrase in question would require quotation marks in English translation.[46] The general drift of Paul's statement, however, is clear enough: he has been seeking to restrain certain excesses he has perceived in their common life. Wherein those excesses consist becomes clearer as he proceeds.

Throughout these opening chapters Paul has again and again taken them to task for taking sides *in support of one against another*. The particular way in which he now characterizes their partisanship is highly significant. His aim has been to stop them being *inflated with pride*. The form of the verb implies that this is a danger to which they have already succumbed and that Paul's aim is to stop them carrying on in the same way. Not only have they been making inflated claims on behalf of the leaders of their choice, they have themselves become 'inflated with pride' or 'puffed up', to use the AV rendering.[47]

This word, *physiousthai*, 'to be inflated', 'to be puffed up', triggers off the thought of the rest of the paragraph. As we noted in our comments on 3.9b–17, Paul sees in this condition a major root of the community's malaise. As Paul sees the situation, the Corinthians have over-realized their eschatology. This expression, 'you are inflated, you are puffed up', describes that condition in a nutshell.

4.7   Paul now proceeds to draw a sarcastic contrast between the pretensions of the Corinthians to be something, to have arrived, and the actual situation of the apostles whose disciples they are so proud to be. He begins with a series of abrupt rhetorical questions. Couched in the second person singular, they are addressed to the Corinthian Everyman. There is some uncertainty about the precise translation of the first question, but again the thrust of the question is clear enough. Paul is not denying for a moment the reality of their endowment with the grace of God, to which he has alluded in the opening paragraph of the letter and to which he will return in chapters 12 and 14. What the Corinthians must recognize is that any spiritual endowment they may have is a gift from God, not something to boast of, as if it were their own achievement. *If you received it as a gift*, Paul asks, *why take the credit to yourself?* In the kingdom of God there are no self-made men or women.

4.8   The abrupt questions of v. 7 now lead into a sustained contrast between the way the Corinthians see themselves and Paul's own experience of what it means to be an apostle. As the Corinthians see themselves, they are already blessed with everything God has to give, spiritual millionaires, kings. They have arrived. No need for any more effort. No more painful tension between what they have and what they hope for. *No doubt*, Paul exclaims, *you already have all you could desire; you have come into your fortune already! . . . you have come into your kingdom.*

But there is no mistaking the sarcasm in Paul's tone. If the Corinthians see themselves as kings already, enjoying the kingdom of God in its fullness, heaven on earth, let them count Paul out, and with him every other apostle of the Lord. The reality of apostolic ministry is something far removed from a heaven on earth. It is rather one of ignominy, weakness, dishonour, hardship and persecution.

But Paul is not content simply to set side by side the Corinthians' perception of the Christian life and his own perception of what it means to be an apostle, as if to say, 'Everything has gone your way. I wish I had half your luck.' As he will make clear in 11.1 and even clearer in his second epistle, apostolic existence is Christian existence writ large, and Christian existence is a matter of being conformed to the dying of Christ. Therefore this belief of theirs that they are already in heaven on earth is an illusion. *How I wish*, he says, *you had indeed come into your kingdom; then you might share it with us!*

4.9   Here, in reality, he goes on to say in the following verses, is the royal lot that God reserves for apostles, not to be treated like kings but as the lowest of the low. We are like those condemned criminals who are brought on at the end of a gladiatorial show to fight for their lives either with one another or with gladiators or with wild beasts, *like men condemned to death in the arena, a spectacle to the whole universe – to angels as well as men*. Paul speaks here as if he were one of the participants in a vast gladiatorial show, with angels as well as men and women as spectators.

4.10   Paul now sets side by side once more, with biting irony, the perception of the Christian life entertained by his readers and his own experience of the reality of apostolic ministry: *We are fools for Christ's sake, while you are sensible Christians! We are weak; you are powerful! You are honoured; we are in disgrace!* Words like 'fools', 'sensible', 'weak', 'powerful', put us in mind of 1.25ff., where we learned that God's wisdom, the wisdom of the cross, is folly in the eyes of the world and God's power, the power of the cross, is weakness in the world's eyes. So Paul may be a fool, but he is a fool for Christ's sake, a fool with Christ. He may be weak, but he is weak with Christ. The Corinthians, on the other hand, are perilously near to being on the side of the world.

As Fitzgerald remarks, in a perceptive treatment of this passage, 'The poor, abject apostles have become "fools for Christ" (4.10), a fact that paradoxically indicates their true wisdom (3.18). Yet, from the world's point of view, the heralds of the "moronic message" appear as ludicrous as the crucified Christ whom they proclaim. And this is their vindication, precisely their humiliation.'[48]

4.11   But Paul has not finished yet. *To this day*, he continues, *we go hungry and thirsty and in rags; we are beaten up; we wander from place to place*. Paul is not fantasizing here, even though he is focusing on only one aspect of his life as an apostle. 2 Cor. 11.23–33 shows that he had undergone all kinds of hardship in the service of the gospel.

Nor is Paul listing his sufferings in order to boast of his prowess in enduring the blows of fortune, in the manner of the Stoics. His intention is simply to throw into relief the misery of his outward circumstances in contrast to the self-sufficiency of the Corinthians.

4.12f.   Furthermore, *we wear ourselves out earning a living with our own hands*. The verb here translated 'wear out' often refers in Paul to the specifically Christian task of founding and caring for churches. Not only is he working hard, even to the point of exhaustion, to earn his living, he is doing all this in addition to his specifically Christian service. In the Hellenistic world it was widely held to be an indignity for a moral teacher to have to support himself in this way, and it is clear from a later chapter (9.4–18; cf. 2 Cor. 11.9; 12.13) that the Corinthians themselves were taking exception to Paul's decision to support himself and not accept support.

Paul's experience of apostolic ministry thus stands in the sharpest contrast to the perception of the Christian life that is currently dominant in the church in Corinth. There is also a sharp contrast between the treatment that he and his fellow-apostles receive at the hands of the world and the response they make in return: *People curse us, and we bless; they persecute us, and we submit; they slander us, and we try to be conciliatory.* It is not Paul's intention here to insist on the Christian grace that he and his fellow-apostles have shown in persistently returning good for evil. He is seeking rather to contrast the treatment he and his fellow-apostles have received with the response they have given.

Paul concludes his account of his ministry with two vivid comparisons: *To this day we are treated as the scum of the earth, as the dregs of humanity.*[49] Paul is sparing no efforts to bring home to the Corinthians that their conception of the Christian life is totally at variance with the reality of apostolic ministry. And, as he has already done in v. 11, he insists that his account of apostolic ignominy is true *to this day*, up to this very moment. There can be no happy ending to the apostolic story in this age. The phrase, 'to this day', stands in pointed contrast to the word 'already', which Paul has used in v. 8 to characterize the Corinthian position.

The cruciform nature of Christian existence is set forth equally powerfully in Paul's Second Letter to the Corinthians, this time in contention with scurrilous opponents. As I remark in my comments on 2 Cor. 4.16–18,

> The scars of suffering that Paul exhibits are signs of the reality of his identification with Christ crucified. They are therefore signs that his life is authentically Christian and authentically apostolic. They are not a contradiction of his apostleship, as his enemies maintain; on the contrary, they are its most compelling vindication.[50]

Father or mentor?
4.14–21

In the previous two paragraphs Paul has drawn a most telling contrast. 'This,' he has said, 'is how you see yourselves: as people already blessed with everything God has to give; but this is what it is really like to be an apostle: it is to experience ignominy, weakness, dishonour, hardship, persecution, utter contempt.' If any of Paul's first hearers had ears to hear, they would have been brought up with a rude shock. 'Here we are,' they might have said, 'proudly claiming to be the followers of this or that apostle, looking up to them as our preceptors in the Christian faith, and yet we have been cherishing an understanding of the Christian life that is totally contrary to the facts of their experience. We have been living in a world of illusion.'

4.14   Paul now senses that this may well be the effect of what he has just said, and so he checks himself: *I am not writing this to shame you, but to bring you to reason; for you are my dear children.*

4.15   It is not as their tutor, or, as we might say, their mentor, that Paul is writing to the Corinthians but as their spiritual father. Here the word 'tutor' should be seen as standing in contrast not only to 'father' but also to the word 'teacher'. The underlying Greek word, *paidagōgos*, was used to denote the person, usually a slave, whose duty it was to conduct a boy of good family to and from school and generally superintend his conduct. The word is also used in a somewhat pejorative sense in Gal. 3.24.[51] But Paul is not the tutor of the Corinthians. Nor is he merely their teacher. He is their father, and therefore he has a unique right to address them not as pupils but as his own dear children. However many tutors in Christ they may have, he and he alone can claim to have 'fathered' their life in Christ, for it was he who first brought them the gospel of Christ and initiated them into the new life in him.

In making this claim, however, Paul is not seeking adulation. In v. 15b, where he claims the Corinthians as his offspring and his alone, the phrases 'in Christ' and 'through the gospel' are thrown forward into an emphatic position.

4.16   On the strength of this unique relationship with his readers, Paul now addresses to them a particular appeal. It was he who first led them to Christ; let them continue to look to him as their example of how to live in Christ (the form of the verb implies the continuation of a pattern of behaviour already adopted, not the adoption of a new one).

Taken out of its context, Paul's appeal, 'Be imitators of me', to use a literal translation, might sound like arrogant self-recommendation, but the next verse makes it clear that Paul is urging his readers to imitate him precisely in his following of Christ. This intention is brought out still more clearly in 11.1. It is still significant, however, that he does not urge them simply to be imitators of Christ, as we might have expected in the light of a passage like Phil. 2.5, where he urges his readers to have that mind among themselves which is theirs in Christ Jesus. As new converts, they are to continue following the footsteps of Paul himself, who first set them on the way. As we noted in our discussion of 4.6–13, one of the fundamental convictions of Paul's that comes to expression in this epistle, and still more in the second, is that apostolic existence is Christian existence writ large.

4.17 Paul now tells the Corinthians what steps he is taking to help them further along the way. He is clearly feeling the pain of separation from the church in Corinth and is taking a further step, in addition to writing this letter, in order to overcome it. As we have noted in the Introduction, there was, in the Hellenistic world, a considerable amount of reflection on the functions of letter writing, particularly as a means of overcoming physical separation. The ideal solution would be for Paul to visit the Corinthians in person, but in the meantime he is sending as his representative a trustworthy member of the circle of his closest fellow-workers in the person of Timothy, who is *a dear son* to him and *a trustworthy Christian.* Timothy's high place in Paul's esteem is well attested; see Acts 16.1–3; 19.22; Phil. 2.19–22. Timothy will remind them of Paul's teaching, that which he teaches *everywhere in all the churches,* and not only teaches but also seeks to put into practice. Hence his description of Timothy's mission as being *to remind you of my way of life in Christ* ('in Christ' here virtually means 'as a Christian'). Here we detect once again an underlying confidence in a congruence between his words and deeds which we have already noted in our discussion of 2.1–4 and which will become a central theme of 2 Corinthians.

4.18 In v. 18 there is an abrupt change of tone from paternal address to severe warning. It may well be that the mention of Timothy's forthcoming visit leads Paul to wonder what sort of reaction Timothy will receive on his arrival, and thus recalls to Paul's mind a disagreeable piece of news that has been brought to him by one of his inform-ants. *There are certain persons who are filled with self-importance because they think I am not coming to Corinth.* Evidently Paul had talked about coming to them but had been delayed for some reason, and this was now being held against him. Some of his critics may well have been circulating the report that he was afraid to visit them in person, and that was why he was sending Timothy instead. The word Paul uses to describe the attitude taken towards him by these persons literally means 'puffed up'. It is the same word that is used in 4.6 and that, as we noted above, describes in a nutshell a major root of the commu-nity's malaise. Here the reference seems to be not so much to theologi-cal error as to an attitude of self-importance. It is this which has led them to distance themselves from Paul and belittle his authority.

4.19   Paul's response is decisive: *I shall come very soon, if it is the Lord's will.* Furthermore, this visit will inevitably lead to a confrontation with these dissidents, which will expose what Paul describes as their 'power', that is, the real worth that underlies all the big talk. He will *take the measure of these self-important people, not by what they say but by what they can do.*

4.20   It is not easy to determine the exact force of the following verse: *for the kingdom of God is not a matter of words but of power.* What is clear is that it is linked with the previous verse by the terms 'words' and 'power' and that it is intended as some sort of substantiation of that verse. Paul has just said that his visit will show up whether the dissi-dents have any real power, any real worth, any substance, or whether they are all talk. The appeal to the kingdom of God appears abrupt but probably involves an allusion to v. 8. By making this declaration about the kingdom, Paul may well be hinting that the exposure of the dissidents, to which he has referred, will make it clear whether they are indeed, as they would have others believe, part of the kingdom.[52]

4.21   The chapter, and the whole opening section of the letter, ends with a final appeal. At the beginning of the paragraph, Paul has assured the Corinthians that he is not writing to shame them but out of fatherly concern, but, from v. 18 on, it has hardly been the note of fatherly concern that we have heard but something more like the intent to shame. But that is because at this point Paul is addressing people who have belittled his authority and, in effect, no longer recognize him as their father in Christ. Now he says in effect, 'You have heard me speak with two voices, as a father and as a strict mentor. In which role am I to come to you, *with a rod in my hand, or with love and a gentle spirit? It is for you to choose.'*

It is clear that disaffection is beginning to take root in the Corinthian community and that Paul has already been the victim of a campaign of rumour. Whatever the extent of the trouble, it is but a foretaste of what lies in store. Already, however, we see something of the vigour with which Paul responded to such disaffection. Verses 18–21 could almost be lifted out of the last four chapters of 2 Corinthians. His response may strike us as being unduly sharp, but at least he cannot be accused of being reluctant to face unpleasant facts.

Moral Anomalies in the Church
5.1—6.20

Spare not the flesh, that the spirit may be saved
5.1–5

Paul evidently considers that he has said enough by way of rebuke to the Corinthians for their divisive partisanship, but the problems to which he now turns are not unrelated to the themes of the first four chapters.

Underlying much of the argument of the opening chapters is the question of Paul's authority as an apostle, although that authority has not yet been attacked as openly as it was to be later. In 5.1–13, 6.1–11 and 6.12–20 he singles out three instances of Corinthian conduct that fall far short of what he believes should be expected of a Christian community. In urging the Corinthians to put things right, he strongly asserts his apostolic authority. The theme of authority thus links these two chapters to chapters 1—4.

5.1 The first problem Paul takes up is one of which he has heard a report, presumably either from the three visitors named in 16.17 or from Chloe's people. To his dismay, Paul has heard reports of *sexual immorality, immorality such as even pagans do not tolerate: the union of a man with his stepmother.*

The Greek word underlying 'immorality' is used to cover all types of sexual irregularity. Paul does not call it adultery, which makes it likely that the offender's father was either not living or else had divorced his wife. Paul does not use the word 'incest', so that the woman was probably the offender's stepmother. One's 'father's wife' is a designation in the Old Testament and rabbinic literature for a stepmother. If that is what is envisaged, then such a marriage is forbidden both in the Old Testament (see Lev. 18.8; 20.11) and in Graeco-Roman law.[53]

5.2 What dismays Paul still further is the attitude taken to this irregularity by the Corinthians themselves. Far from going into mourning and turning the offender out of the community, as they should have done, they are actually proud of themselves. Underlying the rendering 'proud of yourselves' is a Greek word that, as we have already noted in our comments on 1 Cor. 4.6 and 4.18, is frequently used by Paul in this letter to characterize what he considers to be the characteristic Corinthian malaise. It appears that the rest of the community were, for the most part, viewing this aberration with complacency, seeing it as a sign of their new freedom as spiritual persons to set aside the conventions and taboos of society.

5.3–5 Though absent in body, Paul has already reached his judgement on how the offender is to be dealt with. When they are *all assembled in the name of our Lord Jesus*, Paul himself being with them in spirit, they are to pass judgement on the offender *through the power of our Lord Jesus* and carry out the sentence.

In declaring himself to be present 'in spirit', Paul evidently has in mind a more dynamic presence than the use of this phrase in contemporary speech would suggest. In the next verse he speaks (in the literal rendering of the RV) of 'ye being gathered together, and my spirit', and seems to think of himself being actually present. It appears that he is thinking of his presence being communicated to them by the Spirit through the reading of his letter.

As for what is to take place at this gathering, the whole tone of the discussion, together with the procedure described, suggest that we are dealing with a judicial act of some kind and the execution of a sentence. Yet it would be anachronistic to think of an ecclesiastical court. What Paul is directing the church to do is to pronounce what he is convinced is the verdict of God and thereby set in motion a process of judgement that will be completed by God. Käsemann traces the origins of this procedure back to the time when the church was dominated by the expectation of an imminent end, a time when prophets were believed to be empowered to announce in advance, and thereby set in motion, the verdict of the Lord in the imminent final judgement.[54] On this view, Paul is acting on this occasion as a prophet, yet the action he calls for is not to be his alone. The community as a whole has to take action.

The sentence Paul enjoins is a severe one but one that envisages ultimate deliverance. They are to *consign this man to Satan for the destruction of his body, so that his spirit may be saved on the day of the Lord.*

The act of consigning the offender to Satan clearly implies solemn exclusion from the community but, more than that, a handing over of the man to the sphere where Satan rules.

The next phrase in v. 5 literally reads 'for the destruction of the flesh'. The precise meaning of the word 'flesh' here, as well as of the word 'spirit', is a matter of some debate. The REB rendering, *for the destruction of his body,* implies physical death, and this view has been accepted by many interpreters, ancient and modern. One argument in its favour is the fact that in Acts 5.1–10 Ananias and Sapphira, who have deceived the Holy Spirit, die as the result of a curse (cf. Acts 12.23). In 1 Tim. 1.20, on the other hand, Hymenaeus and Alexander are *consigned to Satan, in the hope that through this discipline they might learn not to be blasphemous.*

The view that Paul intends the death of the offender is vulnerable on several grounds. It would follow, to begin with, that Paul is using the terms 'flesh' and 'spirit' to mean the physical body and the essential self. But that would imply a dualistic understanding of human nature, according to which body and soul confront each other as opposites. Such an understanding was clearly prevalent in Corinth but is foreign to the unitary tendency of Pauline anthropology.[55]

It would also follow that Paul envisages the Christian community playing no part whatever in the ultimate redemption of the offender, once it has expelled him from its ranks, and that is hard to believe. In 2 Cor. 2.5–11 Paul calls for forgiveness to be shown to someone who has insulted him in a particularly hurtful way. There is no mistaking his concern there that the erstwhile offender be now reinstated, lest he be overwhelmed by his distress.

What then does Paul mean by 'the destruction of the flesh'? According to Paul's normal usage, the words 'flesh' and 'spirit' refer not to a part of the personality but to the whole person considered from two different points of view: the person in his or her creatureliness and frailty, on the one hand; and the person as capable of fellowship with God, on the other. This suggests that 'the destruction of the flesh' refers to the process of doing away with the old self-centred style of life, expressed, in this instance, by an attitude of complacency and self-congratulation. In a similar way, Paul speaks in Gal. 2.19f. and 5.24 of the crucifixion of the *ego* and the crucifixion of the old nature with its passions and desires (cf. 2 Cor. 5.14f.).

But how can Paul be so confident that the act of expelling the offender from the community will produce this effect? There is some reason to believe that he is assuming that the judicial procedure he is recommending will be accepted by the offender in a spirit of penitence. At several points, 1 Cor. 11.27–34 runs parallel to the present passage. In 11.32 Paul writes that *when we do fall under the Lord's judgement, he is disciplining us to save us from being condemned with the rest of the world*. The use of the word 'discipline' implies that the judgement referred to in that passage is not being seen as automatically ensuring deliverance from condemnation at the last day. It will ensure deliverance only if it is effective as discipline, that is, if it brings the church to a penitent acceptance of God's judgement. In the light of this passage, it would seem that in chapter 5 also Paul is enjoining an act of pastoral discipline, in the hope of bringing, not only the offender but the whole church, to its senses.

As Schrage remarks, all the weight of the passage seems to fall on v. 5b. This is the most extraordinary statement in this extraordinary section, namely, that the handing over to Satan is not to end simply with the destruction of the flesh, thus allowing the offender to sink into nothingness, but is to be carried out *so that his spirit may be saved on the day of the Lord*. It is a question of the spirit being saved, by whatever means, from final destruction.[56]

Become what you are – unleavened
5.6–8

Paul now moves to more general exhortation prompted by the reprehensible attitude which the Corinthians have taken up towards the case of the incestuous man.

5.6 Once again Paul alludes to the misplaced pride which the Corinthians have taken in this sign (as they see it) of their new freedom as spiritual persons: *Your self-satisfaction ill becomes you*.

Paul now develops a complex argument to show that what the Corinthians have seen as a sign of new life and freedom is in fact a remnant of the old age. He begins by quoting what appears to be a proverbial saying: '*A little leaven leavens all the dough*' (cf. Gal. 5.9). The image of leaven was widely used to describe something apparently insignificant but capable of permeating and affecting a much larger entity of which it was part. Readers of the Gospels are familiar with the use of the image of leaven to describe a beneficent influence. In literature contemporary with the New Testament, however, the image was normally used to describe a maleficent one. That is how it is used here. The toleration, and worse, shown by the Corinthians to the scandalous situation in their midst is a sign of a moral blind spot which is capable of corrupting the life of the whole community.

5.7   Paul now combines the thought of a moral blind spot acting like leaven to corrupt the whole community with an allusion to the Jewish Feast of Unleavened Bread, which is further interpreted as having been fulfilled in Christ.

Part of the ritual of the feast consisted of cleansing the house of all old leaven. This action is here regarded as a symbol of purging one's life of evil ways. The Corinthians are to *get rid of the old leaven*. The primary reference in the context is to the removal of the incestuous man, but the image is to be given a broader application in v. 8.

The whole complex of Passover and Feast of Unleavened Bread is now represented as a type pointing to Christ and fulfilled in him. Thus Paul can say that *Christ has been sacrificed as our Passover lamb*. Because he is the fulfilment of the old order, the moral cleansing to which the cleansing of the household of old leaven points is already accomplished fact. Therefore Paul can assure his readers that they already are *unleavened dough*.

Yet to leave the matter there would be to reinforce the over-realized eschatology that is the real corrupting leaven in the spirituality of Corinth. And so, in the same breath, indeed before he mentions the corresponding indicative at all, Paul urges the Corinthians to *get rid of the old leaven*, so that they may be what they already are, namely, *a new batch of unleavened dough*. The motif that is so characteristic of Pauline exhortation, namely, 'Become what you are,' is nowhere stated more clearly than here.

5.8   The next verse reinforces the call to live out in practice the new moral life available in Christ, in whom the old order, particularly Passover and the Feast of Unleavened Bread, find fulfilment. The Christian life is here represented as the lifelong celebration of a festival, the festival of unleavened bread of the new order. Like the old festival of unleavened bread, this new Christian 'festival' also calls for a clean-out, a clean-out of *the leaven of depravity and wickedness*, and a commitment to living in *sincerity and truth*.

INDICATIVE AND IMPERATIVE

Attempts have sometimes been made to weaken the force of one side or the other of the Pauline paradox, 'Become what you are.' It has been suggested, for example, that Paul realizes that, while the indicative may be a fine ideal, it needs to be corrected by empirical reality. But there is no hint that Paul is not taking both sides with full seriousness. Christians are actually unleavened (7c). They belong to the new age (Gal. 1.4) and have been freed from the power of sin (Rom. 6.22). And at the same time they are actually and earnestly exhorted to live as new creatures within the old age. Indicative and imperative must be held together.

Indeed, the indicative provides the grounds for the imperative. The conjunction that Paul uses to link the two together in v. 7 is not *although* but *as*. In similar fashion, the Philippians are exhorted to work out their own salvation not *although* but precisely *because* it is God who is at work in them, inspiring both the will and the deed, for his own chosen purpose (Phil. 2.12f.).

Discipline the community; leave the world to God
5.9–13

Paul judges that this is the moment to clarify the intent of an earlier letter that he had sent to Corinth. Part of this earlier letter, usually known as the Previous Letter, is thought by some scholars to be embedded in 2 Cor. 6.14—7.1, though this theory is no longer as popular as it once was.[57] This earlier letter was evidently not written in response to the scandalous situation that Paul has just been discussing, but he refers to it here, because it has a direct bearing on the case. It is also very likely that the Corinthians themselves had referred to Paul's letter in their letter to him. This would explain the rather abrupt introduction of the former letter into the present argument. Indeed, they may well have taken exception to what they took to be its sweeping prohibition of contact with immoral people in general. It is often assumed that their misunderstanding of his letter had been unintentional, but in the light of the reference in 4.18 to people who were belittling his authority, it seems quite likely that some had used the lack of specificity in his letter as a pretext for disregarding it entirely.

Whatever the causes of the misunderstanding, Paul now makes his position unmistakably clear and then proceeds to apply his earlier directive to their present situation.

5.9ff.   In his earlier letter Paul had laid down that the Corinthians *must have nothing to do with those who are sexually immoral.* He now makes it clear that this earlier direction was not meant as a blanket prohibition of contact with *any* immoral person, or, for that matter, with any extortioner or swindler or idolater. Underlying the word 'extortioner' is a Greek word that is widely used both in Classical Greek and the New Testament to describe a person who is shamelessly rapacious and reckless of the rights of others.

To avoid all contact with such people, the Christians of Corinth would have had *to withdraw from society altogether.* But that is not what Paul had meant. The intent of his admonition had rather been that they must have nothing to do with *any so-called Christian* who lived in such a fashion, and he refers to slanderers and drunkards, as further illustrations of the kind of misconduct he has in mind. With anyone like that they should not even eat.

5.12f.   To reinforce what he has just said, Paul now clarifies the area of the church's disciplinary responsibility. It does not extend beyond the Christian community, and he himself disclaims any desire to pass any judgement on those outside it. *God is their judge.*

But the church has the right and the duty to discipline its own members. The responsible exercise of this discipline sometimes calls for the exclusion of an errant member from the fellowship, and it is precisely that sort of situation that the Corinthians are facing now. Appropriating the language of Deut. 17.7, Paul urges them to *root out the wrongdoer* from their community.

Paul's words in this chapter may sound harsh, coming as they do from the author of the hymn to love in chapter 13. What has become of the love that keeps no score of wrongs? Yet the contemporary church urgently needs to be reminded that discipline is an essential ingredient of love.

Consider, for example, the situation of a priest or minister who is found to be guilty of sexual harassment. When such situations have occurred, the reaction of church authorities has all too often been to hush the matter up, counsel the priest or minister concerned to be more careful in future and move him on. Alternatively, they may have treated the offender as a sick person in need of therapy rather than as a sinner who needs to repent. Certainly those who advocated firmer action, closer to that advocated by Paul in this passage, have often been accused of vindictiveness and witch-hunting.

Yet failure by church authorities to exercise effective discipline in such situations really amounts to a failure in love both towards the offender himself, his past and potential victims, and the church as a whole. Bonhoeffer's warning against the corruption of the gospel into a message of cheap grace is as timely today as it ever was.[58]

No litigation before unbelievers
6.1–11

Paul now takes up with the Corinthians another matter about which he has heard an oral report, either from Chloe's people or from the three visitors named in 16.17. He has heard about a member of the church in Corinth going to law before a pagan court to settle a grievance against a fellow-Christian. There is therefore a link with the previous section in that both passages have to do with the exercise of judgement within the community.

As for the occasion of the dispute, the text itself gives us few hints, but the verb translated 'defraud' in v. 8 suggests some sort of property or business dealing. Recourse to the law was habitually practised only by the wealthier members of society. The Roman legal system was, in practice, heavily biased in their favour. Wealthy litigants were able to hire professional orators to argue their case and could also bribe the judges.[59]

6.1 Paul goes straight to the point, expressing his dismay at the thought that anyone in such a situation should have the effrontery, the 'face', to take such action, instead of having the matter resolved within the Christian community.

6.2 Paul now takes the community itself to task for allowing such a thing to happen. What makes the incident the more outrageous is the fact that it is their vocation, as part of God's people, to participate in the judgement of the world.

Literally this verse begins, 'Do you not know that . . .?' – a form of expression that Paul regularly uses to remind his readers of something they already know or ought to know. The fact that Paul uses this rhetorical device ten times in the present letter (see the commentary on 3.6) illustrates once more how defective, in Paul's eyes, was their grasp of Christian truth.

The belief that the people of God are to judge the world is widely attested in Jewish apocalyptic writings and probably stems originally from Dan. 7.22.

Paul now develops an a fortiori argument: *If the world is subject to your judgement, are you not competent to deal with these trifling cases?*

6.3f.   To underline still further the incongruity of the action that the church has allowed to be taken, Paul asks a further rhetorical question: *Are you not aware that we are to judge angels, not to mention day to day affairs?* How, then, when disputes arise between Christians in day to day affairs, can they possibly look for a resolution of the conflict to *outsiders with no standing in the church*? The word here translated as 'outsiders with no standing' is quite a pejorative one, which has already been used in 1.28 to characterize Christians as having no standing in the world, mere nobodies. It is not Paul's intent here to demean the character of pagan judges. His point is simply that Christians own a different allegiance and are called to live by radically different standards from those of the world.

6.5f.   So deeply is Paul upset that he freely avows the motive that, two chapters earlier, he had disclaimed. He is now seeking to shame them.

The irony of the rhetorical questions that follow (there are no fewer than ten in the first nine verses) should not be missed. Here is a community for which wisdom represents its primary aspiration, and yet there is not to be found among them a single person wise enough to give a decision in a fellow-Christian's cause. And so *Christian* has to *go to law with Christian – and before unbelievers at that.* Arbiters had a recognized role in the society of the day, and it should not have been difficult for Christian communities to appoint their own.

6.7f.   Whatever the outcome of such a suit may be, the mere fact of their *going to law with one another at all* represents a defeat, both for the men involved and for the church as a whole. If the very community that claims to be the object and instrument of the reconciliation of God is itself unreconciled, its credibility is called in question.

Paul now addresses more directly the initiator of the legal action, although his use of the plural form of the verb shows that he still has at least half an eye on the community. Would it not be much better, he asks, to submit to wrong and let oneself be defrauded than to take such action? Paul may be recalling here the teaching of Jesus in Matt. 5.38–42, but this is not certain. Similar sentiments are to be found in pagan authors, such as Plato (*Gorgias* 509 c).

The focus of Paul's attention now appears to shift once more, this time to the perpetrator of the original wrong, as he expresses his dismay at the thought of a Christian injuring or defrauding a Christian brother. Once again, however, his use of the plural form of the verb indicates that his indignation is directed equally at the community, which has allowed this scandalous train of events to run its course.

Paul's indignation throughout this passage may seem extreme, but it is the other side of a deep conviction that, as we have said repeatedly from 2.1–5 on, underlies the whole Corinthian correspondence, namely, that the conduct of Christian believers must square with the truth of the message they bear.

6.9f.   Once again Paul uses the formula, 'Do you not know?' (REB: 'Surely you know') to remind his readers of another truth he fears they may have forgotten. This time it is the truth that *wrongdoers will never possess the kingdom of God*.

To drive the point home, Paul then gives ten instances of what he means by 'wrongdoers'. The REB runs items 4 and 5 together under the rendering 'sexual pervert'. The first of these two words can be used to describe someone as 'soft' or 'effeminate', but, in association with the following word, probably denotes the passive partner in a male, same-sex liaison. The second word denotes the active partner in such a relationship, which was usually between an older man and a youth. In the Greek, the echo of Lev. 18.22 is unmistakable. The translation, 'homosexual', however, is anachronistic, inasmuch as there is no evidence that biblical authors were aware of any distinction between homosexual behaviour and a homosexual orientation.

Since the list of wrongdoers has points of contact with contemporary pagan and Jewish lists of vices, Paul may well be using traditional material at this point, but, as the next verse makes clear, traditional material which tallied with his own observation and convictions.

6.11   Paul now goes on to remind his readers that such was the kind of life that some of them were living before their first encounter with the gospel. But they have now been converted, and their conversion meant being cleansed; being sanctified, that is, being drawn into the divine life; being justified, that is, being brought into right relationship with God. The word translated in the REB 'dedicated to God' is traditionally translated 'sanctified', for which see the commentary on

1.2. For 'justification' see the commentary on 1.30. The focus of Paul's thought seems to be the total event of conversion, which included as a matter of course baptism (cf. the expression 'washed clean') and incorporation into God's people. The 'Once . . . but now' pattern is traditional in early Christian exhortation. For a particularly clear example see Ephesians 2.

The implication of this threefold reminder is clear: from such a transforming experience there should flow a transformed moral life. We might well have expected, therefore, an explicit direction to the Corinthians to become what in Christ they already are, but Paul is apparently content to let them draw that inference for themselves. The movement from warning to assurance is a common one in Paul. There is a particularly clear example of this movement in 1 Cor. 10.13. Here too Paul has chosen to end the section with an indicative rather than an imperative, with 'you have been' rather than 'you are now to be'. Nevertheless, it is clear that for him, if not for the Corinthians, grace and obedience are inseparable. Anyone who, having experienced the grace of God, engages in the kind of wrongdoing described earlier in the chapter can only be blind to the meaning of what God has done for them.

Christian materialism: honour God in your body 6.12–20

Paul now engages in a critique of the permissive sexual morality prevalent among members of the Corinthian church. He begins by calling in question the understanding of freedom, as well as of the body, that underlies their practice.

The contrast between successive statements is at times so sharp as to make it highly probable that at these points Paul is quoting slogans current in Corinth, in order to correct them. The REB implies that this is what Paul is doing in vv. 12 and 13, by putting certain words in quotation marks and adding, 'you say'. This is also the view taken by most modern translations and commentaries, though there is some disagreement about the limits of the actual quotations.

6.12 We may take it therefore that v. 12 begins with a statement of a Corinthian slogan, *I am free to do anything.* Having quoted the Corinthian slogan, Paul immediately qualifies it. Yes, I am free to do anything, *but not everything does good.* It is true that the believer is not required to observe certain rules in order to obtain salvation, yet he or she is not free to say of any proposed course of action, 'I don't mind if I do,' and leave it at that. On the contrary, the believer stands under the constant obligation to consider the well-being of the brother or sister, to ask, 'Will this action I am contemplating build up the church?' It is already becoming clear that for Paul Christian freedom is not simply freedom from, although a freedom of that kind is involved, but also freedom for – freedom for the other. This understanding of freedom is reinforced by the later discussion of food offered to idols (see especially 8.8–13).

But Christian freedom must also be limited not only by concern for the other but by concern for one's own true well-being. It is possible to exercise one's freedom in such an irresponsible way that one becomes the slave of another or even of the craving for freedom itself. This possibility is alluded to in the latter part of the verse, in which Paul indulges in a word play that is rendered rather neatly by the REB: *No doubt I am free to do anything, but I for one will not let anything make free with me.*

6.13 The next verse probably begins with the quotation of another Corinthian slogan, referring this time to what one may eat. Some scholars also assign to the quotation the following statement that God will one day put an end both to the belly and to food. On the one reading of the verse, this is Paul's own statement; on the other, it is a statement of the Corinthians, which he does not dispute.

In the second half of the verse Paul affirms that *the body is not for fornication; it is for the Lord – and the Lord for the body*. In the light of the dialogical nature of the argument thus far, it is very likely that Paul is now contradicting a further Corinthian slogan. It seems that the Corinthians were arguing that since the physical body is mortal, sexual relations were therefore a matter of indifference, being of no more importance than what one chooses to eat. Therefore they were free to have relations with a prostitute. As we satisfy the body's need for food, so we may satisfy the body's need for sex.

Implicit in this argument is a dualistic understanding of human personality. According to such a view, the soul and the soul alone is capable of salvation, the body and its functions being of minimal importance, so that one is free to form a sexual liaison with anyone one may choose. The Corinthian response to the message of resurrection, which is the occasion of chapter 15, also seems to have been informed by a dualistic understanding of human nature.

It is significant that, as he moves from the question of food to that of sexuality, Paul introduces the term 'body'. The Corinthians were evidently arguing that, just as food was for the belly, so sex had to do with the sexual organs, and that was that. But Paul says, 'No. Sex involves the *sōma*.' For this critically important word, which is used eight times in the present passage, the translation 'body' is not quite adequate. The rendering 'embodied person' comes somewhat closer to it. The word denotes not just the physical body but the person as capable of relationship. That is why Paul can say that *the body is for the Lord*. Bodily existence, as he understands it, is existence *for* others, existence in relationship.

It is the dimension of relationship with another that differentiates sexuality from eating. Eating is something that affects myself alone. Sexual relationship always involves a partner.

This aspect of Paul's understanding of *sōma*. (body) is stressed particularly by Schweizer and Käsemann. Thus Schweizer speaks of Paul understanding *sōma*. as 'that side of our total existence by which we contact others, meet them, serve them, build up a congregation, or enter into fellowship with the world'; and again as 'man in his openness to God and his neighbours'.[60] Similarly, Käsemann writes of the body being for Paul 'the possibility of communication', and adds, 'As body, man exists in relationship to others.'[61]

At the same time, the aspect of physicality is not lost sight of, so that we might define *sōma* not only as *'the embodied person'* but also as *'the person as embodied'*.

6.14   Furthermore, the body is destined not for extinction but for resurrection, even if, as Paul himself insists in chapter 15, it is to be transformed. It is significant that in affirming the destiny of the body in v. 14 Paul switches from 'the body' to 'us' – a clear indication that by 'the body' he means something like 'the person'.

6.15   Paul now spells out in greater detail the nature of the relationship between the believer's body and Christ, as well as the incompatibility between that relationship and union with a prostitute. The relationship into which the believer enters with Christ is so close that Paul can say that *your bodies are limbs and organs of Christ*. Underlying 'limbs and organs' is a single Greek word traditionally rendered 'members'. There is here a hint of the concept of the church as the body of Christ, which is to be developed in 10.16f.; 11.27–34; and 12.12–31. Here, however, the focus of Paul's concern is not the relationship of the members to one another but rather the relationship of the individual believer to the Lord. The point is that as body, that is, as a person capable of relationship, each believer is drawn into union with Christ and called and gifted to perform a service for the community that Christ indwells. In this sense each Christian 'body' becomes a limb or organ of his 'body'.

The exercise of sexuality also involves 'the body', that is, the whole person with a capacity for relationships. Paul does not advocate an ascetic rule of life for all believers. He does not say that union with Christ is incompatible with any form of sexual union, though some people in Corinth had evidently drawn that conclusion (see 7.1–5). He is affirming, however, that since sexual union involves the whole person, the choice of a partner is of critical importance and that for a believer union with a prostitute is not permitted. Paul does not see any necessity to argue this point. He simply underlines the intolerable nature of such a union by declaring that it is tantamount to taking parts of Christ's body and making them over to a prostitute.

6.16 Using once again the formula, 'Do you not know?' (REB: *You surely know*), Paul now gives a new twist to his argument that sexual union has to do not just with a part of the body but with the whole embodied person. Recalling the text from Gen. 2.24 quoted in Mark 10.8 (and parallels) that *'the two shall become one flesh'*, Paul declares that *anyone who joins himself to a prostitute* becomes one body. 'Body' here means something like a single, interpersonal unity. The REB translation, *becomes physically one with her*, possibly directs attention too much to the physical side of the relationship. Paul's point is not so much that sexual intercourse effects a physical union as that it affects the whole embodied person (*sōma*), by bringing into being a new *sōma*. His argument here requires that 'one body' and 'one flesh' be taken as equivalent.

6.17 Over against that sort of union stands the union into which the believer is drawn with the Lord. It is significant that, although in v. 13 Paul has stated that the body belongs to the Lord, he does not say in v. 17 that 'anyone who joins himself to the Lord is one body' but rather 'one spirit' (REB: *one with him spiritually*). Perhaps Paul wished to make clear that this relationship was not exactly on a par with union with a prostitute. It cannot be his intention, however, to imply that one's relationship with Christ involves only an immaterial, spiritual part of one's personality. That would be quite inconsistent with v. 13b.

At the same time, Paul's choice of the expression 'one spirit' supports our interpretation of the phrase 'one body' in the previous verse. There must be a fundamental similarity between the relationships denoted by these two terms. Otherwise his argument about the mutual incompatibility of the two relationships would not hold. But, if so, then 'one body' can hardly refer to a purely physical relationship; it must, as already suggested, mean something like a single, interpersonal unity, comparable to 'one spirit'.

There are differences, however, in the nuances of 'body' and 'spirit', 'spirit' emphasizing more the person as open to God and open to salvation.

6.18 Having summed up the drift of the paragraph in the terse command, *Have nothing to do with fornication*, Paul now appears to draw a distinction that is not easy to sustain: *Every other sin that one may commit is outside the body; but the fornicator sins against his own body.* The word 'other' is not in the Greek but is deemed to be necessary by many modern translators in order to make sense of the sentence. But how can Paul say that only fornication represents a sin against one's own body? What about the sins of drunkenness or gluttony or self-mutilation or suicide? According to Allo, this problem has occasioned 20 to 30 solutions.[62]

It eases the problem somewhat, if, along with a number of commentators, one takes the statement as yet another slogan of the Corinthians that Paul is quoting in order to contradict it. On this reading of the verse, the Corinthians were saying that the domain of sin lay beyond the merely physical; the physical domain was morally neutral; therefore one could do what one liked with one's body, including visiting a prostitute. By contrast, Paul is asserting that *the fornicator sins against his own body.* We might still argue that there are other ways of sinning against one's own body, while agreeing with Paul that fornication strikes at one's 'body' in a peculiarly direct way. As Byrne has written,

> The immoral person perverts precisely that faculty within himself that is meant to be the instrument of the most intimate bodily communication between persons. He sins against his unique power of bodily communication and in this sense sins in a particular way 'against his own body'. No other sin engages one's power of bodily personal communication in precisely so intimate a way.[63]

6.19 To underline still further the incompatibility of fornication with Christian discipleship, Paul now speaks of the union between the believer and the Holy Spirit. Picking up again a metaphor already used in 3.16, he uses the 'Do you not know?' formula yet again to remind his readers that their body is *a temple of the indwelling Holy Spirit*, who is *God's gift* to them. Some scholars punctuate this verse so that everything is included within the question.

This declaration cuts right across the Corinthian view of the body as destined for destruction and therefore having no lasting significance. As 'spiritual' people, the Corinthians despised everything bodily, but for Paul the presence of the Spirit signifies not the negation of the body but rather its affirmation. Once again, as in vv. 13f., Paul switches from the word 'body' to the personal pronoun 'you'.

As for the relationship of intimacy yet not identity between the Spirit and the risen Christ, see the commentary on 2.10b–16.

6.20 Whether they are viewed as united with Christ or as indwelt by the Holy Spirit, believers do not belong to themselves but to God. To clinch his argument, Paul looks back to the event which effected the transfer: *you were bought at a price*. This reference to a single, costly transaction is clearly an allusion to the death of Christ. It would be pedantic and overliteral to ask, To whom was the price paid?

The upshot is that believers belong 'body and soul', as we would say, but, as Paul says, as bodies, that is, as embodied persons with a capacity for relationship, to God. They are therefore under the obligation to place themselves wholly at God's disposal, for God to cleanse, rule, shape and use. By so doing, they will glorify (REB: 'honour') God in their body.

This final injunction amounts to another pointed attack upon Corinthian dualism. For the Corinthian pneumatics the very idea of glorifying God *in their body* must have represented a contradiction in terms. How could the contemptible body be the means of glorifying God? But for Paul it is precisely in the bodiliness, that is, in the inter-relatedness, of human existence that God is to be served and glorified. It is not surprising that later generations of copyists blunted the force of Paul's position by adding to the phrase, 'in your body', the further words, 'and in your spirit'.

Sex, Marriage and Divorce
7.1–40

Paul now begins to take up in turn the various matters on which the Corinthians had sought his advice in their letter to him. His reference here to their letter is quite explicit. At later points in the letter (five in all) where he begins a sentence with the phrase, 'Concerning this or that', we may reasonably assume that he is picking up further matters that they had referred to him.

Paul appears to begin by disparaging all sexual relations between men and women. A literal translation of v. 1b would read, 'It is good for a man not to touch a woman,' but it is clear that Paul is alluding to sexual relations. In the light of later verses, however, especially v. 3 and v. 7, it is very hard to believe that v. 1 represents Paul's own mind. It is therefore held by the great majority of contemporary scholars that the initial statement in v. 1 is another Corinthian slogan,[64] very probably a quotation from their letter to him. Hence the use of quotation marks in the REB. It is clear from later chapters that the Corinthians had not been content merely to ask for guidance. They had also put their own case, probably in response to Paul's Previous Letter to them, mentioned in 5.9.

The chapter as a whole suggests that considerable pressure was being put on those who were married to dissolve their marriages or at least to abstain from sexual relations with their partner, while those who were engaged or widowed were being pressured not to marry at all. Such pressure could hardly be due to Jewish influence, since marriage was regarded as obligatory for Jewish men. It is rather an expression of an asceticism that is of a piece with the over-realized eschatology and the dualism that we have repeatedly found to be characteristic of Corinthian Christianity. If the Corinthians, or at least the most vocal among them, supposed themselves to be living already the life of heaven, one can understand that they would have seen sexual relations as belonging to the present age, which is passing away. And if they believed themselves to be spiritual persons, one can understand that they would have repudiated the physical expression of sex.

The most striking feature of Paul's response to the Corinthian position is the frequency with which he urges the Corinthians to stay as they are. This note is sounded eight times in the course of the chapter.

In urging this course of action, however, Paul is clearly contradicting the position of the ascetics in Corinth. The label 'ascetic' has often been pinned on Paul himself, but, if our interpretation of v. 1, and the chapter as a whole, is on the right lines, then the label 'ascetic' properly belongs not to Paul but to the Corinthian extremists whose views he is here seeking to correct.

We shall also find in the chapters that follow that, as Paul takes up one by one the other items listed in the letter from Corinth, he takes exception to their position at point after point.

Celibacy and marriage – equally honourable vocations
7.1–7

7.1f. At first sight, the opening verses read like a rather grudging admission of the acceptability of marriage, and of sexual relations within marriage, on the grounds that since people are likely to form illicit sexual relations, if they are forbidden to marry, it is better to let them marry. It is quite likely, however, that Paul has in mind a particular situation that has arisen at Corinth. If there were men who were being deprived of sexual relations by their 'spiritual' wives, it is understandable that some of them should have resorted to prostitutes. It also becomes clear, as the chapter proceeds, that Paul rates marriage more highly than the lesser of two evils (see especially v. 7), and that such reservations as he has about the advisability of marriage stem largely from his conviction that the time is short and the end near (see especially vv. 29–31).

7.3f. The next two verses make it clear not only how highly Paul regards marriage but also how he sees it as a fundamentally equal partnership. He expresses himself with a certain delicacy and allusiveness, but there can be no doubt that in speaking of each giving the other what is due to them he is referring to sexual relations. The fact that some texts read 'the kindness that is her due' instead of 'what is due to her' shows that some in the early church found even Paul's allusive language here too earthy.[65] Paul's position is clear. Husbands and wives have sexual responsibilities to each other. This may seem a rather joyless way of speaking of the consummation of human love, but v. 3 must be read in the light of v. 5, which shows that some were depriving their spouses of sexual relations. Besides, as Fee observes, 'Paul's emphasis is not on "You owe me" but on "I owe you."'[66]

The truth is, Paul continues, that the husband cannot claim his body as his own; it is his wife's.

What is especially striking about these verses is Paul's unqualified assertion of the equality of husband and wife. Each time he addresses himself to both husband and wife, even to the point of tautology and awkwardness. This mutuality is maintained throughout the chapter. Twelve times, in all, the argument alternates between men and women, and each time they are placed on exactly the same footing, with equal rights and duties. Such mutuality diverges sharply from the ethos of the surrounding culture, which tended to see everything solely from the point of view of male rights and convenience.[67]

7.5 It follows that husband and wife should not deny themselves to each other. The verb here translated 'deny' is the same verb that is translated 'defraud' in 6.7f. It refers to the taking away of what rightfully belongs to another.

If husband and wife do refrain from intercourse, it should be first of all by mutual consent. It should also be only for a limited time, in order that they may devote themselves without distraction to prayer, and afterwards they should resume relations as before. Otherwise, because of their inability to control their sexual drive, they may be tempted by Satan to enter an illicit relationship. This verse suggests in passing that there were people in the early church who devoted themselves from time to time to continuous prayer, uninterrupted by other normal pursuits.

7.6 Paul now indicates that something he has just said amounts to a concession not a command. That is to say, it does not represent the ideal, it is rather an attempt to meet them half way. But to what exactly is he referring? Much the most likely view is that he is alluding to the second part of the previous verse, in which he allows abstinence from sexual relations only for a limited time and under strict conditions. The next most likely view is to take 'this' as referring to the whole of the previous paragraph, which would mean that Paul regarded sexual intercourse between husband and wife as the lesser of two evils. Such a reading of the verse is hard to reconcile with vv. 3 and 4, which are quite unequivocal.

7.7   The next verse may again appear to qualify Paul's acceptance of the legitimacy of sexual relations. He would like everyone to be as he himself is, that is, presumably, to refrain from sexual relations, as he himself was evidently doing, either because he was unmarried or, what is more likely, given his Jewish background, because he was a widower. Does this therefore mean that sexual abstinence is the ideal, which only a few are able to attain? It might seem so, but the second half of the verse introduces a decisive qualification of the first half. Paul speaks of each person having *the gift God has granted him, one this gift and another that.*

Underlying the word 'gift' is the Greek word *charisma*, which is central to the argument of chapter 12. What is distinctive about Paul's use of the word in that chapter is the way in which he links *charisma* with ministry, vocation (see especially the commentary on 12.4–11). To receive a *charisma*, according to that chapter, is to receive the empowerment needed to perform a service for the good of the community.

Here too the word *charisma* has clear overtones of vocation. One person has both the empowerment and the calling to live like this, that is, to live a celibate life; the other has the empowerment and the calling to live in another way, that is, in marriage. It follows therefore that marriage should not be regarded as the lesser of two evils, to be entered upon only by those who do not have the inner strength to follow the harder road of abstinence. It is rather the way that some are *called* to follow.

If the Corinthian enthusiasts were proposing that all Christians should renounce marriage, or at least the physical expression of sexuality, Paul here pricks the bubble of their ascetic idealism. Married people should not allow anyone to bully them into thinking that sex is evil or that marriage is wrong in and of itself. If at certain points in this chapter, like v. 7a, Paul expresses a preference for the single state, it is partly because he believes that the time is short and partly because he opts for the extended family of the church rather than the natural family.

It is equally important to note, however, Paul's insistence that the single state may also be a *charisma*. Life as a single person is not, as is implied by so much popular culture, a second-best for those who have the misfortune to be unable to find a partner. Some people are actually called, and empowered, to live a single life.

Better to stay as you are
7.8–11

Having clarified his own response to Corinthian asceticism, Paul now addresses different groups in the Corinthian community in turn: in vv. 8f. the unmarried and widows; in vv. 10f. the married; and in 12–16 'the rest'. With 'the unmarried' Paul seems to be thinking of all categories of unmarried men but particularly, in view of the parallelism with widows, of widowers.

7.8f.   Turning to the first group, Paul expresses a preference for them emulating his own example and staying as they are, that is, without a partner (cf. v. 7a). However, this is not to be taken as a rigid rule. *If they do not have self-control, they should marry. It is better to be married than burn with desire.*

Once again the suspicion is aroused that Paul has a distaste for sexual relations. Does he consider marriage to be nothing better than a second-best option, appropriate only for those who lack the necessary self-control? It may seem so, but the main reason why he prefers the single to remain single will become apparent in vv. 25ff., where he refers to the present as a time of stress before the end.

Moreover, v. 9 almost certainly amounts to a modification of the position of the Corinthian extremists, who were evidently urging those without partners to stay single, however difficult that might be for them. Paul, on the other hand, acknowledges that not everyone has the gift to live as a single person (cf. v. 7).

7.10f.   Paul now addresses those who are married and, in doing so, makes it quite clear that the advice he is now giving is not his but the Lord's. *A wife must not separate herself from her husband . . . and the husband must not divorce his wife.* The change in terminology from 'separate herself' to 'divorce' may be deliberate and may reflect the differences between the legal rights and social status of men and women. Under Jewish law, the rights of a wife to initiate divorce were extremely limited. In Graeco-Roman society, women were legally entitled to divorce their husbands, but in practice only those who were able to support themselves did so.[68]

Once again Paul's directive almost certainly amounts to a qualification of the position taken by the Corinthian extremists, who were evidently urging those who were married either to separate or to practise a purely 'spiritual' marriage without sexual relations.

The Gospels show that Jesus was opposed to divorce among his followers (see Mark 10.1–12 and parallels; Matt. 5.31f.; Luke 16.18), and Paul appeals to his teaching as a counter to the Corinthian position. At the same time, he tries to spell out how the principle enunciated by Jesus is to be applied in practice and does so in a way that exhibits both realism and rigour. *If the wife does separate herself from her husband* – a clear acknowledgement that this may be unavoidable in certain circumstances – *she must either remain unmarried or be reconciled to her husband.* Presumably, though this is not stated, the husband who separates is under the same obligation.

Paul does not alter or weaken the word of the Lord, but at the same time he clearly acknowledges that Jesus's prohibition of divorce may prove, for some, impossible to adhere to. In the face of marriages that have failed or are failing, he does not espouse some metaphysical principle of indissolubility. Faced with the demands of the Sermon on the Mount, no one, whatever their marital status, can imagine they have reached, or can reach, the point where they can say, 'I have done all I ought to do; I am all I ought to be,' without deluding themselves.

Stay with your non-Christian partner – if you can
7.12–16

Paul now addresses a third group, whom he calls 'the rest'. It soon becomes apparent, however, that he has in mind Christians who are married to non-Christian partners. At this point he is not relying on the remembered teaching of Jesus but giving them his own word, in the confidence that he is being guided by the Spirit of God (see v. 40).

Almost certainly the Corinthians had included in their letter to him a question about Christians who were married to non-Christian partners. There must have been many such people in the Corinthian community, as in any missionary situation, and no doubt they were beginning to discover the difficulties inherent in such a relationship. Ought they to maintain the relationship, in spite of the difficulties, or should they separate? It is highly likely that there were voices in the community calling for such mixed marriages to be dissolved, so that believers might not be contaminated by daily cohabitation with pagan partners. What was Paul's mind?

Paul's response is notable for its realism, its flexibility and its evangelical optimism.

7.12f.   First of all, he distinguishes between non-Christians who are willing to continue living with their Christian partners and those who are not. These two situations are quite different, and from the Christian side different responses are in order.

Paul's ruling on the first situation is that the Christian partner must not initiate a separation. This holds both for the Christian man married to a non-Christian wife and for the Christian woman married to a non-Christian husband.[69] The mutuality of Paul's instructions, which we noted in the first paragraph of the chapter, is maintained throughout this paragraph also.

7.14   Paul now offers a reason for this ruling: *the husband now belongs to God through his Christian wife, and the wife through her Christian husband*. Indeed, the same thing is true of the children of such a marriage. They too *belong to God*.

The Greek word here translated 'belongs to God' is translated in the AV 'is sanctified', while the statement about the children is translated 'are holy'. As was noted in the commentary on 1.2, the basic idea denoted by the words 'sanctify' and 'holy' is that of God setting people apart for God's own purposes and drawing them into God's own life. What is unusual about this passage is that the objects of sanctification are non-believers, not Christians. However, it is not necessary to conclude, as some commentators do, that the word is being used here in a sense essentially different from Paul's usage elsewhere. Nevertheless, the emphasis falls very much on the initial act of God setting these people apart. The REB rendering in terms of belonging is therefore an appropriate one. The words of the 'sanctify' word group imply both initiation into a special relationship with God and moral transformation by God. Sometimes the emphasis is on the one, sometimes on the other. Here it is on the relationship.

There is probably also a polemical point to Paul's use of these words at this juncture. The Corinthians could well have argued, in their letter to him, that Christians who continued in a marriage to a non-Christian were allowing themselves to be defiled. No, says Paul, it is not that the believer is defiled by the relationship but rather that the unbeliever is sanctified. As Schrage remarks, in opposition to a bunker- or separation- mentality, Paul trusts the sanctifying power of Christ.[70]

In other words, God works on a person's heart through whatever means are available, before that person responds in conscious commitment. The marriage of a non-believer to a Christian provides God with the opportunity to exercise such an influence, and so the Christian should maintain the marriage, if at all possible, so as to let God have God's way.

This is a passage that depicts in a striking way the prevenience of grace. For this reason it can be appealed to in support of infant baptism. To claim it as evidence for the actual practice of infant baptism in Paul's time, however, would be to outrun the evidence.

7.15   Paul now turns to the case of the non-Christian who *wishes for a separation* from the Christian partner. Their wish is to be granted; *in such cases the Christian husband or wife is not bound by the marriage.* The word here translated 'bound' literally means 'enslaved'. The implication is that persistence in the marriage under such circumstances would amount to enslavement. Heroic self-sacrifice on the part of the Christian partner, in the uncertain hope of converting the non-Christian partner, is not required. At this point Paul exercises a remarkable freedom to adapt the teaching of Jesus in circumstances that Jesus had not envisaged.

It is not certain which sort of marriage partner Paul has in mind when he adds that God's call is a call to live in peace. A partner who wishes to separate or one who is willing to stay? If the former, Paul is saying that it is better to accede to their request than to resist and provoke strife. If the latter, he is urging his readers to preserve their marriages in the hope of their partner's eventual acceptance of the gospel. In view of v.15a, the former interpretation seems more likely.

7.16   Paul ends with a further expression of confidence in the sanctifying effect that Christians may have upon their non-Christian partners. Ultimately it is only God who can save anyone, but those Christians who are able to sustain the relationship with their non-Christian partners have reason to hope that, by so doing, they are providing a channel through which God's saving grace may flow. Thus the paragraph ends on a note of evangelical optimism. Once again, man and wife are treated throughout the entire passage as complete equals.

Stay as you are (if you can) is a good general rule
7.17–24

Again and again in the previous paragraphs, as well as in the paragraphs which follow, we hear Paul enunciating the maxim, 'It is a good thing to stay as you are,' and this in opposition to the enthusiasts of Corinth, who held it to be more in keeping with their new 'spiritual' existence to change their present status. At the same time he does not treat this maxim as a rigid rule. In the rest of the chapter Paul applies the maxim to his readers in respect of their marital relationships. In the present paragraph Paul gives the maxim a different application. The distinctions he now has in mind are not those between married and single or male and female but between circumcised and uncircumcised and between slave and free. Once again, however, the maxim, 'Stay as you are,' is not applied in a rigid fashion, at least in relation to slaves. At the same time Paul goes out of his way to minimize the differences between the components of each pair. The linking of male and female, Jew and Greek, slave and free person, echoes Gal. 3.28, which is widely held to be a pre-Pauline formula.

7.17 Paul begins by stating the principle that has underlain his advice so far. Whatever their condition may have been, when God called them, they should continue in it. Indeed, they should accept it as *the lot which the Lord has assigned* to them, as the sphere which God has appointed for the living out of their calling. Here, as throughout the paragraph, conversion is envisaged as a response to God's call to commitment in Christ.[71]

Paul adds that this is the rule he gives in all the churches. This is one of four passages in this letter in which he appeals to what is happening in other churches, no doubt in order to make the point that it is the theology and practice of the Corinthians that are eccentric, not his own.

7.18 The rule, 'Stay as you are,' is now applied to the distinction circumcised/uncircumcised. This is the only time in this chapter that Paul gives this ruling without allowing for any exceptions.

7.19 Paul also reinforces his ruling by minimizing the importance of the distinction. *Circumcision or uncircumcision is neither here nor there; what matters is to keep God's commands.*

Any Jewish reader would have been mystified, if not horrified, by this statement. Was not circumcision commanded in Scripture? How then could Paul place it in opposition to keeping God's commands? Was it not the God-given sign of membership of God's people? How could Paul declare it to be 'neither here nor there'? But for Paul this represents a fundamental principle, reiterated twice in different words in Galatians (5.6; 6.15). The one thing needed for membership of God's people is now faith in Christ. But faith in Christ is not antithetical to obedience but expresses itself in keeping the law as redefined by Christ, that is, in keeping the law of love (see Gal. 5.6; Rom. 12.8–10).

7.20f.   After a further formulation of the principle already enunciated in v. 17, Paul now applies it to another distinction, the distinction between slave and free, but not without qualification.

The main thrust of his advice is, as before, that it is better for people to stay as they are, but, no doubt in order to avoid any suggestion that slaves are free to choose their status, he varies his form of expression and counsels the slaves among his readers not to let their status trouble them.

The latter part of the verse is understood by the REB translators as a qualification of what has just been said. Hence their preferred rendering: *though, if a chance of freedom should come, by all means take it.* But it is grammatically possible to understand this clause as intended to dissuade a slave from seeking freedom. Hence the alternative rendering in the REB footnote: *but even if a chance of freedom should come, choose rather to make good use of your servitude.* Scholars and translators have been fairly evenly divided on this issue, but, in our judgement, Fee has shown that a stronger case can be made for the option for freedom.[72]

7.22   Once again, as in v. 19, Paul now minimizes the importance of the distinction to which he has just referred. The truth is that when any slave is called, he or she becomes the Lord's freed person, and, equally, when a free person is called, he or she becomes Christ's slave. Each person belongs to Christ and each is called to 'the service which is perfect freedom'.

7.23   Paul probably has both of these groups in mind in making the further comment, *You were bought at a price*, since the word 'bought' could apply either to purchase for freedom or purchase for service as a slave. But the point still holds that in Christ both groups are both free and enslaved; free precisely because they have become the slaves of Christ. It follows that they must not allow themselves to become slaves of any human being.

7.24   There is at the moment no urgent necessity to develop the preceding admonition, though this will no longer be true in the later stages of the Corinthian correspondence, and so Paul concludes by reiterating once again the general principle: *everyone is to remain before God in the condition in which he received his call.* The last phrase is a further reminder that what matters is that we all belong to God and are to live as in God's presence.

Sit lightly to everything – the world is passing away 7.25–31

Paul now returns to marital issues, after the broader discussion of the previous paragraph. The use once more of the phrase 'About...' indicates that he is responding again to a specific question raised by the Corinthians in their letter to him, but this is one of the passages where our lack of access to the Corinthian letter proves most frustrating. More than ever we feel that we are listening to one half of a conversation.

Paul has already counselled those who are married, those who are unmarried and those who are widowed. The word he uses to designate the group he now has in mind is usually translated 'maidens' or 'virgins', but its precise meaning here has been much debated. One view that has been quite widely held is that Paul is referring to couples who had committed themselves to each other in a spiritual marriage and were living together but without sexual relations.

While there is evidence of this practice in subsequent centuries, there is no firm evidence for it at this early stage, and on balance it seems more likely that Paul is referring to young women who were betrothed. If, as we have argued, Corinthian spirituality had an ascetic bias, such women, along with their fiancés, would have been under pressure not to go through with their marriages. It seems reasonable to assume that the word 'virgin' is being used in the same way in vv. 34 and 36–38.

7.25   In turning to this group, Paul stresses that he has no direct command from the Lord but is offering his opinion *as one who by the Lord's mercy is fit to be trusted.* It is a striking fact that he should appeal to his experience of the Lord's mercy as authenticating his advice in the present instance. The assumption seems to be that one who has been so signal a recipient of Christ's mercy as he has been can be trusted to give merciful, that is, humane advice.

7.26   Paul now gives the substance of his advice in the form of the very general statement that it is best for people to stay as they are. There is an awkward repetitiveness about the sentence in the Greek, which makes it likely that, as in 6.12f. and 7.1, he is quoting words used by the Corinthians themselves.

These words express Paul's own position, already stated in the earlier part of the chapter, but, as he is to make plain in vv. 28, 36 and 38, for him it is a matter of preference not, as it evidently was in some circles in Corinth, of rigid rule.

Moreover, Paul's position rests on different assumptions from those that shaped the Corinthian position. One of these is indicated by his reference to *a time of stress like the present*. This appears to be an allusion to present sufferings understood, in accordance with apocalyptic thought, as the necessary prelude to the end. Paul's thought is controlled here by the thought of the imminence of the Day of the Lord. B. W. Winter has drawn attention to contemporary evidence of a severe grain shortage in Corinth at this time, and has suggested that Paul could well have seen this shortage as one of the hardships that were to precede the end.[73] Paul's point is that, in the light of the sufferings that Christians have, of necessity, to undergo before their final redemption, who needs the extra burden of marriage?

7.27f.   With v. 27 the question arises once again, Who is it exactly whom Paul is now addressing?

The REB implies that he is addressing the married and the divorced, but, if so, v. 28 becomes impossible to reconcile with v. 11.

More widely accepted is the view that he is now speaking in general terms to the married and the unmarried.

But it is also possible and, in our judgement, more likely that he is still speaking directly to the situation we have posited behind vv. 25f. The word 'loosed' is commonly used in the papyri for discharging someone from the obligations of a contract. This being so, Paul could be addressing first of all men who are under obligation through betrothal to a woman and then all who are free from such obligations, that is all who are single.

Paul's advice to both these groups is that it is better if they stay as they are, but once again he qualifies this advice. Anyone who does marry is not doing anything wrong. This may seem like a grudging concession on Paul's part, but it is likely that he is picking up Corinthian language and contradicting it. People who do decide to go through with marriage are to be affirmed in their decision, not made to feel guilty.

Paul's overriding concern in counselling them to stay as they are is the desire to spare them hardship, and *those who marry will have hardships to endure.*

7.29–31   Paul now states in more precise terms than he has used so far the reason why it is better for people to stay as they are, whatever their present condition: *the time we live in will not last long* (v. 29); and again: *the world as we know it is passing away* (v. 31).

In between these two statements about the impermanence of the present world we have a moving description of what should be the effect on believers of living in the brief interval before the End. Recognizing the impermanence of every relationship, every mood, every possession, they should sit lightly to all these things and live 'as though they had not'.

It cannot be Paul's intention that these 'as if' clauses be taken literally. He cannot mean that husbands and wives, for example, should from henceforth live a celibate life. That would contradict what he has already said clearly in vv. 2–6. The fourth and fifth admonitions demonstrate Paul's intent most clearly. Believers may continue to buy the goods they need, but they are not to hold on to their possessions with clenched fist, so to speak. They are to use the things of the world but not squeeze them out to the last drop. They are to live in the world but not allow themselves to be totally absorbed by it.

With its encouragement to look not to the things that are seen, which are transient, but rather to the things that are not seen, which are eternal, this passage must have brought hope again and again to believers who found themselves trapped in a seemingly hopeless situation. However, people who have lived through times of persecution may well wish to modify Paul's conclusion, on the grounds that suffering of any kind can be faced more easily, if one is living in a committed partnership rather than as a single person.

Free from other cares, caring for the things of Christ
7.32–35

7.32f.   The main thrust of the next four verses is that it is better for those who are not married to stay as they are. It is primarily this group that Paul appears to have in mind at this point rather than the whole community, but, since he has just been addressing the whole community, the 'you' of v. 32a should probably not be limited to the unmarried. Paul wants all of them to be *free from anxious care.*

The Greek noun used here, *merimna*, is cognate with the verb used in the section of the Sermon on the Mount in which the disciples are bidden not to be anxious (Matt. 6.25ff.). These Greek words can have both a positive and a negative meaning, denoting both a legitimate concern and a distracting and debilitating anxiety. In the following verses Paul appears to have deliberately exploited this ambiguity, which partly accounts for their difficulty. He wants them to be free from *merimna* in the sense of distracting anxiety, so as to be able to make the things of the Lord the focus of their *merimna* in the sense of their undivided concern.

This is difficult for the married man, who is inevitably *concerned with worldly affairs*, namely, how to please his wife, so that *he is pulled in two directions*. The unmarried man, on the other hand, is free to concern himself with the Lord's business, with pleasing him. Certainly, being single does not automatically ensure that one will so concern oneself, but at least one is free to do so.

7.34 Paul now draws a similar contrast between the situation of the unmarried woman or betrothed virgin (literally, 'virgin', but the meaning seems to be the same as in vv. 25–28) and that of the married woman. The former *is concerned with the Lord's business*, with being *dedicated to him in body as in spirit*, whereas the married woman, like the married man, is concerned with worldly affairs, with pleasing her husband.

Paul's point appears to be simply that married people 'have more things on their plate', so to speak. There are more demands upon their concern. It is in this sense that they are 'pulled in two directions'.

If this correct, Paul seems to be falling short of the insight expressed in v. 7, namely, that for some people marriage is a *charisma*, a state to which they are both called and empowered. If marriage can be a *charisma*, how can Paul contrast a concern to please one's wife with concern for the Lord's business? If marriage is my *charisma*, or at least part of it, am I not concerning myself with the Lord's business precisely by caring for my wife?[74]

7.35 Paul now makes it quite clear that, in speaking like this, he is simply giving the Corinthians the advice that he thinks to be in their best interests. He has no wish to keep them *on a tight rein*, that is, to put a halter around their necks. At this point he borrows from the language of hunting or warfare an expression that evokes the image of lassoing an animal or an opponent in order to catch or immobilize them.

In disavowing any such intention, Paul may well be drawing an implicit contrast between his own practice and that of the dominant party in Corinth. We can well imagine them laying down the rigid rule that anyone who married was acting in an unspiritual way. Not so Paul. His overriding concern is that their behaviour should be above reproach and that they should adhere faithfully to the Lord without distraction. His own opinion is that, especially in the present crisis, this is easier for those who are unmarried, but he refuses to lay down any law.

All are winners, but especially the single
7.36–40

Paul now addresses directly once again those who are engaged to be married, and makes it crystal-clear that they do indeed have two options open to them. He has already expressed a preference for people remaining single and he continues to hold that opinion, but let no one suppose that he is forbidding, or even discouraging, marriage. His advice to widows is similar.

7.36   Paul considers first the case of the man who is engaged and who *feels that he is not behaving properly* towards his fiancée, by not going through with the marriage. It makes best sense to assume that the word 'virgin' is being used here in the same sense as in vv. 25, 28 and 34, but other interpretations have been held and are reflected in some of the versions.

Paul then describes more precisely, in a second if-clause, the sort of man he has in mind: it is one who finds that *his passions are strong and something must be done*. This expresses what seems to be the meaning of a Greek word not found anywhere else, but the clause can be construed as referring not to the man but to the woman and to a woman who is past her prime, no longer in the bloom of youth. This interpretation is also reflected in some versions, such as the AV.

Whatever the status of the woman may be, Paul's direction to the man is clear: *let him carry out his intention by getting married; there is nothing wrong in it*. Once again Paul is almost certainly countering the more rigid position of the dominant party in Corinth, which appears to have been actively discouraging marriage.

7.37   Paul now considers, by way of contrast, the situation of the man who is also engaged but has decided in his own mind to respect the virginity of his fiancée and is standing firm in that resolve, being under no compulsion ('compulsion' seems better than 'obligation', as in the REB) and having his own desire under control. Such a man will do well to refrain from going through with the marriage. However, the way in which Paul piles up synonyms as he describes the man for whom such a course of action is appropriate shows that he is well aware of its difficulty. His own preference is for celibacy, but he does not underestimate the strength of the natural desires and drives. His repeated insistence that such a man should be convinced *in his own mind* is also evidence of the pressure to which such men were being subjected in Corinth from those of a 'spiritual' persuasion.

7.38 Summing up his stance on the issue, Paul affirms that both options are open to the Christian man. Neither entails sin. Both he who marries and he who refrains from marrying are doing well, but he who refrains will do better.

We would be doing Paul an injustice, however, if we described him as representing one state as inherently better than the other. It is primarily his conviction that the time is short and the end near that leads him to prefer the single state.

7.39 In the final two verses of the chapter Paul offers similar advice to widows. He has already affirmed the binding nature of marriage in v. 11. Now he makes it clear that the wife is subject to this bond as long as her husband is still alive. *If the husband dies, she is free to marry whom she will.* Only let the marriage be *within the Lord's fellowship.* The literal rendering of the RV reads: 'she is free to be married to whom she will; only in the Lord', but Paul is almost certainly recommending the choice of a partner from within the Christian community.

7.40 Once again Paul expresses his preference for the single state. His own opinion is that the widow will be better off (literally, 'happier') as she is. By choosing the word 'opinion' (already used in v. 25), he makes it clear once again that he has no wish to impose a law. Nevertheless, he is confident that his opinion is informed by the Spirit. The words 'I too' are probably added with a view to the claim being made by the Corinthian Christians to be Spirit-filled. Paul does not deny their claim but he is firm in asserting his own.

Food Offered to Idols
8.1—11.1

Was it, or was it not, permissible for a Christian to eat meat that had passed through sacred rites in pagan temples? This was an issue which was not confined to the church in Corinth. In Rev. 2.14 and 20 the churches of Pergamum and Thyatira are taken to task for 'eating food sacrificed to idols' (cf. Acts 15.28f.).

The modern reader may well be inclined to regard this as a question of cuisine, with no bearing on faith, but it was not so for the Christians of Corinth. Most of the meat available for purchase came from animals that had been offered on the altar of a pagan god. Whatever was left over, after portions had been set aside for the gods, the priests and the person making the offering, was sold in shops. It is sometimes said that all of the meat available for purchase had passed through a temple, but 10.25 and 28 imply that not all of the meat available for consumption was derived from such a source.

Moreover, it is no exaggeration to say that the whole public and social life of a city like Corinth had a cultic setting. State festivals were regularly associated with meals in honour of the gods. Indeed, business, social and family life at all levels was bound up with cultic meals. Archaeologists have uncovered the ruins of dining rooms attached to temples, which could be used for private parties.[75] It appears that these facilities were widely used by people who had something to celebrate, in much the same way as we nowadays would go out to a restaurant. Probably most of the Gentile Christians of Corinth had been attending such banquets all their lives.

The poorer members of the Corinthian church, however, will have had fewer opportunities to participate in such occasions. For them, meat was a luxury, and they survived mainly on grains, whereas, for the wealthier members, participation in temple banquets will have been a regular part of their social life.

For Jews, there was no issue. All branches of Judaism were united in their rejection of meat that was connected in any way with pagan worship. Moreover, they were permitted by the civic authorities to slaughter and sell their own meat. No doubt there were in Corinth Jewish Christians who argued that the prohibitions to which Jews were subject were also binding on the church. It also seems clear, however, that their position was repudiated by other 'enlightened' members of the church, on the grounds that an idol has no real existence. The fact that these temple banquets were both religious and social occasions at one and the same time must have complicated the issue considerably.

Paul raises the issue now in response to their letter, but the combative tone of his response makes it unlikely that they had simply asked for his advice. Besides, there is, as we shall see, reason to think that he is quoting slogans of theirs, which would imply that they had already advanced their own opinions on the matter. What seems most likely is that he had spoken against the eating of meat in his Previous Letter and that in their letter to him they had taken exception to his prohibition.

Paul deals with this problem directly in chapters 8 and 10, and indirectly in chapter 9. In 10.1–22 it seems clear that he is prohibiting participation by Christians in any cultic meal, on the grounds that such participation involves partnership with demons. In 10.23—11.1, however, it seems equally clear that he is addressing a different aspect of the problem, namely whether Christians were free to eat sacrificial meat that had been sold in the marketplace and was being served at a meal in a private house. His judgement on this issue is much more permissive: Christians are free to eat such meat, unless someone else present at the meal draws attention to its connection with pagan sacrifice.

Which aspect of the problem then is Paul dealing with in chapter 8? Many scholars have taken the view that he is primarily concerned here with the problem of marketplace food, but this view labours under serious difficulties. For one thing, v. 10, the only reference in the chapter to actual practice, refers to participation in a cultic meal in a temple. Besides, the tone of chapter 8 is much less permissive than that of 10.23—11.1. Whereas in chapter 8 Paul discourages the eating of the food in question, in 10.23—11.1 he actually encourages it, unless someone points out that it has been offered in sacrifice. It seems therefore that in both 8.1–13 and 10.1–22 Paul is addressing the one issue, namely, whether Christians have the right to participate in cultic meals.

It is very likely, however, that there was considerable variation in the degree to which such meals had a distinctly religious focus. Some of the meals to which Christians were invited in the precincts of the god Asclepius, for example, will have been expressions of gratitude for healing from sickness, while others will have been primarily social occasions. This may account for the difference in tone between Paul's advice in 8.1–13 and 10.18–22. In 8.1–13 he seems to regard the incident that he envisages as harmful only in so far as it could cause distress to a 'weak' fellow-Christian, whereas in 10.18–22 he represents the mere act of participation as intrinsically harmful, in that it brings the participants into partnership with demons.

The primacy of love over knowledge
8.1–6

8.1   The similarity of the opening phrase of the chapter to the opening of 7.1 makes it clear that in broaching the question of meat offered to idols Paul is addressing a further problem that the Corinthians had raised in their letter to him. However, he does not proceed immediately to tell the Corinthians whether they are free to eat such meat or not. He begins rather by affirming some fundamental ethical principles, in conscious correction of what he perceives to be the characteristic Corinthian standpoint.

Of course, he says at the outset, *'We all have knowledge,' as you say*. Literally, v. 1 reads, 'Concerning things sacrificed to idols, we know that we all have knowledge.' The formula, 'We know', is one that Paul uses in several letters in passages where he is stating what is or ought to be common ground between himself and his readers (cf. Rom. 2.2; 3.19; 7.14; 8.22, 28; 2 Cor. 5.1). The REB therefore is justified in treating it as a quotation of a Corinthian slogan.

The REB translators have detected a further quotation in v. 4, again with good reason. We can surmise that, in their letter to Paul, the Corinthians had made, in effect, the following statements: 'We are free to eat meat, for we all have knowledge and know that no idol has any real existence in the world and there is no God but one.'

How, it may be asked, could they have said, 'We all have knowledge,' when they represented only a part of the Corinthian community? Perhaps their answer to this question would have been, 'All ought to think as we do, and anyone who is weak needs to be enlightened.'

But Paul immediately goes on to qualify severely the value of knowledge: *Knowledge inflates a man, whereas love builds him up*. The word here translated 'inflate' is one which has already been used four times in this letter (see 4.6, 18, 19; 5.2) and which we have seen to express in a nutshell a major cause of the community's malaise. As for knowledge, it is abundantly clear from the opening chapters of the epistle what store the Corinthians set by wisdom. It is likely that they set equal store by knowledge. Thus wisdom and knowledge are singled out for special mention in the thanksgiving in 1.5.

8.2   Here Paul makes a further qualification of the worth of knowledge: *If anyone fancies that he has some kind of knowledge, he does not yet know in the true sense of knowing*. The tension between these two statements in vv. 1b and 2 and Paul's initial concession in v. 1a that 'we all have knowledge' confirms the supposition that in v. 1a he is quoting a Corinthian slogan.

Verse 2, however, leaves the reader with a question. If the person who fancies that he has knowledge does not have the real thing at all, how is true knowledge to be attained? Furthermore, what sort of knowledge is Paul talking about? It is a natural presumption that he is talking about the knowledge of God, but that has not yet been clearly stated.

8.3   These questions are all clarified by v. 3: *But if anyone loves God, he is known by God*. Now it becomes clear that Paul is talking about the knowledge of God. It is also made clear that it is the person who loves God who truly knows God. It is significant, however, that Paul substitutes for the active voice, 'knows God', the passive, 'is known by God'. The truth is that whatever knowledge we have of God is due to God's loving initiative. Thus it can be said both that we love God only because God first loved us and that we know God only because God first knew us. Paul has welded these two thoughts together in a short epigrammatic sentence. The second verb literally means, 'has been known by God', the perfect tense denoting a present state resulting from a past action. For a similar statement of the dependence of our knowledge of God on God's knowledge of us see Gal. 4.9. In both passages the word 'know' carries overtones of choice, intimacy and engagement consistent with its use in the Old Testament. The Corinthians surely needed to be reminded of this truth, given the high premium they obviously put upon knowledge of an intellectual rather than an ethical kind. No doubt they considered such knowledge to be the only arbiter in ethical problems. But just as Paul redefines the meaning of 'wisdom' in the opening chapters, so here, at least by implication, he redefines the meaning of 'knowledge'.

8.4f.   Here Paul turns to the particular issue named in v. 1: *Well then, about eating this consecrated meat: of course, as you say, 'A false god has no real existence, and there is no god but one.'* Once again Paul uses the formula, 'We know', and once again the REB interprets this as a sign that he is quoting a slogan of the Corinthians themselves. It is not immediately apparent, however, whether the statement of v. 4, with its clear denial of the existence of pagan gods, does in fact express exactly Paul's own position. Verse 5a appears to echo this denial by speaking of *so-called gods, whether in heaven or on earth*, but v. 5b appears to concede that they do have a real existence and are not mere fictions or projections.

8.6   A single short phrase at the beginning of v. 6 helps to clarify Paul's position, the phrase 'for us'. 'For us' there are no other beings in heaven or earth that may rightly be called God or Lord, apart from God the Father and the Lord Jesus Christ, but for others such beings do exist. There are the gods of traditional Greek religion, Apollo and Dionysus and the like, and also 'lords', by which term Paul evidently means the deities of the mystery cults. The devotees of these religions and cults, Paul implies, *confer* divinity on these figures by worshipping them.

May we also say that they confer *reality* on them by believing in them? The latter statement does not seem to be a correct statement of Paul's position in the light of chapter 10, where he clearly states the belief that anyone who participates in a heathen rite is not simply engaging in something meaningless but is, on the contrary, in touch with some sort of power. And yet in this chapter Paul insists with great emphasis that there is only one God, namely, the Father, and only one Lord, namely, Jesus Christ.

This verse is of particular interest because of the light it throws on Paul's Christology. By his choice of prepositions, 'from' and 'for' being applied to the Father, 'through' being reserved for Christ, he makes a clear distinction between the roles of Father and Son. Indeed, he refrains from calling Christ God, and yet clearly places Christ on the other side of the dividing line between God and humanity. Thus he ascribes to Christ the role of mediator in both creation and redemption, yet without any sense of incompatibility between such a belief and the affirmation of one God.

The practice of love
8.7–13

8.7 Paul has just conceded the truth of the position maintained by the 'enlightened' Christians of Corinth, namely, that *a false god has no real existence*. He now points out that *not everyone possesses this knowledge*.

Here Paul seems to be alluding to Christians who believe with the top of their minds that an idol is no god but are not yet able to believe this truth with the bottom of their hearts. If such Christians act as if they had fully assimilated this truth, the effect upon themselves will be not only distressing but destructive. Whatever their heads may tell them, their hearts will continue to believe that the meat they are consuming has been consecrated to an idol and that the mere act of consuming it amounts to participation in an idolatrous rite. Such Christians cannot eat such meat without violating their conscience or, as Paul puts it, without their conscience being defiled.

8.8 To be sure, Paul continues, it is not that the meat in itself automatically has this destructive effect upon anyone who eats it. Stating the point in general terms, he concedes that *food will not bring us into God's presence*, so that *if we do not eat, we are none the worse, and if we do eat, we are none the better*. Nevertheless, for some Christians, those whose conscience is 'weak', such meat is not mere meat but meat which is inseparably associated with pagan worship.

In insisting on this point, Paul shows a remarkable insight into the power of belief to determine the effect of an action on the person performing it.

'But surely,' Paul's readers in Corinth may have objected, 'this business about the meat being consecrated to an idol is all in the minds of these weak brethren.'

'Certainly,' Paul replies in effect, 'it is they who confer destructive power upon the meat by their residual belief, just as pagans confer divinity upon gods and lords many by worshipping them, yet that destructive power is real nonetheless.'

8.9 Enlightened Christians must therefore take heed that their liberty to eat whatever is set before them, say, at a temple banquet *does not become a pitfall for the weak*. The way Paul speaks of 'this liberty of yours' suggests that he is picking up a Corinthian catchword, and indeed the verbal counterpart to the noun denoting 'liberty' that is used here occurs in the Corinthian slogan cited in 6.12, 'I am free to do anything' (cf. 10.23). For the Corinthians liberty had become the highest good; for Paul it is love, love that freely renounces rights for the sake of others.

8.10 Here Paul describes how the thoughtless exercise of one's own liberty may lead to the downfall of a fellow-Christian. *If one of them (the Christians of weak conscience) sees you sitting down to a meal in a heathen temple – you with your 'knowledge' – will not his conscience be emboldened to eat meat consecrated to the heathen deity?* This verse shows that there were Christians in Corinth who not only ate the meat in question either at home or with their friends but also took part in meals in the temple precincts. Paul evidently has in mind meals eaten in the temple restaurant. The weak would not be likely to go into the actual sanctuary and see the strong sitting there.

8.11 Paul now describes the effect of such thoughtless conduct upon the weak Christian in even stronger terms than he has used in v. 7. The effect will be destructive, destructive of his faith, destructive of him as a Christian. That Paul is envisaging an outcome as serious as this and not simply an internal going to pieces is clear from his use of the word 'destroy' elsewhere. The word consistently refers to eternal ruin. What he evidently has in mind is a former idol-worshipper falling back into the grip of idolatry.

Yet, Paul continues, this weak Christian, whom you, my enlightened friend, so readily despise, remains *a fellow-Christian* (literally: a brother) *for whom Christ died.*

8.12 This fundamental truth imparts to your sin against any of your brothers and sisters an altogether new dimension. *In sinning against your brothers and sisters in this way and wounding their conscience, weak as it is, you sin against Christ.*

The switch between v. 11 and v. 12 from sinning against the fellow-Christian for whom Christ died to sinning against Christ who died for that fellow-Christian provides striking evidence of Paul's profound sense of Christ's identification with the church.

8.13 Such a disastrous sequence of events as Paul has just described can only be averted if Christians allow their actions to be governed not primarily by liberty or knowledge but by love, love that would rather abstain from eating meat altogether than cause the downfall of a fellow-Christian. *Therefore, if food be the downfall of a fellow-Christian, I will never eat meat again.*

It is a renunciation of meat altogether that Paul is talking about here, not just a renunciation of meat offered to idols. But abstinence from meat, or from any other kind of food, must not be made an absolute rule. There are circumstances, as in the situation Paul alludes to in Gal. 2.11–14, when eating becomes a duty.

In retrospect: while the actual word 'love' is used only in vv. 1 and 3, the concept in fact determines the argument of the whole chapter.

Paul's apostolic rights
9.1–12a

Chapter 9 begins abruptly with a string of four questions, shortly to be followed by ten more, and a protestation of the validity of Paul's apostleship as something which ought to be recognized by the Corinthians, if by anyone, as beyond question.

All this has no immediately obvious connection with what precedes or follows, but, as becomes clear in vv. 12–15, Paul is citing his own case in order to show that it can be an admirable thing to do not to claim rights or liberties to which one is entitled. In the light of his example, the Corinthians ought to be prepared to forgo some of their liberty, out of consideration for their less emancipated brethren.

Some scholars take the view that Paul's apostolic status was actually being called in question in Corinth, but it seems more likely that he is stressing his apostolic authority in order to make more pointed the example he had set by not claiming his apostolic rights. If he, whose apostolic status could not be questioned by the Corinthians, had chosen not to claim his privileges, how much more ought the Corinthians be ready to relinquish some of theirs.

At the same time, there is an apologetic edge to the chapter. By refusing to accept material support, Paul had given offence to some of the well-to-do members of the community. In the Synoptic Gospels the disciples are sent out by Jesus as missionaries and bidden to take neither money nor pack but to depend on such hospitality as may be offered them. There is reason to believe that these instructions were still being literally followed by itinerant missionaries in Paul's time and for decades to come.[76] Paul, however, who worked as a tentmaker to support himself (Acts 18.1–3), did not fit that mould.

Indeed, by remaining financially independent, Paul was flying in the face of contemporary conventions of friendship, as well as the social institution of patronage (on which see the excursus at the end of this section, *Paul and Patronage*).

9.1   Paul's main concern in this chapter is to assert both his right to accept support from the church and his right to forgo that right, in order to give a clearer witness to the gospel of the grace of God. He begins with a vigorous assertion of his apostolic status. The first question, *Am I not free?* has to be understood in the light of the chapter as a whole. He is affirming his freedom to accept or renounce the material support of the congregation, rather than the freedom to eat or reject any kind of food. He has every right to claim such freedom, by virtue of his calling to be an apostle.

The next question but one states an essential qualification of an apostle, namely, that he or she should have *seen Jesus our Lord*. Not that all those who had seen the risen Lord were counted as apostles. In 1 Cor. 15.5–8 'all the apostles' clearly form a group within the larger group of those who have seen the Lord. A direct commission from the risen Christ is also necessary (cf. Gal. 1.16).

9.2   Paul is not content, however, to rest his claim to apostleship upon such credentials. *Are you not my own handiwork in the Lord?* he exclaims. And again, *In the Lord you are the very seal of my apostleship.* In other words, their very existence as Christians is evidence of his exercise of truly apostolic functions. The work that Christ has wrought through him speaks for itself, and the Corinthians, if anyone, ought to recognize it.

9.3f.   Paul now takes up the controversial issue of his refusal to accept material support. By means of a string of rhetorical questions, ten in all, he affirms with great emphasis that as an apostle he has the right to claim such support.

9.5f.   In passing, he mentions other rights, particularly *the right to take a Christian wife* about with him, but it is clear that the real question at issue is his right to accept support and not to have to work for his living. The reference to Barnabas in v. 6 implies that he too followed Paul's policy.

9.7   Here he presses home the point by a series of analogies from military service and farming. As the founder of the church in Corinth,

89

he has as much right to their support as a soldier has to his pay or a farmer to the produce of his vineyards or fields.

9.8ff. Next he appeals to the law, interpreting the command, *You shall not muzzle an ox while it is treading out the grain*, as applying to Christian ministers, particularly apostles. His point is that the writer of Deuteronomy was wiser than he knew and that under the inspiration of the Holy Spirit he was stating a command the full significance of which would only become apparent under the Christian dispensation. Paul's dismissal of a literal interpretation of Deut. 25.4 in vv. 9f. is in line with Philo's principle that the law of God has to do with higher things than creatures without the power of reason.[77] But this is one of the most attractive of the kindly laws of the Old Testament, and Paul's dismissal of the literal interpretation surely has to be called in question today. Unwittingly, he has given support to that disregard of the natural world that has plagued Christian history through so many centuries.

9.11f. Paul ends the paragraph with a reaffirmation of his rights and a double a fortiori argument. As people who have sown a spiritual crop in Corinth, the apostles have the right to claim a material harvest. If others (probably Apollos and Peter) have been recognized as having the right to such support, a fortiori Paul and his companions have that right.

Paul and Patronage

Patronage has been described by John K. Chow as 'the cement that held Roman society together'.[78] A great many people in a city like Corinth were linked together in the relationship of patron and client.

Patronage is also described by Chow as 'an asymmetrical exchange relationship'.[79] It entailed mutual obligations. The patron gave the client hospitality, legal protection. In return, the client was expected, for example, to act as an informant on his patron's behalf or to support him in candidature for public office. But patron and client did not relate as equals. The relationship was not horizontal but vertical, not a true friendship, more of a lopsided friendship.[80]

There is good reason to believe that the well-to-do members of the church in Corinth were patrons in secular society and expected to continue to exercise that sort of role in the church. It is also clear, from this chapter as well as from 2 Cor. 11.7–11, that some members of the church offered Paul material support and were slighted by his refusal to accept it. Acceptance of the support of these people would have resulted in Paul being seen as their client and would have made it impossible for him to function as their father in Christ (1 Cor. 4.18).

In chapter 12 Paul distances himself still further from the patron–client ideology by choosing as his main metaphor for the church the body. He thereby offers a horizontal model of community in place of the vertical model of patron and client.[81]

Freely received, freely given
9.12b–18

In the previous paragraph Paul has asserted with considerable emphasis his right as an apostle to accept support from the church. Now he attempts to show his critics why he has not availed himself of that right. He has chosen not to claim it in order to bear more effective witness to the gospel of Christ. We catch a glimpse here of Paul's consuming passion to be the most credible, effective witness to the gospel that he can possibly be. As Fee puts it, 'Paul is a man of a single passion, "the gospel of Christ."'[82] It is significant that in the present paragraph the word 'gospel' occurs five times and the corresponding verb, 'to preach the gospel', three times.

9.12b *Rather than offer any hindrance to the gospel of Christ*, he is ready to put up with everything that comes his way. Would that the Corinthians would show a similar concern not to put any hindrance in the way of fellow-Christians with a weaker faith (cf. 8.9, 13; 10.32)! The word translated 'put up with' is not Paul's usual word for 'endure'. He seems to be referring not to sufferings in general but to the sort of hardships concomitant with working with his own hands and evangelizing at the same time. There could also be a contrast intended with the itinerant teachers of various creeds and philosophies who could be found in any Mediterranean city peddling their teaching and who supported themselves by finding a patron.

9.13f. Instead of proceeding to elaborate the statement he has just made, Paul pauses to reaffirm what he has been asserting throughout the previous paragraph, namely, his right to receive support from the church. His first argument is an appeal to analogy. *Those who are engaged in temple service eat the temple offerings, and those who officiate at the altar claim their share of the sacrifice.* In the same way, *those who preach the gospel should get their living by the gospel.* Indeed, the Lord himself gave specific instructions to that effect. At this point Paul is probably alluding to the saying of Jesus recorded in Matt. 10.10 and Luke 10.7 that *the worker deserves his keep* or *pay.* The vigour with which Paul reiterates his right to material support shows how severely his position on this issue must have been criticized in Corinth.

9.15   Paul now comes back to the main theme of the paragraph, that he has *never taken advantage of any such right,* and furthermore has no intention to claim his rights in this letter. He would rather die than do so. The structure of the sentence is broken in a way that often happens when he is writing under strong emotion. It is his boast that he has never claimed such a right – a boast that no one is going to make null and void.

It is striking to note how the very word that can denote an attitude that is the very antithesis of faith can also be used by Paul to designate an authentically Christian stance. Thus on the one hand the gospel of God's free grace received by faith alone rules out all boasting, all reliance on what one is or has or has done (Rom. 3.27; 4.2). Henceforth Paul can boast no longer of any achievement of his own, only of the cross of Christ (Gal. 6.14) or, as far as he himself is concerned, of his weaknesses, in so far as they are the means to a deeper experience of the power of Christ (2 Cor. 12.5–10).

Yet there is, after all, a legitimate form of Christian boasting, a pride that the Christian minister may legitimately have, not in what he or she has accomplished in their own strength but in what God has accomplished through them, in this case in what God has been able to achieve through his renunciation of the right to support. Just how that act of renunciation has been used by God becomes clearer in v. 18.

9.16   On the other hand, simply having preached the gospel affords no grounds for boasting. The truth is that Paul has no choice, he can do no other. It would be agony for him not to preach.

Commentators aptly draw comparisons with the call narratives of the prophets, such as Moses (Exod. 3.11f.); Amos (Amos 3.8); Jeremiah (Jer. 1.5f.); and Jonah (Jonah 1.2ff.).

9.17f.   Paul now chooses to illuminate the sense of constraint under which he stands by means of a word that can be translated either by 'pay' or by 'reward' (*misthos*). In v. 17 'pay' seems the more appropriate translation, in v. 18 'reward'. The point is that Paul's situation is not that of a free agent who enters into a contract, voluntarily undertaking to carry out an assignment in return for pay from an employer (or reward from God). His situation is rather like that of a slave entrusted with a responsibility. He therefore has no choice, he is simply discharging a trust. The word here translated 'trust' is related to the word translated 'steward' in 4.2.

And yet Paul does after all receive a reward. Paradoxically, his reward consists in his proclamation of the gospel without reward. By not exercising his right to claim material support as an apostle, he is able to offer the gospel free of charge and therefore in a way that is congruent with its content, congruent with the message of free grace. As Fee puts it, 'In offering the "free" gospel "free of charge" his own ministry becomes a living paradigm of the gospel itself.'[83]

Here once again is an expression of a theme to which we drew attention in 2.1–5 and which dominates the whole argument of 2 Corinthians, namely, the inescapable necessity for a congruence between message and messenger, between the content of the gospel and the style and spirit in which it is proclaimed.

The dominant impression, however, that this paragraph leaves with the reader is probably one of overwhelming constraint. It is hard to match the power of the AV rendering of v. 16b: 'Woe is unto me, if I preach not the gospel!' And yet this sense of constraint is not experienced as something oppressive or crushing. It is rather a matter of an overwhelming longing on Paul's part to serve the proclamation of the gospel with every fibre of his being in gratitude to God for the overwhelming bounty of God's grace.

G. K. Chesterton has written in his life of St Francis of Assisi that the key to all the problems of Franciscan morality consists in the discovery of an infinite debt.

It is the highest and holiest of the paradoxes that the man who knows he cannot pay his debt will be for ever paying it. He will be for ever giving back what he cannot give back, and cannot be expected to give back. He will be always throwing things away into a bottomless pit of unfathomable thanks.[84]

All things to all people
9.19–23

The previous paragraph began and ended on the same note: Paul's willing renunciation of his apostolic rights for the sake of the gospel. It seems that his conduct has appeared to some to be inconsistent and contradictory. Any apparent inconsistency, however, is solely due to his one overruling aim, to be the most effective witness to the gospel that he can possibly be. Now he sees an opportunity to show how other apparent inconsistencies in the pattern of his life have the same explanation. As he is to explain in the following chapter (10.23–33), it is his practice to eat or not eat marketplace food, depending on the situation. This stance probably laid him open to the charge of inconsistency.

Paul's defence is, in essence, that people cannot be evangelized at arm's length. To bring the gospel home to men and women and win them to Christ's allegiance, the evangelist must sit where they sit. Paul is willing to shed every vestige of his inherited Jewish life-style and adopt the lifestyle of anyone at all, or, on the other hand, to resume Jewish manners and customs, in order to do just that. Such is his passion for the gospel.

9.19   He begins by describing this evangelical adaptation as a deliberate acceptance of slavery. Though he is free and owns no master, he has made himself *everyone's servant* (literally, 'I have enslaved myself to all'), *to win over as many as possible*.

Paul's paradoxical understanding of freedom is nowhere expressed more clearly than here. For him, true freedom means freedom *from* oneself, *for* service, for *love*.

9.20f.   He now elaborates this thought with reference to Jews and Gentiles: *To Jews I behaved like a Jew, to win Jews; that is, to win those under the* law . . . *To win those outside that law, I behaved as if outside the law.*

In each case, his decision to live like a Jew or a Gentile has been a willing act. It is not because he is himself still under the law that he has on occasion behaved as if under the law. His conduct has been wholly motivated by his evangelical passion. Similarly, it is not because he is a Gentile, outside God's law, that he has on occasion lived like a Gentile. Once again his conduct has been wholly motivated by his passion to communicate the gospel.

A literal translation of v. 20a would read: 'To Jews I became as a Jew.' But how can a person who was born a Jew say such a thing? Because in Christ there is neither Jew nor Greek (Gal. 3.28), Paul, though born a Jew, is no longer simply a Jew but becomes one, in order to win Jews.

The way in which Paul describes his relationship to the law of God in these two verses is extremely subtle. On the one hand, he is not himself 'under law', that is, obliged to fulfil the law in order to secure his relationship with God. But neither is he 'lawless', in the sense of owing God no moral obligation. He is, so to speak, 'Christ's en-lawed one', owing moral obligation to God through him. Here as in other letters, particularly Galatians and Romans, Paul's paradoxical statements become more intelligible, when one realizes that he is viewing law from different standpoints. Considered as a way of salvation, the law is terminated by Christ. From this standpoint, Christ is the end of the law (Rom. 10.4) in the sense of its termination. But considered as an expression of the will of God, the law is fulfilled by Christ. From this standpoint, he is the end of the law in the sense of its goal. As Christ's servant, therefore, Paul can describe himself as his 'en-lawed one'.

9.22 *To the weak*, Paul continues, *I became weak, to win the weak.* Who are 'the weak'? Most commentators believe he is referring to the sort of people mentioned in 8.7ff., who are not yet persuaded that idols have no real existence. However, since he is speaking here of potential converts, he may well have in mind the socially vulnerable, the sort of people whom he champions in 11.17–22, who, because of their menial status, were unable to come to the eucharistic meal on time. To all such, as well as to 'the strong', Paul has *become everything in turn, so that in one way or another* he might save some.

9.23 This verse reiterates Paul's determination to be governed in everything he does by the gospel, not simply in order to share it with others but in order to *share* with them *in its blessings*. The basic idea of the root underlying the word 'share' is that of participation in something in which others also participate. Indeed there is a hint of the idea which will be developed in v. 27 that it is only by sharing the gospel that he himself participates in it.

The Christian athlete
9.24–27

The thought hinted at in v. 23, namely, that Paul's own salvation is not assured, is now developed in the form of an exhortation to strenuous spiritual discipline. It is not Paul's primary concern in this paragraph to justify his own apostolic practice but rather to warn the Corinthians against presumption, by way of preparation for the following chapter. Nevertheless, there is still a connection with the early part of chapter 9. His willing surrender of his privileges for the sake of the gospel is one form of the discipline he has undertaken.

9.24   Paul begins with the reminder that in any race only one of the contestants wins the prize, and then urges his readers to run in such a way that they will win. The analogy, however, cannot be pressed. The Christian life is not a race in which only the top competitor wins a prize and all the others get nothing, however hard they may have striven. Perhaps that is why Paul does not develop his athletic metaphors in quite the same way in the subsequent verses.

9.25   Another athletic metaphor is taken up to make the same essential point: *Every athlete goes into strict training*. Before they could compete in the Isthmian Games (held outside Corinth), athletes had to undergo ten months of strict training. *They do it to win a fading garland; we, to win a garland that never fades*. In other words, the Christian life calls for total commitment. The *garland that never fades* is eternal life.

9.26f.   Paul now gives expression to his own ardour to practise the spiritual discipline he has just been urging upon his readers. *For my part, I am no aimless runner; I am not a boxer who beats the air*. On the contrary, *I do not spare my body, but bring it under strict control, for fear that after preaching to others I should find myself disqualified*. Paul here quite clearly articulates the possibility that he may find himself excluded from the salvation he has preached to others.

The sentiments Paul expresses here acquire a sharp polemical point, when one recalls that they are addressed to a community of people who supposed that they had arrived. On the contrary, he and they are engaged in a contest the result of which is not assured. No Christian, not even an apostle, not even Paul himself, who has renounced his apostolic right to community support and spent himself in the preaching of the gospel, becoming everything in turn, so that in one way or another he might save some, may regard his salvation as certain. The most unstinted sacrifice of his rights and energy does not do away with the possibility that he may yet find himself rejected. Let the Corinthians therefore be warned.

Yet it is not Paul's intention that his last word to them should be one of warning. That is rather the word they need to hear, so long as they remain in a state of illusion. His aim is not to induce a state of despair but rather one of penitence leading to chastened hope.[85] This intent of Paul's finds clearer expression in the following chapter.

Secure in God's grace alone
10.1–13

Paul's intention to deflate Corinthian presumption now becomes explicit. He is shortly to give his readers a clear directive: no participation in cultic meals in pagan temples (vv. 20–22). Evidently some of the Corinthians had argued that they could participate in such occasions with impunity. It is clear from 8.4 that they would have justified this position on the grounds that an idol has no real existence. It now appears that they were also relying on their participation in the sacraments. The references to supernatural food and drink (literally, 'spiritual food and drink') in vv. 3–4 are probably borrowings from Corinthian language. 'We', they said, 'have partaken spiritual food and spiritual drink; therefore we are secure.'

It is this false security based upon a super-sacramentalism that Paul now seeks to demolish. He does so by drawing an elaborate comparison between the situation of the Israelites in the wilderness under Moses and the situation of the church, which is in Christ. Such a homiletic exposition of biblical narrative falls within the category of midrash.

The main emphasis of the passage falls on the fundamental similarity between the situation then and the situation now, with the intent of warning the Corinthians not to provoke God's anger as the Israelites did.

We find in Jewish apocalyptic an expectation of an enhanced repetition of the miracles of the wilderness period, which makes it more understandable that Paul should allude to this Old Testament story. The miracles of that period were pointers to greater miracles yet to come.

10.1–4 These verses emphasize that those who belonged to the wilderness generation all alike experienced God's presence and liberation. Indeed, the word 'all' occurs six times in the first four verses. *Our ancestors were all under the cloud, and all of them passed through the Red Sea.* It is striking how, in addressing this predominantly Gentile-Christian community, Paul describes the wilderness generation as 'our fathers', thereby drawing the Corinthians into continuity with the Israel of the first covenant.

Indeed the people of that generation experienced counterparts to the Christian sacraments of baptism and eucharist, in that *they all received baptism into the fellowship of Moses in cloud and sea* and *all ate the same supernatural food, and all drank the same supernatural drink.*

They were even in living relationship with Christ himself, *for they drank from the supernatural rock that accompanied their travels – and that rock was Christ.*

There is evidence of the belief within Judaism that the rock with its well of water accompanied Israel through the wilderness. This belief was spun out of a combination of Num. 20.1–13 and 21.16–18. As for the identification of the rock with Christ, there could be a link here with Philo's identification of the rock with Wisdom,[86] but the likeliest explanation is that Paul has associated with the image of the rock at Horeb passages like Deut. 32.15, 30f., where God is described as the Rock of Israel's salvation.

10.5 Yet the possession of such privileges had not been a guarantee that God would continue to show favour to the children of Israel, however they might choose to behave. On the contrary, the majority had incurred God's displeasure and punishment, so that *the wilderness was strewn with their corpses.* According to Num. 14.30; 26.64f., only two people of the wilderness generation entered the Promised Land, Joshua and Caleb.

10.6 Paul now drives home the application. In allowing these things to happen, God had in mind not only that generation but our own. *These events happened as warnings to us not to set our desires on evil things as they did.*

10.7 In specifying more precisely the nature of the evil things on which the wilderness generation set their desires, Paul passes over to exhortation: *Do not be idolaters, like some of them; as scripture says, 'The people sat down to feast and rose up to revel.'* The verb underlying 'revel' suggests 'letting the hair down', dancing before the golden calf and engaging in sexual excesses. The NIV translates, 'to engage in pagan revelry'.

This warning against idolatry is directly relevant to the problem Paul is addressing in chapters 8—10. It is important to note that the people of Israel ate in the presence of the golden calf. There is thus a parallel between their misconduct and the eating of cultic meals in the idol's presence in Corinth.

10.8 *Let us not commit fornication; some of them did, and 23,000 died in one day*. This warning is also acutely relevant to the Corinthian situation, in view of the irregularities castigated in 5.1–5 and 6.12–20. Num. 25.9 speaks of 24,000 casualties, but this discrepancy could be due to confusion with Num. 26.62.

10.9f. *Let us not put the Lord to the test as some of them did; they were destroyed by the snakes. Do not grumble as some of them did; they were destroyed by the Destroyer*.

These warnings are not so obviously relevant to the Corinthian situation but probably are relevant nevertheless. Verses 21f. imply that persistence in attending cultic meals would amount to putting Christ to the test. Perhaps Paul envisages the Corinthians grumbling against himself and his prohibitions, as the Israelites grumbled against Moses, thereby grumbling against God. Perhaps too he anticipates them grumbling about the food they will have to forgo, by not participating in cultic meals.

Paul now repeats the assertion made in v. 6 that the things that happened to the Israelites in the wilderness happened for our benefit. They were thus, in a sense, *symbolic*. But the Greek word underlying this rendering is cognate with the word translated as 'warnings' in v. 6, and so Paul adds that these things *were recorded as a warning for us*. Paul knows that the whole church needs to heed the warning implicit in the Old Testament story, not only the enthusiasts of Corinth. Hence 'us' not 'you'. All of this remains true, even though it can be said of us, what could never be said of them, that we are those *upon whom the end of the ages has come*. Here is another carefully formulated correction of Corinthian eschatology. Rather than suggesting that the end time has arrived in its fullness, Paul's expression implies that what they have experienced is an anticipation of the end. The sacraments provide no guarantee that one is already secure in the possession of one's salvation.

10.12   The Corinthians must therefore let the experience of the wilderness generation serve as a warning to them. They must be warned of the peril of presuming upon the grace of God. *If you think you are standing firm, take care, or you may fall.*

10.13   Yet it is not Paul's intention to leave his hearers in a state of fear and trembling, and so v. 13 marks a sudden switch of mood. Having demolished a false self-reliance, Paul now seeks to build up a proper confidence, a confidence not in themselves but in God, who will not allow them to be overwhelmed by trial. *God keeps faith and will not let you be tested beyond your powers, but when the test comes he will at the same time provide a way out and so enable you to endure.*

One with Christ and one another
   10.14–17

10.14   It appears that some of the Corinthians had been arguing that they were free to participate in cultic meals in pagan temples on the grounds that their participation in the Christian sacraments made them secure. Paul has sought to demolish this false security. Now he gives his readers specific direction: *So then, my dear friends, have nothing to do with idolatry.*

10.15   Having done that, however, he corrects himself to the extent of appealing to their own good sense and urges them to *form your own judgement on what I say.* Much as Paul wishes to assert his authority, it is the assent of the Corinthians that he is seeking, not their blind, uncritical obedience.

10.16   The main point of v. 16 is clear: participation in the Lord's Supper brings about a particular bond with Christ. It is thus designed to lead up to vv. 20–22, where Paul will assert that participation in pagan sacrifices brings about a particular bond with demons, and then draw the conclusion that these two bonds are incompatible. He formulates this thought in conscious reminiscence of the words spoken by Jesus over the bread and the cup at the Last Supper, which, in the form quoted in the following chapter, run: *This is my body, which is for you . . . This cup is the new covenant sealed by my blood.* However, the words Paul uses here in chapter 10 are, in their exact parallelism, more reminiscent of the Marcan form of these sayings, namely, *This is my body . . . This is my blood, the blood of the covenant, shed for many* (Mark 14.22, 24).

Paul makes the point in the form of two parallel questions which expect the answer, 'Yes'. *When we bless the cup of blessing, is it not a means of sharing* in *the blood of Christ? When we break the bread, is it not a means of sharing in the body of Christ?* He clearly expects his readers to agree with what he is saying here. This fact, together with the exact parallelism of the two halves of the verse, suggests that we are dealing with two levels of text in vv. 16 and 17: pre-Pauline tradition in v. 16 (probably a liturgical text) and Paul's own reinterpretation of the tradition in v. 17.

The primary idea expressed by the Greek word underlying 'means of sharing', namely, *koinōnia*, is that of participation in something in which others also share. In the following verse the emphasis falls on the significance of participation *with* others, here it falls on the significance of participation *in* the blood and body of Christ. In vv. 18 and 20 Paul will use the cognate noun, *koinōnoi*, that is, 'sharers together'.[87]

But what exactly is meant by *sharing in the blood of Christ*? The fact that Paul uses a cognate word, *koinōnos*, in an analogous way in v. 18 gives us a clue. In v.18 he speaks of those who eat a Jewish sacrificial meal being *partners in the altar*. This is clearly a figure of speech, and the sense appears to be that they participate in the benefits that come from the altar. If we take v. 16a in the same way, it follows that Paul is thinking of the share all Christians enjoy, and enjoy together, in the benefits of Christ's passion, in other words, in the new covenant sealed by Christ's blood (11.25).

In what sense then is the breaking of the bread a means of sharing in the body of Christ? In view of the parallelism of the two sentences, it is natural to suppose that Paul is still thinking of sharing in the benefits of Christ's death. At the same time the sentence suggests further levels of meaning. As we shall see in connection with 11.23–26, the Aramaic word, *guphā*, which probably underlies 'body', means the person as a whole, the self. On this view, the words 'This is my body,' would have conveyed to the first followers of Jesus after Easter the meaning, 'This is I myself.' They would have been heard as an assurance that the crucified and risen Lord was present, offering to them his 'body', his very self. This interpretation fits the main thrust of the whole section from vv. 14–22, which, as we have seen, emphasizes that anyone who partakes of the Lord's Supper becomes a sharer in Christ.

But there is still more to be said. In the following verse Paul uses the word 'body' to refer not to something in which we participate but to something that we are, that is, the church. It appears that already in v. 16b Paul is thinking of this shift of meaning. That is probably the reason why he has reversed the usual order of the bread and the cup.

10.17   Paul's thought now shifts from participation *in* the blood and body of Christ to participation *with* others. From the fact that *there is one loaf* he draws the conclusion that *we, though many, are one body.*

It may not be immediately obvious what the causal connection is between the existence of one loaf and the conclusion that we, though many, are one body. The missing link must be that participation in the one loaf means participation in Christ. It is because he is one that we, though many, are essentially one and must live out this essential unity in daily life.

As for the precise meaning of *sōma*, 'body', this seems, as already indicated, to shift between v. 16 and v. 17. In v. 16 the body is one in which we participate, in v. 17 it is one that we ourselves are. For another example of the word *sōma* changing its meaning within the space of a verse or two, see Col. 2.17 and 19. In v. 17 it means substance as against shadow, but in v. 19 it denotes the church.

Even if some sort of distinction is intended, however, between the 'body of Christ' in v. 16 and the 'body' of v. 17, it is clear that there is also an intimate relationship between them, since it is precisely by participating in the body (and blood) of Christ that we become one body. It is instructive to compare this passage with Rom. 12.5, which makes it clear that the body of believers is neither to be identified with Christ nor seen as a community apart from Christ but rather as 'one body in Christ'.

For further discussions of the phrase, 'body of Christ', see the commentary on 11.23–26, 27–29; 12.12–27.

The emphasis on the unity of those who participate in the sacrament may not seem relevant to the immediate context but it is certainly relevant to the wider context. We have seen, from chapter 1 on, how seriously the community has been plagued by divisions. The problem discussed in chapter 8 could also be viewed as a problem of division, of division between the strong and the weak. The following chapter will afford further evidence of division, this time on social lines.

You must choose
10.18–22

Paul is now about to develop the warning first sounded in v. 14. He has stressed the reality of the participation brought about in the Lord's Supper, a participation *in* the body and blood of Christ *with* others. Now he is to argue that participation in any cultic meal is not a harmless act but one that relates the worshippers, to their detriment, to some reality behind the rite.

10.18 First of all, he invites his readers to *consider Jewish practice* (literally, to 'consider Israel according the flesh'). *Are not those who eat the sacrificial meal partners in the altar?* As has already been indicated in connection with v. 16a, we take this to mean a sharing in the benefits of the altar. The word translated here and in v. 20 as 'partners' is cognate with the word translated 'means of sharing' in v. 16.

10.19 Paul now anticipates that his readers will guess his next move, namely, that participation in a pagan cultic meal has a comparable effect to participation in a Jewish or Christian meal. He pictures them asking whether he is seriously suggesting that *meat consecrated to an idol is anything more than meat, or that an idol is anything more than an idol.* Evidently the Corinthians have been justifying their participation in pagan cultic meals on the grounds that an idol has no real existence, so that any meat offered to an idol is no more than mere meat. And has not Paul himself already agreed that *a false god has no real existence, and there is no god but one* (8.4)? Is Paul now going to deny what he asserted two chapters earlier?

10.20 Paul is adamant that any food offered on a pagan altar is not offered to any being worthy of the name of God, but this does not mean that the worshippers are not in touch with anything at all. On the contrary, they *become partners with demons* – for Paul, an intolerable state of affairs. He is here echoing a belief expressed in a number of Old Testament passages that pagan sacrifices, as well as the sacrifices made to pagan gods by apostate Jews, are in fact offered to demons (see especially Deut. 32.17).

10.21 It follows that the two forms of sacred meal, the Lord's Supper and the pagan cultic meal, are incompatible. *You cannot drink the cup of the Lord and the cup of demons. You cannot partake of the Lord's table and the table of demons.*

10.22   To do otherwise would be *to provoke the Lord*, to put him to the test of a trial of strength. It is clear from 8.9–12 that the dominant party in Corinth thought of themselves not only as enlightened, mature and spiritual but as strong, in contrast to other Christians who were, in their eyes, unenlightened, immature, unspiritual and weak. Strong you may be, Paul says to them, but you are surely not so foolhardy as to take on God.

This passage raises deep questions for ourselves as we seek to apply Paul's words to life as we know it. What are we to make of Paul's assertion that *pagan sacrifices are offered . . . to demons and to that which is not God?* What are we to make of Paul's references to demons? Or to his references to Satan? Does he at this point become the spokesperson of a world-view that we can no longer share?

Without, I trust, oversimplifying an extremely complex question, I suggest that there are manifestations of evil that can hardly be adequately accounted for without recourse to the category of the demonic. I cite two examples.

How did it come about that a significant proportion of the citizenry of Germany, a country with a rich and deep Christian tradition, as civilized a country as any in the world, the homeland of Luther, Bach and Goethe, became mesmerized by the hate-filled rhetoric of Adolf Hitler?

I also cite the experience of pastors and social workers who have worked among drug addicts. One such pastor, Rudolph-P. Borawski, has drawn striking parallels between the story of the man of Gadara in Mark 5.1–20 and the life histories of the drug addicts among whom he has worked, people who could be described as 'possessed' by the craving for alcohol or drugs.

> These people had been 'chained' by their craving. It had subjected their lives to domination by an alien power, destroyed their peace of mind, driven them to lonely places, completely changed their personalities and left them sick in body and soul.[88]

Thiselton follows a different line of interpretation, suggesting that the demons can be thought of as social constructs, but constructs that decisively shape people's lives.[89]

Freedom unqualified – except by love
10. 23—11.1

Paul now begins to draw to a conclusion the long discussion begun in chapter 8. Here, however, the question at issue is not whether believers may participate in cultic meals served in temple precincts but whether they may buy meat that is being offered for sale in the market and, further, whether they may eat meat that is being served at a private house.

10.23f.   The opening words of v. 23 are identical with the opening words of 6.12, apart from the omission of one word. Here, as there, there is good reason to believe that Paul is first quoting, and then qualifying, a Corinthian slogan, as is implied by the punctuation of the REB: *'We are free to do anything,' you say. Yes, but not everything is good for us.*

We found reason to suppose that in chapter 8 also Paul begins by quoting a Corinthian slogan. The intent of Paul's correction of the Corinthian position here is very much in the spirit of chapter 8. There he qualifies their claim to have knowledge by affirming the priority of love. Here he qualifies their claim to be free by urging that *each look after the interests of others*, not their own, and in this way build up the community. This is, in fact, the dominant emphasis of the whole passage, that the believer's conduct must always be determined by consideration for the neighbour's spiritual welfare, the neighbour's conscience, so that the church may be built up (cf. vv. 28f., 32f.).

10.25f.   Out of consideration for the neighbour, the Christian will be willing to set aside his or her freedom, but that freedom is still a reality, and Paul now strongly affirms it. *You may eat anything sold in the meat market without raising questions of conscience.*

As was noted at the beginning of our discussion of chapter 8, the available evidence suggests that not all the meat that was sold at the meat market had been previously sacrificed. It also appears to have been possible, at least in some instances, to find out whether a particular cut had been sacrificed. Otherwise Paul's injunction to his readers in this verse not to inquire too closely into the origin of what was for sale would have no point.

Paul's advice to believers who may be hesitating to buy meat at the market is that to enquire too closely into the meat's origin would represent an unnecessary scrupulosity. In taking this stance, he places

himself unambiguously among 'the strong' and clearly implies that
the meat in itself is harmless, whatever its immediate origin. The meat
that has passed through pagan temples is still part of God's good
creation and is to be accepted with gratitude.

Paul here distances himself decisively from comparable rabbinic
prescriptions. In the early church in general, also, his position was not
maintained, as is evident from the Apostolic Decree recorded in Acts
15.29. Contrary to Luke's account, Paul was probably not present on
the occasion when this decree was passed.[90]

10.27 In the same way, whenever believers are invited to the home
of a non-Christian for a meal, they are to eat whatever is put before
them, *without raising questions of conscience*. In other words, they may
eat it with a perfectly clear conscience.

10.28 Yet, if on such an occasion somebody should say, *'This food has
been offered in sacrifice*,' then they are not to eat it, out of consideration
for the other person and their conscience.

The question naturally arises, What sort of person does Paul envisage proffering this information? The host? A non-Christian fellow-
guest? Or a fellow-believer? Paul's use of the indefinite pronoun,
'somebody', makes it unlikely that he is thinking of the host. On the
other hand, the precise word Paul uses here to describe the meat has
not been used before and lacks any pejorative nuance. This suggests
that he can hardly be thinking of a fellow-believer. There remains the
possibility that Paul has in mind a pagan fellow-guest, who is trying to help the Christian out of an embarrassing situation. What Paul
does make clear is that under such circumstances a Christian ought to
abstain from eating the meat referred to, not because the act of eating
would be harmful in itself but rather because of the effect of the action
upon the conscience of the other. The other person would be led to
believe that the Christian guest was in no way concerned to distance
himself or herself from idolatrous worship, and in this way the distinction between true worship and idolatry would be blurred. As a
result, their conscience would be at risk.

10.29f. At this point there are some awkward jumps in Paul's argument, and no interpretation is without its difficulties. Thiselton lists no
fewer than six different explanations.[91] Verse 29b appears to reject any
idea of my freedom being curtailed or *called in question* out of consideration for *another's conscience*, while v. 30, though cryptic, reads like

an assertion of my freedom to eat whatever I like, so long as *I partake with thankfulness,* and express that thankfulness by saying grace. The problem is: in whose name is Paul speaking at this point?

Some commentators take the view that Paul suddenly feels compelled to justify his own liberal stance, arguing that the language used here recalls Paul's defence of his own conduct in chapter 9. But, if this were the thrust of these questions, we would expect them to be placed after v. 26 or v. 27, rather than in their present position.

The view taken by the REB translators, which was advocated by Lietzmann, is that Paul now anticipates an interjection from the Corinthian side, and is pursuing still further his dialectical engagement with the Corinthian position, begun in v. 23. Something that can be said in favour of this view is that a Corinthian Christian can readily be imagined expressing such sentiments. Something that counts against it is the fact that vv. 31 and 32 amount to a somewhat indirect rejoinder to such a hypothetical interjection.

10.31f.   Paul's rejoinder to this anticipated interjection, if that is what it is, is to say, in effect, 'Yes indeed, you may eat and drink whatever you like, so long as you say grace and mean it. For to say grace is to bless God, the Giver of all good. If you say that and know what you are saying, you will surely acknowledge an obligation to seek the glory of God not only in what you eat and drink but in everything you do. So long as you do act from that motive, you are indeed free. On the other hand, how could you claim to be honouring God by acting in a way that gave *offence to Jews or Greeks or to the church of God*?'

Paul normally uses the word 'church' (*ekklēsia* in Greek) to refer to the local Christian community, but here 'the church of God' seems to denote the whole Christian community. 'Giving offence' here clearly means something more serious than hurting someone's feelings. It means acting in a way that would make it difficult for another person either to hear the gospel or to remain a believer.

This injunction to be careful to give no offence should not be understood as something additional to the preceding injunction to do everything to the glory of God but rather as part of its explication. This is something that Paul has to impress upon the Corinthians again and again, that the service of God and the service of others are inextricably associated.

10.33   To clinch the argument, Paul cites his own behaviour, as being one who seeks to live by the rule he has just stated. Consideration for his neighbour's spiritual welfare is his constant concern, *the good of the many* rather than his own good. The word translated here by the REB as 'good' is cognate with the word translated by 'is good for us' in v. 23.

11.1 This being so, Paul has every right to urge the Corinthians to follow his example (literally, to 'be imitators of me'), as he follows Christ's. As in 4.16, he does not urge them to follow Christ directly but to take himself as a guide to what following Christ means. The word 'as' here in the phrase, 'as I follow Christ's', has something of the force of 'inasmuch as' but also of 'in so far as'. It is only in so far as Paul does in fact follow Christ's example that he can claim to be setting an example for others to follow. Read in this way, Paul's injunction is not so breathtakingly immodest as appears at first sight.

This verse clearly belongs with the preceding passage, not the following one. The traditional chapter division is here unfortunate.

Order in Worship
11.2–34

Let men be men and women be women
11.2–16

Paul now moves to a new topic, appropriate behaviour in worship. More precisely, he enunciates the principle that when women pray or prophesy, as when men pray or prophesy, they should do so appropriately attired, so that there is no blurring of the distinction between women and men. He returns to the subject of worship in chapter 14, where he discusses the relative value of certain spiritual gifts that are exercised in worship.

We cannot say for sure what has occasioned this discussion. The absence of the phrase, 'Concerning . . .' suggests that Paul has been led to take up the topic not by anything said by the Corinthians in their letter to him but by reports he has heard by word of mouth. On the other hand, the number and diversity of the arguments he employs indicate that he was conscious of challenging some strongly held convictions, and it may be that these convictions had been conveyed to him in the letter from Corinth.

Hays suggests that the Corinthians had raised the subject and had described certain practices they had adopted, confident that these would meet with his approval. He also offers a highly plausible reconstruction of what they may have said.[92]

Whatever its immediate occasion may have been, this is a passage that abounds in obscurities. Since Paul's addressees were fully acquainted with the manner in which worship was being conducted in Corinth, he is content to allude to certain practices with a brevity that modern readers find tantalizing. As a result, there is far from being a consensus among scholars over the actual practice alluded to in vv. 4 and 5. There has also been considerable debate over the meaning of certain words, particularly 'head' in v. 3, 'glory' in v. 7 and 'authority' and 'because of the angels' in v. 10.

109

According to a long-standing reading of the passage, Paul is here upholding the right of men to exercise authority over women. Women therefore are to wear veils or head coverings as a sign of their submission to male authority. It is now widely held, however, that this view is largely untenable. It rests upon particular interpretations of the controversial words already referred to, but at point after point the linguistic evidence points decisively in another direction. This view also misstates the main thrust of the passage, which, as stated above, is that when men or women pray or prophesy they should be appropriately attired.

Nevertheless, it cannot be denied that there is a certain tension in the passage. This is probably due to Paul being confronted yet again by advocates of an over-realized eschatology, for whom sexual differentiation no longer had any meaning. On the one hand, Paul wants to affirm the equality of women and men in Christ, on the other, to put the 'liberated' women of Corinth in their place. The tensions in the passage may also be due in part to Paul's abhorrence of anything moving even slightly in the direction of homosexuality.

11.2 Paul begins with a word of commendation for the Corinthians for always keeping him in mind and maintaining the traditions he had handed on to them. However, the fact that he proceeds immediately to give definite instructions on the appropriate manner in which women and men are to be attired for worship suggests that in this area their behaviour has not been conforming to the standards he had set.

11.3 He now makes a basic theological statement about the mutual relationships of God, Christ, man and woman from which, presumably, later directives are derived, namely, that *while every man has Christ for his head, a woman's head is man, as Christ's head is God*. The problem is to determine the precise nature of the relationships in question, and that hinges on the precise meaning of 'head'. In vv. 4–7 the word is used repeatedly in its literal sense, though the 'head' on which the man or woman may bring shame may well be the metaphorical 'head'. In v. 3 'head' is equally clearly being used in a metaphorical sense. But how exactly?

It was widely assumed by commentators up to Barrett that the word was being used here to mean 'ruler', so that the point of the verse was that just as God rules Christ so Christ rules man and man rules woman. However, the use of *kephalē* to mean ruler is not a native Greek idiom. Liddell and Scott do not give the meaning 'ruler' as a subcategory within the metaphorical usages of the word. The Hebrew word for head, *rosh*, is used in the Old Testament to denote a ruler, that is, the ruler of a community, but, when it is so used, the Greek translators of the LXX usually render it by *archōn* or *archēgos* rather than by *kephalē*, the word they regularly use whenever the physical head is intended. Fee's judgement is that out of 180 occurrences of the word *kephalē* in the LXX there are only six in which it clearly carries the meaning 'ruler'.[93]

There is, however, an idiomatic use of *kephalē* in Greek to denote a source. If the word is understood in this way, then Paul is thinking not of hierarchies of rulers and ruled but of a series of relationships of derived being. That is certainly the kind of relationship implied by the creation story of Genesis 2, which is clearly in Paul's mind in vv. 8 and 9.

The case for the rendering, 'source', however, is not as strong as some of its advocates have claimed, and, in view of the subordinationist strain in v. 7, the sense of pre-eminence or dominance cannot be ruled out. Schrage's conclusion is that a clear solution is not yet in view,[94] while Thiselton takes the unusual step of enclosing an alternative translation in brackets, thus, 'Man is foremost (or *head? source?*) in relation to woman.'[95]

11.4f.   Paul now states his main thesis, that *a man who keeps his head covered when he prays or prophesies brings shame on his head; but a woman brings shame on her head if she prays or prophesies bareheaded.*

This translation reflects the traditional understanding of what was going on at Corinth, according to which Paul is objecting to the way in which some women were praying or prophesying without wearing a head covering or a veil. On this view, Paul is asserting the propriety of men wearing such a covering and of women refraining from doing so. The actual Greek phrase, however, is not precise and there is an alternative view, which is also quite widely held, that Paul is objecting to some women having their hair hanging down, unloosed. It is also possible that Paul is asserting the propriety of men having their hair short and not long. On the whole, the view reflected by the REB seems more probable.[96]

The 'head' that man is capable of shaming by wearing inappropriate attire appears to be, at one level, the physical head, and, at another, the metaphorical head, Christ. If the second meaning were not present, the principle stated in v. 3 would play no part in the argument. If so, 'head' is being used in a double sense in v. 5 also.

11.5bf.   Paul now reinforces the rule just laid down for the behaviour of women. If a woman prays or prophesies bareheaded, *it is as bad as if her head were shaved*, and that, it is implied by v. 6, is generally recognized as something shameful. But why should it be shameful? It may be because a shaven head was recognized as a mark of a prostitute or, what is more likely, that a woman with a shaven head was considered to have lost her femininity. The Corinthian women, it seems, were acting as if distinctions between the sexes no longer existed. Such behaviour would be entirely consistent with the over-realized eschatology of Corinth. If the age to come was already present in its fullness, did it not follow that distinctions between men and women had been eliminated?

11.7   Paul now seeks to provide further theological justification for his contention that, when praying or prophesying, women and men should be distinctively attired. *Man is the image of God, and the mirror of his glory* (literally, 'the image and glory of God'), *whereas a woman reflects the glory of man* (literally, 'is the glory of man').

But why should Paul speak only of man being the image (and glory) of God, when Gen. 1.27 states explicitly that it was as male and female that humankind was created in God's image? Fee suggests that Paul is thinking of the two creation stories together, 'in a somewhat harmonized way', so that the order of creation as narrated in Genesis 2 has precedence in his thinking.[97] Wire, on the other hand, is adamant that Paul identifies the privileged male as God's image and the female as man's glory.[98] Critical as we are of much of Wire's argument, we find it difficult to avoid the conclusion that at this point Paul is showing a patriarchal bias.[99]

A further problem is to determine the precise force of 'glory' here. A literal rendering of v. 7b would run: 'but the woman is the glory of man'. The REB introduces the notion of reflection, but the use of 'glory' in that sense is hardly attested. Some have argued that 'glory' here means 'that in which one takes delight'. Woman is the glory of man, not in the sense of being his reflection, since she is different from him, but in the sense that she represents his joy and pride, by bringing him an incomparable wealth of which he would otherwise be deprived. She is the helpmeet whom he had sought in vain among the other creatures, his invaluable and irreplaceable complement.

This is an attractive view but it runs counter to the trend of the verse as a whole, which unmistakably assigns a certain priority to the man. The divine glory in which woman too is bathed results from her relationship to the man and is a derived and mediated one. At this point Paul falls short of his deepest theological insights.

11.8f.   Verses 8 and 9 seem to assign some sort of priority to man but a priority that is temporal in nature. *For man did not originally spring from woman, but woman was made out of man; and man was not created for woman's sake, but woman for the sake of man.* These verses support the interpretation of 'head' in v. 3 as meaning source rather than rule.

11.10   Paul now draws the conclusion: *therefore a woman must have the sign of her authority on her head, out of regard for the angels.*

This verse raises two problems. The first is the meaning of 'authority'. There is a long-standing tradition that the word here means a sign of woman's *submission* to authority, namely, that of the man, but there is now a growing consensus of scholarly opinion that the Greek cannot be made to yield any such sense. Neither in Paul's own usage nor in the whole range of Greek literature is *exousia* ever used in the passive sense of an authority to which the subject must submit. The word means not power submitted to but power exercised by someone. 'Authority' here can only mean the woman's own authority, which she herself exercises, not the authority of the man over the woman.[100]

But how exactly does the woman exercise her authority by wearing a head covering? Various suggestions have been made, none of them wholly convincing. The one that coheres best with the context is that the covering is a sign of her right to pray and prophesy in the assembly because she is attired in a manner that reflects her peculiar status as a woman.

The other major problem is what is meant by the phrase, 'out of regard for the angels'. Again various suggestions have been made, but Paul's reference is too cryptic to permit any certainty. Some see an allusion to the story in Gen. 6.1–4 (elaborated in later Jewish tradition) of the seduction of women by evil angels. Alternatively, the underlying thought may be that the angels, as guardians of the created order, would be hostile to women praying and prophesying, in so far as this threatened to obliterate the distinctions between men and women. If so, Paul may be saying, in effect, that women must show by the use of head coverings that they do in fact possess the authority to transcend the subordination to which they were subjected in the old creation.

11.11f.   Paul now appears to reverse the trend of the preceding argument. Whereas vv. 3 and 7–9 appear to attribute some sort of priority to man over woman, these verses appear, equally clearly, to assert their equality both as creatures and as believers. *Woman is as essential to man as man to woman. If woman was made out of man, it is through woman that man now comes to be, God being the source of all.* But this relationship of mutual dependence holds good not only of man and woman as creatures but of man and woman as believers. Each is essential to the other *in the Lord's fellowship.*

11.13   Paul now has recourse to other arguments. He begins with a call to the Corinthians to judge for themselves and an appeal to their sense of what is fitting.

11.14f.   Is it not a fact of nature, he asks, that women have longer hair than men? Indeed, *long hair disgraces a man*, whereas *it is a woman's glory*. This argument is presumably to be seen as reinforcing the conclusion that it is appropriate for women to pray and prophesy with heads covered but for men with heads uncovered.

11.16   Finally, Paul appeals to custom, *custom among us* and the custom of *the congregations of God's people* (literally, 'the churches of God'). His tone is undeniably somewhat peevish. He appears to have recourse to his final argument somewhat reluctantly, only *if anyone still insists on arguing*. Here he seems to have a premonition that his somewhat tortuous arguments will not convince all of his hearers or readers.

Even though this passage has yet to surrender all of its secrets, it is still of considerable interest. It contributes to our picture of the Corinthian community and further illustrates the propensity of the Corinthians to suppose that God had given them all God had to give. As elsewhere, Paul seeks to check their enthusiasm, but his main concern is that when women (or men) exercise their God-given gifts in worship they should do so in a way that does not obscure the continuing differences between them.

The passage is also important because it shows that Paul clearly accepted the right of women to pray and prophesy aloud and in public. It is true that prayer may be a private matter but prophecy is public by its very nature. In the new creation men and women know that they belong together as members of the one body of Christ, celebrate worship together and exercise their gifts for their mutual upbuilding. It is the difference between man and woman that is in the foreground, not the subordination of the woman or the authority of the man.

Not the Lord's Supper
11.17–22

Paul now takes up another aspect of the worship life of the Corinthian community, the manner in which they are celebrating the common meal.

In this case, the source of his information is clear: oral report (see v. 18).

It is also clear that Paul regards this as a much more serious matter than the one with which he has just been dealing. The practices that he has just been deploring and that he believes have been occurring in Corinth amount to nothing worse than impropriety (see v. 13). But the matter he is now addressing is much more serious than that, something that strikes at the heart of both the gospel and the church.

To feel the force of Paul's strictures, we need to reconstruct, as far as we are able, the nature of the occasion he is talking about. There is good reason to believe that the earliest celebrations of the Lord's Supper consisted of a complete meal, which began with the breaking of the bread and ended with the sharing of the cup. This order would correspond to Jewish custom not only at the Passover but at any meal to which guests were invited. There is, moreover, what is likely to be a trace of this order in the phrase, 'after supper', which in both the Lucan and the Pauline accounts is attached to the saying over the cup but not to the saying over the loaf.

It is possible that by this time the act of breaking the bread had been moved to the end of the meal and associated with the sharing of the cup, so that the celebration now consisted of two parts, a fellowship meal followed by explicitly sacramental actions. However, we lack the evidence to draw this conclusion with confidence. What we can be sure of is that the explicitly commemorative acts are being performed in conjunction with a communal meal. Schrage reconstructs the sequence of actions in Corinth at this time as follows: private meal; sacramental breaking of bread; *agapē*; sacramental sharing of the wine.[101]

11.17   Paul has no criticisms to make of the sequence of actions at their celebration but he is severely critical of the manner of it. He begins with a general statement that their coming together is doing *more harm than good*. It is not conducive of community but rather destructive of it.

115

11.18   He now proceeds to name the first disquieting piece of news he has heard that has led him to this severe judgement: *I am told that when you meet as a congregation you fall into sharply divided groups.*

The word here translated 'meet' is used five times in vv. 17–22 and 33–34 and clearly represents one of the key concepts of the whole passage.

It appears that the divisions Paul is referring to here are social rather than theological. In chapter 1 he speaks of factions that have formed around four names; here only of two groups, the 'haves' and the 'have-nots'.

The REB rendering of v. 18b, *I believe there is some truth in it,* does not quite convey the likely rhetorical force of Paul's statement. Margaret Mitchell has argued persuasively that Paul resorts to 'mock disbelief' as a way of expressing his shock at what he has heard.[102]

11.19   Paul's next statement, that such divisions serve to show which of the members are genuine and which are not, reads like a wry comment on his part but is probably an expression of the conviction that a process of divine judgement is already at work in the church.

11.20   He now makes an even sharper condemnation of their liturgical celebrations than in v. 17: *when you meet as a congregation, it is not the Lord's Supper you eat.* In other words, they are celebrating the supper in a way that denies its very nature. Does he mean that their breaking of the bread and sharing of the cup have become a mere form with no substance to them? That, far from them receiving the body and blood of the Lord, Christ is not really present at all? As he will make clear in vv. 27–34, that is not how he thinks of the consequences of their unworthy celebration. His belief is rather that Christ is indeed present, where the sacrament is celebrated unworthily, but present as Judge rather than as Saviour.

11.21   Paul now gives further evidence of the unworthiness of their celebration of the Lord's Supper. What ought to be a visible expression of their oneness and equality in Christ has become an occasion at which the less privileged members of the community are degraded and humiliated. For one thing, it is clearly a case of every man for himself. This aspect of the meal is brought out clearly in the REB rendering: *each of you takes his own supper.*

It is quite likely, however, that there is also a suggestion that each one is in a rush to eat his own supper, without bothering to wait till all have arrived. The underlying Greek verb can have that meaning, and the likelihood that it has that force in this context is enhanced by the fact that in v. 33 Paul urges the Corinthians to wait for one another (assuming that the verb carries its usual force), when they meet for the common meal. The result of their inconsiderateness is that one goes hungry and another has too much to drink. Those who have too much to drink are clearly those who are going ahead with their own supper. Those who are going hungry must be those who are arriving late. The sort of people Paul is referring to here were probably slaves or poor freedmen or freedwomen. Such people would not have been free to go out to such a gathering until they had completed the tasks assigned to them. Furthermore, the slaves would not have had the same freedom as free citizens to take their own supper along with them but would have been dependent on the generosity of other Christians. But, because other, more affluent members of the community are not bothering to wait for them, these poorer Christians have been finding, when they do eventually get to the gathering, that all the food has gone.[103]

Jerome Murphy-O'Connor has suggested that the Christians of Corinth would have met in villas that, to judge from the remains of Corinthian villas excavated by archaeologists, would have accommodated only nine or ten people in the *triclinium* or dining room, while the other guests would have had to eat in the *atrium* or courtyard. Under these circumstances, the host would naturally invite to the dining room only people from his own class. Thus the limited space available made discrimination between the wealthy and the less well off inevitable. David Horrell, however, has argued persuasively that we know too little about the shape or size of the spaces in which Christians met to be able to provide an architectural explanation for the divisions that arose in the church.[104]

There is also evidence, however, that Roman writers who depended for their existence on the support of a wealthy patron were well used to being treated like poor relations at meal times.[105] No doubt there were affluent Christians in the church at Corinth who took it for granted that such differentiations were part of the nature of things. Nor is it difficult to think of nominally Christian societies in modern times that have accepted similar divisions based on race or class as inevitable.

It is important for the interpretation of the following paragraphs to note that it is the slighting of the less privileged members of the community and that alone that evokes Paul's censure in the present paragraph.

That slighting points to a blind spot of which we have seen evidence again and again. Theirs is a community that is torn apart by competing factions (chapters 1—4). They have been taking one another to court (chapter 6). They have taken delight in parading their Christian freedom, reckless of the effect it might have on weaker brethren (chapter 8). And now we learn that they have been failing to wait for latecomers at the eucharistic meal. This lack of love has perverted the whole occasion, so that it is no longer the 'Lord's Supper'. As Thiselton remarks, paraphrasing Theissen, 'Is it the Lord's own supper which is being held, or that of the host and his most favoured guests?'[106]

11.22 Paul now launches into a series of rhetorical questions, as he seeks to arouse in his hearers a sense of shame. *Have you no homes of your own to eat and drink in?* The point of this question is clarified by v. 34a, where he writes, *If you are hungry, eat at home.* That is to say, they are to see to it that they do not come to the gatherings of the community so hungry that they cannot bear to wait a moment longer.

With his next question Paul lays his finger on the fundamental fault of which they are guilty: *Are you so contemptuous of the church of God that you shame its poorer members?* Indeed, he is so distressed that he confesses himself to be at his wits' end. *What am I to say? Can I commend you? On this point, certainly not!*

Do this in memory of me
11.23–26

Although Paul has just declared himself to be at his wits' end over the way the Corinthians are abusing the Lord's Supper, he now sees a way of making a positive response, by reminding them of the tradition of the institution of the supper, which he had himself received and duly passed on to them. We note briefly, to begin with, the diversity of the different accounts of the supper in the New Testament.

The New Testament contains four accounts of the supper: Matt. 26.26–29; Mark 14.22–25; Luke 22.15–20 and 1 Cor. 11.23–26. These, however, appear to derive from three main traditions. The accounts found in Mark and Paul are the two that differ from each other most noticeably, and therefore provide the clearest evidence of the existence of separate traditions. Matthew's account reproduces Mark's with minor modifications. Luke seems to have drawn not only on Mark and the tradition known to Paul but also on another tradition now embodied in Luke 22.15–18 and 24–30. This tradition is characterized by an intense longing for the coming of the kingdom of God.[107]

11.23 *For the tradition which I handed on to you came to me from the Lord himself.* Here, as later in 15.1 and 3, Paul is using words that are regularly used in the New Testament of the reception and transmission of tradition. The point in the context is probably that the tradition he passed on to the Corinthians came from the Lord in the sense that Jesus himself was its ultimate source. Paul could have received this tradition in Damascus or Jerusalem or Antioch, but it is hard to envisage this not being one of the first things that he learned, so that Damascus seems most likely.

11.24 There is good reason to believe that, whatever else Jesus may have said, he uttered over the loaf the words, 'This is my body.' These words are the only constant elements in all accounts of the supper. What is he likely to have meant by them? There is good reason to postulate behind the Greek word for 'body' the Aramaic word, *guphā*, which means the person as a whole, the self, much as the stem 'body' is used in the English words, anybody, everybody, somebody.[108] If so, the words, 'This is my body,' would have conveyed the meaning, 'This is I myself.' Certainly in the worship of the early church these words would have been heard as an assurance that the risen Lord was himself present, offering himself to his followers. But even at the Last Supper they could have conveyed an assurance of self-giving, since, for the Jews, a meal was in a very special sense a means of fellowship, a means of giving oneself to another and sharing in a common life.

In their present context in the New Testament, however, where they stand in close proximity to the cup saying with its reference to Christ's blood, these words of Jesus convey the further connotation: 'This is I myself, I who am given to death for all.' That is the clear implication of the various additions: 'for you' (the preferred text of Paul); 'broken for you' (some mss. of Paul); 'given for you' (the longer text of Luke).

Further resonances are also likely. Whether or not the Last Supper was an actual Passover meal, it is clear that it was celebrated in the context of the Passover season. In the Passover tradition as preserved in Pesahim X.4, there is a reference to 'the body of the Passover (lamb)'. The words of Jesus should probably be understood in the light of that reference as conveying the implication that this is the new Christian Passover.

119

The command, *Do this in memory of me*, is found in both Paul and the longer Lucan text in connection with the loaf, but Paul also repeats it in connection with the cup.

What precisely is meant by the words, 'Do this'? Since the verb used is quite general in its meaning, 'this' must be taken to include the blessing, breaking, distributing and eating.

In many biblical passages 'remembering' means more than a mental looking back or calling to mind. In 1 Kings 17.18, for example, the widow of Zarephath says to Elijah, in the rendering of the NRSV, 'You have come to me to bring my sin to remembrance, and to cause the death of my son!' What she is afraid of is that her sins will come back out of the past into the present, in living power.

While these overtones are certainly present in many passages, they do not seem to represent Paul's particular emphasis here. Here the emphasis falls on memory and hope rather than on the living presence of Christ here and now.

11.25   What of the cup saying? At this point the tradition embodied in Paul and the longer Lucan text, on the one hand, and the tradition embodied in Mark (and Matthew) differ quite clearly. Whereas, in Paul's version, Jesus says, *This cup is the new covenant sealed by my blood*, in Mark he says, *This is my blood, the blood of the covenant, shed for many*. However, the form of words found in Paul is likely to be closer to the actual words of Jesus. Paul's account was probably written down some 15 years before Mark's and was, as he himself tells us, received by him from older Christians within what must have been a very few years after the death of Jesus.

Moreover, Mark's version exhibits a greater parallelism between the bread saying and the cup saying than Paul's. It is more likely that the two sayings would be assimilated to each other in the course of transmission than that an original parallelism would be discarded.[109]

But what exactly is meant by 'this cup'? It is natural to assume that 'the cup' here means the contents of the cup, namely, the wine, but it is hard to see how the wine could be equated with the new covenant. If, however, we take the reference to be not to the contents of the cup but to *the cup as passed from hand to hand*, then we get good sense, thus: this circulating cup represents the new covenant; therefore the community that passes this cup from hand to hand is the community of the new covenant. But this covenant is sealed by my blood (literally, is 'in my blood'); that is, it is founded upon the death of Jesus.

In Paul's version, Jesus now repeats the command to *do this in memory of me,* prefixing them with the words, *Whenever you drink it.* There is good reason to think that Paul is now beginning to move from the quotation back to his own argument. If so, it is likely that these words, which are peculiar to Paul, represent his addition to the tradition. If so, they are a clue to where his present concern lies. He is seeking to bring home to the Corinthians that *every time* they eat this meal it is to be for the remembrance of Christ.

Many scholars consider that the words, *Do this in memory of me,* were not actually spoken by Jesus himself but were added by the church in the attempt to clarify his intentions. The main argument for this view is that the words are absent from Mark's account. However, if Jesus did see his death as inaugurating a new covenant and this meal as a means by which his followers were to appropriate its benefits, it is highly probable that he also envisaged that act of appropriation being constantly renewed. If so, then the words, *Do this in memory of me,* can be accepted as a guide to Jesus's intentions at the Last Supper, even if they do not represent his actual words.

11.26 This verse is probably also Paul's own elaboration of the tradition. If so, then we have a further pointer to the main focus of his concern in citing these traditions. The aspect of the supper that he particularly wants to stress is that it is a means of proclaiming Christ's death. In the Greek, the words, *the death of the Lord,* are placed in an emphatic position in front of the verb. The verb 'to proclaim' probably does not mean that the meal in itself is the proclamation but that during the meal there was a verbal proclamation of Christ's death.

The Corinthians are at fault because they have lost sight of this in their celebration of the supper. In proclaiming Christ's death, they are declaring the good news that Christ has made them all one, but by their manner of celebrating the meal they are humiliating the less privileged members of the community and therefore contradicting the meaning of the whole occasion.

Moreover, while the eschatological setting of the supper was apparently not particularly stressed in the tradition with which Paul was familiar, he himself now underlines it. Every time the Corinthians eat the bread and drink the cup, they *proclaim the death of the Lord, until he comes.* The Lord's Supper is celebrated in this age by people who wait and hope. It is not yet the heavenly meal of the blessed but iron rations for people on the way.

Not discerning the body
11.27–34

The following passage is dominated by the thought of judgement. Judgement terminology is found in vv. 27, 28, 29, 31, 32 and 34. Paul speaks not only of the fact of present judgement but of the possibility of final judgement and of the consequent need for critical self-examination. While he speaks in general terms, to begin with – *anyone who eats the bread, everyone must test himself* – it becomes quite clear from v. 30 on that these warnings are directed against the Corinthians themselves. Therefore, when he speaks at the beginning of unworthy participation, he has the Corinthian situation in mind.

11.27ff. Throughout the present section of the letter Paul has taken them to task for one sin and one sin only, their failure to show consideration towards underprivileged members at the common meal, a failure that amounts to contempt for the church of God (v. 22). This then must be what he is referring to, when he speaks in v. 27 of *anyone who eats the bread or drinks the cup of the Lord unworthily. Such a person,* he goes on, *will be guilty of offending against the body and blood of the Lord.* In somewhat similar fashion, he declares in v. 29 that *he who eats and drinks eats and drinks judgement on himself if he does not discern the body.* These two verses have occasioned a great deal of discussion, so that they are best considered together.

Generations of scholars have taken Paul's words in v. 29 about not discerning the body to refer to a failure to discern the body of Christ in the elements, that is, a failure to distinguish the bread and wine of the Lord's Supper from the common food of a normal meal. On this view, the 'body' here means the risen body of Christ present in the elements. Some translations reflect this view. Thus the RSV rendering of v. 27 (not the NRSV) speaks of 'profaning the body and blood of the Lord'; the NEB of 'desecrating the body and blood of the Lord'.

This interpretation, however, fits neither the letter as a whole nor this passage in particular. Nowhere in the letter does Paul charge the Corinthians with disregard of the sacrament. On the contrary, they appear rather to have been super-sacramentalists (see 10.1–13; 15.29). As for the present passage, both in vv. 17–22, as we have seen, and in vv. 33–34 Paul taxes them with one sin and one sin only, namely, their failure to take seriously the common meal.

In the light of all this, the phrase about not discerning the body is most naturally understood as referring primarily to the church. The

Corinthians are failing to appreciate that what makes this meal different from any other is the fact that here they are constituted one body,
the body of Christ. They are failing to discern that body as represented
by the members of the church, particularly the least and lowliest. But
this does not exclude the possibility of a further level of meaning.
Such a possibility is suggested by v. 27.

The warning in v. 27 against offending against the body and blood
of the Lord is best understood as a reference to Christ who died for
these brothers and sisters. The thought of the presence of the risen
Christ is not prominent, as we have seen. On the other hand, an allusion to the church is ruled out by the reference to the blood. To be
guilty of offending against (literally, guilty against) the body and
blood of the Lord must mean, therefore, to take the side of the powers
that crucified Jesus. A similar thought is expressed in Heb. 6.6.

On this view of the passage, there is a transition from a christological
use of 'body' in v. 27 to a primarily ecclesiastical use in v. 29. But
this has an exact parallel in 10.16–17. Indeed, 10.17 can be seen as an
anticipation both of the present passage and of chapter 12.

There is also a similar movement of thought in 8.11–12. In that passage Paul declares that whoever sins against a weaker brother sins
against Christ, who died for that very brother. In the present passage
he allows the thought of the Eucharist to shape his terminology and
speaks of sinning against the body and blood of the Lord but means
the same thing.

In the light of v. 27, however, with its clear reference to the death
of Christ, it is reasonable to find a further level of meaning in v. 29,
according to which 'not discerning the body' also implies not discerning the body given for you (cf. v. 24), that is, shutting your eyes to the
meaning of the death of the Lord for you and for everyone. Failure to
recognize a fellow-Christian for what he or she is, namely, a brother or
sister for whom Christ died, is *ipso facto* failure to discern the meaning
of the cross.

11.28   Each member is therefore called upon to *test himself before
eating from the bread and drinking from the cup.*

11.30f.   Because the Corinthians have failed to do this, they have
fallen under the judgement of God. Furthermore, this judgement is
a deadly serious matter. It has brought upon many of them sickness
and even death.

11.32 And yet the aim of this judgement is salvific. It has been inflicted upon them precisely in order to save them *from being condemned with the rest of the world*. It is therefore a pedagogical work of grace, carried out in order to preserve the church as the church.

Thus there is in this passage a juxtaposition of the ideas of present judgement and ultimate deliverance that closely parallels 5.1–5. In that earlier passage the church is to pronounce a sentence upon the offender not only in order to preserve itself as church but to preserve this man as a Christian and so ensure his deliverance on the day of the Lord.

11.33f. Paul concludes the passage with specific practical directives: *when you meet for this meal, wait for one another*. And if they are so hungry that they cannot wait for latecomers, they are to satisfy their hunger before they leave home, *so that in meeting together* they *may not fall under judgement*.

A case can be made for interpreting the main verb in v. 33 to mean not to wait for one another but rather to receive one another as guests. However, the usage of the verb elsewhere in the New Testament favours the interpretation adopted in the REB.

As for other matters that, presumably, also have to do with the ordering of worship, Paul will settle these when he comes. It is noteworthy that he does not appeal to any church official such as a presbyter to do what needs to be done. This strongly suggests that, contrary to the evidence of Acts (see 14.23; 20.17), there were as yet no such officials in Paul's churches.

As some commentators observe, this passage has had a fateful effect on the history of the church.[110] In the Reformed and Presbyterian tradition particularly it led, in earlier centuries, to a 'fencing of the Table' against unworthy participation, which must have obscured the character of the sacrament as a means of grace and dissuaded many earnest believers from full communication. Nevertheless, we do well to be reminded that the God of whom Paul speaks is not the 'dear God' who of course forgives all his erring children but the holy and the true, the Lord, whose offer of forgiveness and new life runs counter to everything we have a right to expect. Such an offer is to be received joyfully but never casually.

Paul's closing statement in v. 34b that he will settle the other matters, when he comes, implies that he sees this letter as a substitute, in the meantime, for his presence in person.

Spiritual Gifts
12.1—14.40

Paul now turns to a new topic, gifts of the Spirit. The overall theme of worship remains central, in so far as that is the sphere in which some gifts of the Spirit, notably tongues and prophecy, find expression, but the theme of spiritual gifts or, as Paul prefers to speak of them, gifts of grace (*charismata*), is much wider than worship and is in fact a key to Paul's understanding of the church and its order.

The use once again in 12.1 of the phrase 'About . . .' makes it very likely that this was another issue that the Corinthians had raised in their letter to Paul. In response, however, he does a great deal more than simply supply information. In chapter 14 it soon becomes apparent that he is seeking to correct an exaggerated estimate of the value of speaking in tongues and that he is also urging them to develop the gift of prophecy rather than that of tongues. But chapter 12, when studied carefully in the light of all we know, or can reasonably conjecture, about the Corinthian community, also proves to contain a sharp critique of Corinthian assumptions about the way in which the Spirit makes its presence felt. Central to this critique of Paul's is the term *charisma*.

Chapter 13 may seem at first sight to be a digression. While it may well incorporate thoughts that Paul had composed for some earlier occasion, it nevertheless does have a direct bearing on the themes of chapters 12 and 14, in so far as it sets forth the motive by which any spiritual gift must be controlled, if it is to be of any value for the edification of the church. At the same time this chapter clearly has a bearing on the larger concerns of the letter as a whole.

The presenting problem is, in all probability, an abuse of the gift of tongues, but, in order to deal with it, Paul addresses himself first of all to more fundamental problems. In chapter 12 he considers the manner in which God bestows the Spirit or the gift of grace upon believers, as well as the purpose for which God does this, namely, to bring into being a community in which everyone has a vocation to fulfil and yet is at the same time dependent on everyone else, a community aptly described as the body of Christ. In chapter 13 he celebrates the greatest gift of God, which is withheld from no one and without which even the most spectacular gift is of no avail, love.

Testing the spirits
12.1–3

12.1 The word translated by the REB *gifts of the Spirit* could also be rendered 'spiritual persons'. However, the way in which the word seems to be used interchangeably in the present chapter with *charismata*, gifts of grace, suggests that here the reference is to gifts. The translation, *I want there to be no misunderstanding*, brings out well that Paul is seeking not simply to inform or to instruct but to correct.

12.2 The place of the next sentence in the argument of the passage as a whole is not immediately apparent, but it is clear that Paul is reminding his readers of something they had been familiar with while they were *still pagan*, namely, the experience of being *carried away by some impulse or other* in worship. It is also clear that Paul is stressing that the objects to which they had felt irresistibly drawn had been dumb heathen gods. It is likely that Paul has in mind phenomena common to a number of cults rather than one specific cult.

Strictly speaking, the word translated *pagans* in the REB means Gentiles, the implication being that the Gentile Christians of Corinth have now become part of Israel.

Paul's point in the context appears to be that the mere experience of ecstasy or inspiration by itself proves nothing. As a religious phenomenon, it is, as the Corinthians well know, common to both Christianity and paganism alike. The crucial question is what is the nature of the spirit by which one is inspired and what it is that one is inspired to do and say. In other words, to distinguish between genuine inspiration by the Spirit of God and counterfeit inspiration by some other spirit one needs criteria. In the following verse Paul proceeds to supply a fundamental criterion, which he states first negatively then positively.

12.3 The first part of v. 3, the negative statement, has occasioned endless discussion. Thiselton outlines 12 distinct explanations that have been offered.[111] Is Paul referring to members of a 'Christ party' who had become docetic in their Christology, rejected the man Jesus and professed to know 'Christ after the flesh' (cf. 2 Cor. 5.16) no longer? Or to Christians who felt themselves being overcome by a trance or ecstasy and, in the attempt to ward off the experience, cursed the name of Jesus? Are we hearing an echo of the angry rejections of Christian claims made by some of the Corinthians before their conversion, perhaps even by Paul himself?

All of these views are open to an objection. If Paul had believed that people were actually uttering the words, 'A curse on Jesus!' in any of the circumstances outlined, he would surely have responded at much greater length and with much greater passion. It therefore seems more likely that the expression is a construct of Paul's, an artificial antithesis to the *Kyrios* confession, designed to bring home to the Corinthians, by a kind of shock therapy, the profound implications of uttering the basic Christian creed.

In a positive statement that balances the negative statement of v. 3a, Paul now declares that *no one can say 'Jesus is Lord!' except under the influence of the Holy Spirit*. Thus only the Spirit makes Christian discipleship possible.

The converse of this truth is that no Christian who has made the most elementary confession of faith need be in any doubt about their knowledge of the Spirit. In Acts 19.2 Luke has Paul ask a group of quasi-disciples (probably disciples of John the Baptist), *'Did you receive the Holy Spirit when you became believers?'* For the Paul of the letters, it is impossible to become a believer at all without the action of the Spirit. As we shall see more clearly in the next section, the Spirit for Paul is not the special prerogative of a privileged élite but the common possession of all believers.

Paul applies the term *Kyrios* to Christ no fewer than 220 times.

PAUL'S UNDERSTANDING OF *CHARISMATA*

We have already noted, in the introduction to the previous section, that chapter 12 proves, on careful examination, to contain a sharp critique of Corinthian assumptions about the way in which the Spirit makes its presence felt. Central to this critique of Paul's is the term *charisma*.

The word *charisma* is cognate with the word *charis*, grace, and can be defined as divine grace becoming concrete. Käsemann describes it in an illuminating and seminal essay as 'the manifestation and concretion of the gracious power of God'.[112] Arndt and Gingrich give as its principal meaning 'a gift freely and graciously given, a favour bestowed'.[113] That definition covers quite adequately the meaning of the word in some Pauline passages, such as Rom. 5.15; 6.23; 11.29; 1 Cor. 1.7, but fails to communicate what is distinctive of Paul's usage.

The concept of *charisma* in Paul is closely related to that of the Holy Spirit. Thus in 1 Cor. 12.4 the Spirit is represented as the source of the *charismata* (cf. Rom. 1.11; 1 Cor. 2.12, where the cognate verb is linked with the Spirit). A *charisma* can therefore be defined as a gift of the Spirit.

Now there was an obvious term available to Paul to convey the idea of a spiritual gift, namely, the word *pneumatikon*. He does use that term in v. 1 (though the word here may possibly be in the masculine gender, on which see above), but in v. 4 and subsequent verses (9, 28, 30 and 31) he uses instead the word *charisma*. In v. 1, where he is referring to the letter from the Corinthians, he no doubt uses the word they had used themselves, but it appears that *charisma* is his preferred term.

Paul's evident preference for the term *charisma* over the term *pneumatikon* suggests that he is engaging in a theological critique. It appears that the word *pneumatikon* had become so loaded with misleading associations that Paul found it necessary to replace it with a word of his own choosing. The word *charisma* expresses more clearly the notion of gift, and Paul also gives it a colouring of his own. These hypotheses are confirmed, when we examine Paul's teaching in the chapter as a whole in the light of what we already know, or may reasonably conjecture, about Corinthian assumptions about the way in which the Spirit makes its presence felt.

(i) We may reasonably infer that the Corinthians assumed that the Spirit was given to them for their own enrichment, their personal benefit. We have seen, over and over again, that their community was conspicuously deficient in any sense of mutual responsibility. They were torn apart by competing factions (chapters 1—4). They were taking one another to court (chapter 6). They delighted in parading their Christian freedom, reckless of the effect it might have on weaker brethren (chapter 8). They were failing to wait for latecomers at the eucharistic meal (11.17–34). And yet they had the Spirit. Clearly, for them the Spirit had nothing to do with 'my neighbour'; it only had to do with me, with my enrichment.

(ii) We may also infer that the Corinthians took it for granted that the Spirit made its presence felt chiefly in spectacular manifestations. The care and tact with which Paul disparages any exaggerated estimate of the value of tongue-speaking in chapter 14 shows unmistakably how highly the Corinthians must have prized this particular gift. If so, we may surely infer that they thought of the gifts of the Spirit primarily in terms of things that were abnormal, spectacular, 'out of this world'.

(iii) We may also infer that the Corinthians saw the Spirit as the especial possession of a privileged few, a spiritual élite. We have just found reason to think that they set great store by speaking in tongues. Yet in 12.30 Paul asks the question, *Do all speak in tongues of ecstasy?* and by the form of the question in the Greek clearly expects the answer, 'No'. If not all of them had this gift, then those who did have it must have been seen as especially favoured.

(iv) Throughout the letter we have found ample evidence that the Corinthians had over-realized their eschatology, that they saw themselves as having been lifted out of the present order, marked as it is by temptation, conflict, suffering and risk, and filled with heavenly power, or the power of the age to come, in all its fullness. We may reasonably infer that they attributed this transformation to the gifts of the Spirit. As Schweizer puts it, 'For them the Spirit is the inrush of heavenly power, in which finality is already anticipated.'[114] It is only when we discern these assumptions in the background that we can fully appreciate the sharpness of Paul's critique, for to him each one of them is a distortion of the truth.

(ia) In contrast to the first assumption that the Corinthians were making, Paul affirms that every *charisma* that the Spirit bestows upon the church consists of some sort of capacity to perform a service for the good of others. Thus in vv. 4–6 we have three sentences that are clearly parallel to one another. What is particularly significant is that the word *charismata* in v. 4 is parallel to the word *diakoniai*, forms of service, ministries, in v. 5. Paul follows up this parallelism with the statement in v. 7 that *in each of us the Spirit is seen to be at work for some useful purpose*. Similarly, in Rom. 12.6f., in the same breath as stating that we have different gifts allotted to each of us by God's grace, he exhorts his readers to *use* their gifts, whatever they may be, and once again links *charismata* with *diakoniai*. There is therefore an indivisible connection in Paul's thought between *charisma* and service, ministry or vocation. In this connection, several commentators quote a remark of J.-J. Suurmond that 'It is not so much a matter of *having* a gift as of *being* a gift.'[115]

Right through chapters 12—14, Paul keeps insisting that this is the yardstick by which what is claimed to be a gift of the Spirit must always be measured. All gifts are related to the corporate body, the church, and are assessed in the light of their contribution to that body's proper functioning. The Corinthians are urged to aspire above all to excel in those gifts which build up the church (14.12; cf. v. 26).

(iia) In contrast to the second assumption that the Corinthians were making, Paul makes it clear that the gracious gifts of the Spirit need in no way be striking, spectacular, 'out of this world'. In several places he gives a list of *charismata*, in vv. 8–10 and 28 of the present chapter and also in Rom. 12.6–8. It is especially striking how he places side by side the apostolate and ability to help others, gifts of healing and gifts of administration (1 Cor. 12.28). Similarly, in Rom. 12.6–8 he speaks of works of mercy, almsgiving and helping others in distress. It is safe to say that these were things that it would never have entered the Corinthians' heads to regard as signs of the working of the Spirit. Clearly for Paul extraordinariness is irrelevant as a criterion of the Spirit's presence. This conviction of his is also reflected in his depreciation of speaking in tongues in chapter 14.

This feature of Paul's teaching leads one to ask whether a person's *charisma* consists in a new capacity bestowed upon them by the Spirit or in the heightening and redirection of a natural capacity. Paul himself does not ask this question, but what he does say strongly suggests the answer that some gifts, like speaking in tongues, will appear as new capacities but others, like the ability to help others, as old capacities heightened and redirected.

(iiia) In contrast to the third assumption of the Corinthians, Paul insists that the Spirit leaves no believer ungifted. There is a stereotyped repetition of the fact that God gives to everyone. *In each of us the Spirit is seen to be at work* (v. 7). The Spirit distributes gifts *to each individual at will* (v. 11; cf. Rom. 12.3).

(iva) What of the fourth assumption that the Corinthians were making, namely, that the gifts of the Spirit had lifted them out of this present order? Paul does not make a direct attack on this assumption in the present chapters, as he does in 4.6–13, yet a critique is nevertheless implicit in what he says. His reference in 13.1 to speaking in tongues of men or of angels suggests that the Corinthians supposed that speakers in tongues were speaking the language of heaven. If so, the douche of cold water that Paul pours over their enthusiasm is in line with his consistent correction of their over-realized eschatology. Furthermore, his insistence in vv. 21–26 on the need of every believer to depend upon the gifts of all his or her fellow-believers can also be taken as an expression of his conviction that believers, far from having arrived, are still on the way.[116]

All different but all gifted
12.4–11

12.4–6 Paul begins with three parallel statements, all emphasizing that *there are varieties of gifts (of service, of activity)*, but all are derived from *the same Spirit (the same Lord, the same God)*. This repeated emphasis on the variety of the gifts, also made in vv. 8–10, is probably a response to the Corinthian enthusiasm for the gift of tongues. His stress on the common derivation of all gifts from the one divine source (also made in vv. 8, 9 and 11) may well be aimed at Corinthian assumptions of superiority (postulated in (iii) above.) It is also noteworthy that Paul is not content simply to say that the one God is responsible for the variety of gifts, rather the variety of gifts is a reflection of the variety (in unity) of God. As Fee puts it, 'Diversity within unity belongs to the character of God himself.'[117]

12.7 This verse crystallizes the emphases noted in (ia) and (iiia) above. The verbal form translated in the REB *for some useful purpose* (RSV: 'for the common good') has already been used in 6.12; 10.23, 33.

12.8–10 These verses illustrate the variety of gifts that all derive from the one Spirit. The opening four chapters of the letter have made it clear that the first gifts that Paul mentions, namely, *the gift of wise speech* and *the power to put the deepest knowledge into words*, were gifts by which the Corinthians themselves set special store. Here, as in those opening chapters, 'knowledge' must be understood as insight into the message of the cross, and 'wise speech' as the ability to communicate that message.

'Faith' in v. 9 can hardly mean the faith by which a person is enabled to say, 'Jesus is Lord,' since such faith is a sine qua non of being a Christian at all, whereas the gifts Paul is talking about here are bestowed on some Christians but not on others. So 'faith' here must mean some special gift, probably the kind of faith that is able, if not to move mountains (cf. 13.2), at least to heal the sick. The gifts of prophecy and tongues are discussed in greater detail in chapter 14. As for *the ability to distinguish true spirits from false*, this probably means the ability to differentiate between prophecies, as in 14.29, where the cognate verb is used and understood by the REB to refer to the exercise of judgement upon prophecies that have just been uttered.

12.11   By declaring that *all these gifts*, and any others there may be, *are the activity of one and the same Spirit*, Paul reiterates a major emphasis of the passage before going on to emphasize the Spirit's sovereignty over the gifts that the Spirit bestows.

One body; many organs
12.12–26

In the latter part of chapter 12 Paul makes an extended comparison between the church as a charismatic community and the human body. Since every Christian has his or her own distinctive gift of grace, which consists in the ability to perform a service for the good of the whole, Christians collectively can appropriately be compared with the limbs or organs that together make up a living body. As members of the church, they are 'members' in the original sense of that word, namely, limbs or organs of the body of Christ.

A comparison between a human community and the human body is frequently met with in ancient literature. The best-known example is the fable that Livy (ii.32) ascribes to Menenius Agrippa (c.494 BC). Paul, however, gives the image a new twist. In earlier literature the image is widely used to dissuade the socially disadvantaged members of society from rebellion by persuading them that the more privileged members are not, as might appear, indolent parasites on the body politic but people who perform an indispensable function.[118] Paul uses the image to argue that all the members have a part to play in the life of the church and are therefore all deserving of honour.

12.12   Paul begins by stating his basic thesis: the church in its unity and diversity *is like a single body with its many limbs and organs*. Strictly speaking, it is 'Christ' rather than the church that is here compared to a body, but 'Christ' here is probably a shorthand expression for 'the body of Christ'. The concept of the church as the body of Christ must already have been known to the Corinthians; otherwise Paul's enigmatic brevity here is hard to account for. The use of the phrase, 'one body in Christ', in Rom. 12.5 shows that the concept has not yet crystallized in a fixed terminology. The repetition of the words 'one', 'many', 'many', 'one' indicates where Paul's interest lies, in the church's unity in diversity and diversity in unity.

12.13   Paul now moves from simile to metaphor.[119] He has just said that the church is *like* a body; here he declares that it *is* a body. Those who are baptized are *all brought into one body by baptism*, the body of Christ. The thought of unity and variety remains uppermost. Thus there is a reference to 'one Spirit', 'one body' and again 'one Spirit'. The aspect of the church's diversity that is here underlined, however, is not the diversity of *charismata* but the diversity of race and social status – *Jews or Greeks, slaves or free*. In the new social reality of the church the class antitheses of ancient society are, in principle, overcome. In contrast to Gal. 3.28, however, which is also a baptismal reference, there is no mention of male and female.[120] The statement that *we were all given that one Spirit to drink* is evidently a metaphorical reference to the effect of baptism.

12.14   This verse is like a text for the homily that follows: a body is made up not of *a single organ but many*. This is where the emphasis falls, on the necessary diversity of the functions exercised by the different organs that make up a body, and therefore on the necessary diversity of the functions exercised by the different members of the church.

In vv. 15–26 Paul makes two applications of the principle he has just stated, in order to show that it leaves no room in the Christian fellowship for either envy or arrogance.

12.15–20   Envy first. It would be absurd for the foot to say, *'Because I am not a hand, I do not belong to the body.'* It is equally absurd for any Christian to feel envious of another, for no one is ungifted, and therefore no one is unusable or insignificant.

It is understandable that the foot should see itself as inferior to the hand, the hand being the primary instrument of human creativity. Similarly the ear here seems to be affected by the typically Greek predilection for seeing rather than hearing. By singling out these organs, Paul is seeking to encourage those members of the community who doubt their spiritual gifts and feel themselves to be hopelessly inferior to the more vocal and confident members.

A body that consisted of a single organ, like a foot or an eye, *would not be a body at all* but a monstrosity. In the same way a community of believers that consisted of nothing but tongue-speakers would not be a true church. In calling the church into being to constitute the body of Christ, God has endowed its members with different and complementary gifts, appointing *each limb and organ to its own place*. It follows that each member of the church has his or her own unique contribution to make to the vitality of the whole organism and therefore their own inalienable dignity.

12.21–26   Here Paul makes a different application of the concept of the church as a body. One of the main emphases of vv. 4–11, reiterated in v. 18, is that God gives to each his own as God wills, as God has chosen. As Käsemann has observed, this cuts two ways. On the one hand, it liberates a person from worry and envy, by assuring them that they are not ungifted. God gives individually to each person. No one goes away empty. But conversely no one has too much. The grace that opens up for me a specific avenue of service leaves other avenues closed. Grace both releases me for service and sets a limit to what I may aspire to.[121] In other words, grace gives each Christian a specific competence but gives omnicompetence to no one. And therefore no Christian has any excuse for despising a fellow-Christian; all need one another, all are dependent on one another. This inference is explicitly drawn by Paul in v. 21.

12.22f.   Paul reinforces the exhortation he has just given by means of a further application of the image of the body to the church. He speaks of *parts of the body which seem to be more frail than others*. Probably he has in mind those organs that are not obviously active like the arms or legs, perhaps organs like the liver or spleen. For all their seeming inactivity, these organs are in fact indispensable. Paul does not draw from this observation an explicit conclusion for our understanding of the church, but the point is clear: Christians who are not endowed with striking or spectacular gifts may well be exercising a ministry that is more important to the life of the church than those whose gifts command attention.

12.23f.   There are also parts of our bodies that *we are modest about*, parts that we consider unpresentable. The underlying Greek word here is used with reference to sexual life in Gen. 34.7 and Deut. 24.1, and the reference here too seems to be to the sexual organs, the 'private parts'. In normal civilized society these organs are covered up. Does this mean that we consider them to be objects of shame? On the contrary, says Paul, we are treating these parts of the body *with special honour*, a *special respect* of which *our respectable parts* have no need.

In the same way – so we must conclude – there are members of the church who are in no way in the public eye yet are deserving of special respect. In calling the church into being in such a way that the members form a single organism, God has given *special honour to the humbler parts*, that is, to those who appear to be inferior, to be deprived.

Paul's point here does not appear to be quite the same as in v. 22. The point of v. 22 is that Christians who do not appear to be doing anything important for the church may in fact be doing something essential. What Paul now seems to be saying is that Christians who are in some way deprived are deserving of special concern.

12.25   This leads Paul back to the thought of the church's unity. Throughout the paragraph he has been insisting that the very diversity of the church is to be the means of creating unity. Each member is to recognize that he or she has a unique contribution to make to the life of the whole, and that the same thing is true of every other member. Paul now develops the thought of the duty to love hinted at in v. 24b. There is to be *no division in the body. All its parts* are to *feel the same concern for one another.* Paul here hits out at the tendency of the Corinthians to form rival groups.

12.26   In other words, the members of the church are to recognize that, for all their differences, they really are a single body in Christ. Whatever happens to a Christian brother or sister affects the whole body, of which I too am a part. Thus *if one part suffers, all suffer together; if one flourishes, all rejoice together.* My sister's pain is my pain too, my brother's joy my joy.

In *The Primal Vision* John Taylor has suggested that African Christians understand better than Western Christians the mutuality of which Paul speaks here. In a most moving passage, a description of the mutuality of New Testament Christianity merges subtly into a description of African Christianity.[122]

No one is omnicompetent
12.27–31

12.27 Paul has developed at length his comparison between the church as a charismatic community and the human body. He now sums up the previous paragraph: *Now you are Christ's body, and each of you a limb or organ of it.* The genitive, 'Christ's', is to be understood not as a genitive of definition, 'the body that is Christ', but as a genitive of possession, 'the body that belongs to Christ'.

12.28 Leaving the image of the body behind, Paul now emphasizes once more the leading theme of vv. 4–11, namely, the diversity of gifts needed to sustain the life and mission of the church. He begins by citing eight such gifts. The diversity of these gifts illustrates the fecundity of God's new creation, which parallels the fecundity of the original creation, celebrated by Paul in 15.39–41. Verse 28 is one of the few passages in the authentic letters of Paul (10.32 is another) in which the word 'church' (*ekklēsia* in Greek) refers not to the local gathering but to a wider community.

In our earlier note on Paul's understanding of *charismata*, we have already observed that here he places side by side gifts that are compelling, striking, even spectacular, such as, on the one hand, apostleship or prophecy or healing or *the gift of tongues of various kinds*, and, on the other, gifts that are in no way striking or extraordinary, such as *ability to help others or power to guide them*. The Corinthians need to be reminded that the latter are every bit as much the work of the Spirit of God as the former.

At the same time, certain gifts are given a certain pre-eminence: *Within our community God has appointed in the first place apostles, in the second place prophets, thirdly teachers; then* . . . There is a further break between the first three *charismata* and the remaining five, in that Paul begins by speaking of persons – apostles, prophets, teachers – but thereafter speaks of gifts. This switch is obscured in the REB.

The pre-eminence attributed here to the first three forms of ministry is, no doubt, partly a temporal one, in that apostles are authorized witnesses of the unique foundational event, the resurrection of the crucified one, but more than that seems to be implied.

Not only apostles but also prophets and teachers perform a function that is essential to the church's life. It is not surprising that apostles stand in the first place, in the light of 3.10, where Paul speaks of their role in laying the foundation. Moreover, they alone are directly called and commissioned by the risen one. The primary role of teachers seems to have been that of maintaining and expounding the tradition, whereas that of prophets is to declare to this community what is God's will for them at this time. It is by these three ministries, above all, that the church is established and built up.

12.29f. Throughout the previous paragraph Paul has been concerned to emphasize the diversity of the *charismata*. Now, through a series of rhetorical questions, he stresses that no single gift is the possession of every believer. The Greek word used to introduce each question implies that the speaker is expecting the answer, 'No'. As we observed in commenting on vv. 21ff., the grace that opens up for me a specific avenue of service leaves other avenues closed. Grace gives each Christian a specific competence but gives omnicompetence to no one.

12.31a We have already found reason to believe that the Corinthians set special store by the more striking and spectacular gifts (see the excursus on *charismata*). By now declaring, *The higher gifts are those you should prize*, Paul implies that some gifts are indeed more valuable than others. It has already become clear, however, and will be made even clearer by the following two chapters, that Paul's criterion of value differs sharply from that held by the Corinthians. The essential thing, in Paul's eyes, is that a gift should contribute to the building up of the church. The gifts that the Corinthians should be aspiring to, therefore, are those that do that most effectively. Paul has stressed several times in this chapter that gifts of grace are God's to distribute, as God wills (vv. 6, 11, 28). Nevertheless, there are certain gifts to which believers may legitimately aspire.

12.31b There remains something even more important to be said. No one Christian possesses the totality of the gifts, yet every Christian is called to walk in a *way*, the way of love. Most translations imply that the 'way' Paul is referring to is somehow being contrasted with the forms of charismatic discipleship that he has been talking about throughout the present chapter, but that is a little misleading. To translate literally, Paul is disclosing to his readers 'a way beyond measure'. This is the way that every Christian is called to walk, whatever their *charisma* may be. Indeed, if they fail to do so, then no *charisma* they may possess will be of any value whatsoever. The 'way' is therefore not to be contrasted with the various *charismata* but rather combined with them.

Love, the alpha and omega of the Christian way
13.1–13

As was noted in the introduction to chapters 12—14, chapter 13 may seem at first sight to be a digression. It reads like a set piece, the product of long and leisurely deliberation, and therefore sits rather oddly in the context of a letter that reads for the most part like a running conversation.

This impression that we are dealing with a set piece is strengthened when we count up the number of words the chapter contains that are either not found anywhere else in the New Testament (five) or not found anywhere else in this letter (thirteen).

Nevertheless, the chapter is clearly relevant to the themes of chapters 12—14, in so far as it sets forth the spirit in which any spiritual gift must be exercised, if it is to be of any value for the edification of the church.

Moreover, at several points it has a direct bearing on the situation in Corinth that has occasioned this discussion of spiritual gifts.

We have found reason to believe that the primary problem Paul is addressing at this point is an overestimate of the value of tongues. Paul's insistence in v. 1 on the worthlessness of the gift of tongues, if the gift is not exercised in a spirit of love, speaks directly to that situation. Indeed, his reference to speaking *in tongues of angels* may well echo the Corinthian way of regarding this gift. There is an illuminating passage in the *Testament of Job* 48.3 (first century BC or AD), which purports to tell how the three daughters of Job were given the power of angelic speech and song. This may well have been how the gift of tongues was understood by the Corinthians.

Verses 8–13 also bear directly on the Corinthian situation. We have found abundant evidence throughout the letter that the Corinthians had over-realized their eschatology. These verses draw a sharp contrast between 'now' and 'then', and further define this temporal contrast both in terms of what is transitory and what is eternal and in terms of what is partial and what is complete. In v. 8 prophecies, tongues and knowledge are all assigned to this present time, which will pass away. This is surely a further correction of the position taken by the Corinthians, who undoubtedly prized these gifts, especially tongues and knowledge. The clear implication is that the Corinthians have mistaken penultimate gifts for ultimate ones.

Along with these explicit references to tongues and other gifts prized by the Corinthians, the statement in v. 4 that *love is never boastful, never conceited* also strikes home to the Corinthian situation, since the word underlying 'conceited', literally 'puffed up', is, as we have already noted, used several times by Paul to characterize the distinctive Corinthian malaise (see the commentary on 4.6).

Therefore, if it is indeed a previously composed piece that Paul has inserted here, it must have been composed in circumstances in which he had the distortions of Corinthian piety very much in mind.

As for its literary form, the passage belongs to the genre of eulogy. It is a passage in praise of a particular virtue, comparable with Plato's eulogy of love in his *Symposium* (197 c–e) or with the passage in praise of Wisdom in Wisdom 7.22–30.

The literary structure of the passage is marked not only by the use of a very wide vocabulary but by pronounced stylistic changes and elaborate symmetry.

Verses 1–3 consist of three parallel sentences, each one containing the following essential structure: 'If I have all of this or that gift but not love, I am nothing.' Three times over Paul makes the point that, however remarkable his spiritual gifts may be, they are worthless, if they are not exercised in love.

Verses 4–7 contain 15 verbs of action, which all have 'love' as their subject and are grouped as follows: first, two positive statements about love; then eight negative ones plus a positive restatement of a negative statement; then four verbs with 'all things' as object.

Verses 8–12 consist of a series of five temporal contrasts. The first two and the last two are contrasts between 'now' and 'then', that is, between the present age and the age to come. The middle one in v. 11 is a contrast between the past and the present.

Finally, in v. 13, we have an affirmation in the present tense that makes a less pronounced contrast between love on the one hand and faith and hope on the other.

12.31b The last sentence of chapter 12 links the two chapters together. Paul has just urged the Corinthians to prize the higher *charismata*. Now he states that there is something even more worth pursuing. He does not, however, describe this more worthy object as a *charisma* but as a *way*. Any *charisma* is bestowed on certain Christians but not on all, but all Christians without exception are called to walk in love. Love therefore can be aptly described as a *way*.

13.1–3   The first paragraph of the chapter consists of a series of three sonorous parallel sentences that build up and break like the waves of the sea. We have already noted that these verses have a sharply polemical point in the context of the distorted piety of Corinth. Even if I have the most striking *charismata* and am able to exercise them to the nth degree, so that I can speak in tongues of men or of angels or possess the gift of prophecy and the knowledge of every hidden truth, or faith enough to move mountains but have no love, I am nothing. The words 'mysteries' and 'knowledge' are regularly used in apocalyptic literature to refer to the knowledge of the end time, which is disclosed to the seer. See for example Dan. 2.19–23, 28.

'I' here is not quite interchangeable with 'one' but has rather a subtle rhetorical force. If I, who can speak in tongues better than any of you (see 14.9), were to lack love, I would be worthless. What about yourselves?

According to Vitruvius, bronze vases placed upside down and tilted by wedges were used as resonance enhancers in some theatres. Paul may have such vases in mind in his reference in v. 1 to 'a sounding gong'.[123] Alternatively, the phrase could be simply an image for meaningless noise.

The reference in v. 2 to a faith which is able to move mountains may be a conscious reminiscence of the dominical saying in Mark 11.23 but is more likely to be an independent adaptation of a proverbial expression for doing something which seems impossible.

Verse 3 pushes paradox to the limit. Even the most sacrificial act of 'charity', even the self-surrender of the martyr, is of no benefit to me, if it is not done in love. Paul varies the form of expression here: *I gain nothing by it*. He is not maintaining that the actions here referred to are of no value at all. The first action, at least, will surely be of benefit to the recipients. His point is rather that, if it is not done in love, the action will be of no benefit to the giver.

13.4–7   Paul has just affirmed that the most remarkable feats of piety are worthless without love. In vv. 4–7 he responds to the implicit question, 'What then is love?' It is significant, however, that his response takes the form not of a definition but of a phenomenological description. Love for Paul is a disposition that expresses itself in an inexhaustible variety of actions (15 in all are listed). We may compare 12.31b, where it is represented as a way in which we are called to walk. Love, in other words, is not definable except as a multiform praxis. It *does* this and this and this.

Love is patient and kind. These are qualities that characterize God's consistent attitude to humanity, both in the Old Testament and the New (see e.g. Exod. 22.27; 34.6; Ps. 86.15; Rom. 2.4).

We have already noted that the description of love as *never conceited* echoes a criticism which Paul has repeatedly made of Corinthian spirituality. Other expressions in this list must also have struck the more perceptive among his first readers as uncomfortably relevant to their situation. He has already had occasion to charge them with envy (3.3), and the description of love as *never rude* could well be aimed at the behaviour of certain women alluded to in 11.2–16 or the behaviour of the 'haves' at the Lord's Table described in 11.17–22. The verb means to behave disgracefully, dishonourably, indecently.

The statement that love is *never selfish* recalls earlier teaching in 10.24 and 33.

A striking feature of this section is that there is no explicit reference to the human objects of love. However, the definiteness of Paul's statements implies that love is all-inclusive. There is therefore an aptness about the choice by the REB and other modern translations of 'never' rather than 'not' as a rendering of the Greek word *ou*, thus, *Love is never boastful, never conceited, never rude* . . . In the same way, the repeated use of 'all things' as the object of the verb in v. 7 implies an inclusiveness which is aptly brought out by the REB rendering: *There is nothing love cannot face; there is no limit to its faith, its hope, its endurance.*

At this point the question arises, What sort of love is Paul talking about? Whose love? The answer has to be, God's love in Christ, first of all, for God alone practises love like this in its fullness, but human beings may also embody such love, in so far as they allow themselves to be drawn into the divine life.

13.8–10   The opening sentence of v. 8, *Love will never come to an end,* enunciates the theme of the third section and leads into a series of contrasts that are both temporal and thematic. *Prophecies, tongues of ecstasy, knowledge,* that is, the knowledge we possess in this present order (cf. v. 12), will all pass away, gifts of grace though they are, since they are all partial, and the partial vanishes when wholeness comes.

In v. 8 we have the first of four occurrences in this chapter of the verb *katargeō*, which, as we noted in our discussion of 1.28, is used eight times in this letter to express Paul's conviction that through Christ the present age is already on its way out.

13.11 This verse introduces a different contrast, not between 'now' and 'then' but between the past and the present. It is introduced as an analogous contrast to the dominant contrast of vv. 8–12. Just as the speech, the thought and the reasoning of a child must give place to those of an adult, so also must the gifts of prophecy, ecstasy and our present knowledge give place to the wholeness of the consummation. The verb underlying the rendering 'finished' is the same verb (*katargeō*) that is used in vv. 8 and 10 to describe the passing away of the present order.

13.12 Compared to the knowledge that will one day be ours, the knowledge of God that we have at this present time is no better than a mirror image. Corinth was famous for its bronze mirrors,[124] but even the best mirror image is but a poor substitute for direct vision. What one sees in a mirror is a mediated form of the object, not the object itself. The phrase, *face to face*, recalls Num. 12.8, where God says of Moses, *With him I speak face to face, openly and not in riddles.*

The statement that *my* eventual *knowledge* of God *will be whole, like God's knowledge of me*, suggests the further thought (already expressed in 8.1–3) that we only know God at all because God has already known us.

13.13 This verse is distinct in style from what has preceded but is nevertheless its logical conclusion. In the light of vv. 8–10, it is perhaps surprising that Paul speaks not only of love but also of faith and hope lasting for ever, but we may believe that even the unmediated presence of God will continue to invite trust and hope.

There is clearly a contrast intended between the qualities named in this verse and the gifts especially prized by the Corinthians. There may even be a deliberate contrast with the Corinthian triad of tongues, prophecy and knowledge. The same three qualities of faith, hope and love are also found, in a different order, in 1 Thess. 1.3; 5.8; and Gal. 5.5f.

As Barrett observes, of these three qualities love alone can be attributed to God. Indeed, it is God's essential activity.

> God does not himself trust; if he did, he would not be God. God does not himself hope; if God hoped, he would not be God. But if God did not love, he would not be God.[125]

Tongues are good, prophecy better
14.1–6

Paul now returns to the discussion of spiritual gifts, first broached in 12.1. At the same time he links the present discussion with the previous chapter by the exhortation, *Make love your aim.*

The main thrust of the present chapter is soon clear. At least until v. 25, Paul is primarily concerned to contrast the spiritual gifts of prophecy and speaking in tongues and to represent prophecy as being of greater value because of its intelligibility.

What is meant by these two activities? By 'prophecy' he means primarily a Spirit-inspired declaration of the will of God for this community at this present time (see vv. 3, 24f.). There is an extended example of prophecy in the letters to the seven churches in Revelation 2 and 3.

By 'speaking in tongues' Paul means Spirit-inspired speech, only partially subject to conscious control, which sounds like a normal language but is not identifiable as such. It therefore differs from the miraculous speaking in foreign languages described in Acts 2.

Drawing, no doubt, on experience of contemporary charismatic movements, Tom Wright observes that 'Such speech is experienced as a stream of praise in which . . . a sense of love for God, of adoration and gratitude, wells up and overflows. It is like a private language of love.'[126]

Gerd Theissen, in an illuminating discussion, describes tongues as 'the language of the unconscious, which becomes capable of consciousness through interpretation'.[127]

The contrast Paul draws between prophecy and tongues is so emphatic and so sustained that it must be aimed at the particular situation in Corinth. The Corinthians must have overvalued speaking in tongues and probably also underrated prophecy.

14.1–3   After an injunction to his readers to aspire to all the spiritual gifts but, above all, to prophecy, Paul proceeds to draw a contrast between speaking in tongues and prophesying, in respect of the audience addressed and the benefit to the bystanders.

The speaker in tongues *is talking with God, not with men and women,* whereas the prophet addresses men and women directly.

Again no one catches the meaning of the speaker in tongues, for *he speaks divine mysteries in the Spirit,* whereas the words of the prophet *have power to build; they stimulate and they encourage.*

The word rendered 'stimulate' by the REB conveys the sense both of challenge and of comfort. In older English, as in the New Testament, the nuances of 'comfort' were more bracing than they are today. A. M. Ramsey has drawn attention to a scene in the Bayeux Tapestry which shows William the Conqueror marching behind a column of soldiers, prodding the last man with the point of his sword. The caption below reads, 'King William comforts his soldiers.'[128]

14.4   Picking up the notion of upbuilding, which is quite central to the chapter as a whole (cf. vv. 5, 12, 17, 26), Paul now observes that while *speaking in tongues may build up the speaker himself, prophecy builds up the Christian community*. He is thus continuing to insist on the superiority of prophecy, yet his evaluation of tongues is by no means wholly negative. He acknowledges here that it does build up the speaker himself (the REB's *may build up* is a little too tentative), just as he acknowledges in v. 2 that it is a means of communication with God.

14.5   It is not that Paul is forbidding speaking in tongues. He is happy for them all to do it, but his preference is for prophecy. If, however, the speaker in tongues is able to explain the meaning of his utterance, *and so help to build up the community*, then that is a different situation: accompanied by the gift of interpretation, tongues is equivalent to prophecy. The Corinthians themselves evidently saw no need for interpretation.

14.6   Paul now invites his readers to consider the effect of his coming to them simply as a speaker in tongues, uttering words which contained nothing *by way of revelation or enlightenment or prophecy or instruction*. What good would that do them?

No sharp distinction can be made between the four types of utterance Paul lists here. The important point is that all alike are characterized by intelligibility and therefore serve to build up the church.

Sound must signify
14.7–12

It might be thought that by now Paul has effectively made the point that uninterrupted speaking in tongues, by failing to convey an intelligible message, does nothing to build up the Christian community.

Nevertheless, he now reinforces the point by the use of three analogies. If he has to stress this point at such length, the Corinthians must have been engaging in a veritable riot of tongue-speaking without interpretation.

Common to all three analogies is the use of the Greek word *phōnē*, which has a range of meanings, which Paul exploits skilfully, in order to make his point more persuasively. This word often denotes the human voice, but it can also be used for any sound. Paul's main point is that, whatever the type of *phōnē*, mere sound produces no real effect on the hearer, unless it exhibits some order or pattern or meaning.

14.7   In his first analogy Paul cites flutes and lyres. If the players of these instruments make no clear differentiation of notes, no recognizable tune will be produced.[129]

14.8   The same thing holds good of the *phōnē* produced by a trumpet. A trumpeter who produces no clear, distinct notes will rouse no soldier to battle.

14.9   In the same way, if the utterance of the speaker in tongues yields no intelligible meaning, it is useless. He or she *will be talking to empty air*. The Greek word rendered *meaning* by the REB is *logos*, which is appropriately rendered 'word' in about two out of every three of its occurrences in the New Testament, but, as C. H. Dodd observes, '*logos* as "word" is never the mere word as an assemblage of sounds (*phōnē*) but the word as determined by a meaning and conveying a meaning'.[130]

14.10f.   Paul now takes up a third analogy, foreign languages. *There are any number of different languages in the world*, but unless I understand the force, the intent, of what is being said by a foreign speaker, his words will be to me mere gibberish, as mine will be to him – or, in the more literal rendering of the AV, 'I shall be unto him that speaketh a barbarian . . .'

The fact that speaking in tongues is here *compared* to speaking in a foreign language shows that the two things cannot be identical.

14.12   Paul now draws the argument to a conclusion. Since the Corinthians are eager for gifts of the Spirit, let them *aspire above all to excel in those which build up the church*. There is no mistaking the zeal of the Corinthians, but, like the zeal of those Jews of whom Paul speaks in Rom. 10.2, it needs to be redirected.

'With my spirit, but also with my mind'
14.13–19

14.13 Having made the point, at some length, that speaking in tongues without interpretation fails to edify, Paul now urges anyone who speaks in tongues to pray for the further gift of being able to interpret what they say.

14. 14 Having done that, however, he reverts yet again to the theme of the inadequacy of uninterpreted tongue-speaking. As before, he stresses its ineffectiveness for edification, but first he makes the point that it is of limited value for the speaker himself. This is because it is an activity in which my rational mind is not fully engaged. *My mind is barren.* The AV reads: 'My understanding is unfruitful.' The thought is not simply that his mind is inactive but that no benefit accrues to the community of faith.

The expression, 'my spirit', is sometimes used by Paul in an inclusive sense to refer to my whole being, being thus equivalent to 'me' (see e.g. 2 Cor. 2.13; cf. Gal. 6.18). More fundamentally, however, it refers to myself as capable of relationship with God (see e.g. Rom. 1.9; 8.16). So Paul is saying two things here about praying in tongues: it is the expression of a real relationship with God, yet it does not engage my reason.

This verse also throws some light on what Paul understands by 'speaking in tongues'. It seems that it was primarily an expression of prayer and praise to God, not direct address to the church.

14.15 Most likely Paul is referring here to two distinct activities: on the one hand, praying and praising in tongues; and, on the other, praying and praising in intelligible words. He intends to continue doing both.

14.16f. Paul now reverts to the point already made at length in the first two paragraphs that uninterpreted tongue-speaking does nothing for the bystander. *Suppose you are praising God with the spirit alone.* If an ordinary worshipper *does not know what you are saying*, he will not be edified and not be able to respond with an Amen to your prayer of thanksgiving, however splendid it may be.

Underlying the REB rendering *ordinary person* is a Greek word denoting fundamentally a layman in contrast to an expert or specialist of any kind and hence an uninitiated person. The word is sometimes taken to refer here to Christians who lack the gift of speaking in tongues, but, in view of vv. 23f., where the word is used again, Paul probably means non-Christian sympathizers present as interested guests.

14.18   Paul now makes it clear, in a tantalizingly brief remark, that his disparagement of speaking in tongues is not a case of sour grapes. On the contrary, he thanks God that he is more gifted in tongues than any of his readers.

14.19   Nevertheless, rational discourse, discourse in which my mind participates and which serves to instruct, and thus to build up, my neighbour, is infinitely more valuable for public worship. However, this is not a denigration of tongues per se, as is clear from the way Paul has placed the phrase *in the congregation* in an emphatic position.

Tongues and prophecy – signs and signs
14.20–25

14.20   Paul has talked about the effect of tongues on believers; now he pictures the effect on unbelievers. First of all, however, he tells his readers to grow up in their thinking. In evil they are to be infants but in their thinking grown-up. Here the criticism which has been implicit in verses like v. 14 becomes overt. No doubt these words raised the eyebrows of his readers, who, as we noted at 2.6, clearly prided themselves on their maturity (the Greek word translated 'grown-up' here is translated 'mature' in 2.6; in 13.10 it is translated 'wholeness').

14.21f.   These verses can only be properly understood in the light not only of the Old Testament passage that Paul cites but also of the verses which follow. So we turn to the latter verses first.

14.23–25   The main point of these verses is clear. Paul is inviting his readers to consider the effect upon uninstructed persons, or unbelievers, first of entering a service of worship where all are speaking in tongues, and second a service where all are prophesying. The impression made upon the visitors to the first scene would be that the worshippers were all mad. In the second situation, however, the visitor would hear something that searched his conscience and brought conviction, laying bare the secrets of his heart, and thus be forced to worship and acknowledge that God was in their midst.

These verses show that by prophetic utterances Paul means, above all, direct and penetrating words of judgement, such as we find in the letters to the seven churches in Revelation 2 and 3.

For a note on the word here translated 'uninstructed persons' see the commentary on v. 16. Here Paul seems to have in mind anyone who is untutored in the Christian faith, perhaps even an unbelieving spouse who has come along with their partner to see for themselves.

14.21f. In the light of the clear intent of vv. 23–25, we can now turn back to vv.21f. One thing is already clear: it is Paul's consistent aim not only in vv. 23–25 but throughout the chapter to stress the superior value of prophecy over (uninterpreted) tongues in public worship. Therefore in describing tongues as 'a sign for unbelievers' in v. 22, Paul cannot mean, as some Pentecostals suppose, that tongue-speaking is designed to convert unbelievers.

The precise context and force of the oracle from Isa. 28.11f., which Paul quotes in v. 21, is also important for the interpretation of the passage. According to this oracle, *God will speak to this people through strange tongues, and by the lips of foreigners.* In the context of Isaiah 28, this is God's response to the people's mimicry of Isaiah's preaching, which they have dismissed as *a babble of meaningless noises* (Isa. 28.10). Yet the truth is that through the prophet God was speaking a message of peace. Therefore God will make them hear a truly unintelligible message, the language of the Assyrian conquerors. In completing his quotation, Paul both paraphrases and abbreviates the passage from Isaiah: *and even so they will not heed me, says the Lord.* Paul has here changed the point of the Old Testament oracle somewhat. The main point of the oracle in its original context is that *strange tongues*, that is, the tongues of the Assyrians, will be a sign of God's judgement upon disobedience. Paul's point is that *strange tongues*, that is, tongues of ecstasy, will not lead unbelievers to obedience but to mockery.

14.22 We are now in a better position to understand the difficult statements in v. 22 about tongues and prophecy functioning as signs for unbelievers and believers, respectively. When something becomes a sign to someone in the Old Testament, it may be a sign of God's judgement or of God's blessing, depending on the context. Num. 26.10 and Deut. 28.46 are examples of signs of judgement, as is Luke 2.24; Gen. 9.12 and Exod. 12.13 are examples of signs of blessing. It seems that in this verse Paul is thinking of tongues functioning as a sign in a negative sense and prophecy functioning as a sign in a positive sense.

The Corinthians were probably claiming that tongues were a sign for believers in the sense of demonstrating that the speakers were Spirit-filled. On the contrary, says Paul, tongues are a sign not for believers but for unbelievers, and a negative sign at that. Uninterpreted, they simply confirm unbelievers in their unbelief. It is prophecy that is a sign for believers, and that in a positive sense, in that prophecy leads people to faith, through convicting them of their sins and convincing them that God is truly at work in this community.

There are echoes here of several Old Testament passages, particularly Isa. 45.14; Zech. 8.23; and Dan. 2.47.

Whether Paul's original hearers made much sense out of v. 22 at the first hearing may well be doubted.

Not a God of disorder but of peace
14.26–33a

Paul has completed his demonstration of the superior value of prophecy over tongues in gatherings of the community for worship. Now he proceeds to apply the principles he has been expounding to the Corinthian situation.

14.26 His opening statement could be taken as a description of how things actually are in Corinth rather than of how they ought to be, but, in view of the persistent vein of correction that runs through the whole chapter, the REB is probably right in interpreting the statement in a prescriptive rather than a descriptive sense: one is to contribute *this* gift to the act of worship, another *that*.

The term *revelation* probably refers to prophecy.

Whatever their individual gifts, *all* are to *aim to build up the church* (cf. vv. 3–5, 12, 17, 26).

It is a striking fact that throughout this chapter, as in chapter 11, Paul appears to know no one in Corinth to whom he can appeal, in order to bring about an ordered observance of worship. He can only appeal to the church as a whole.[131]

14.27f. Paul now gives precise instructions to regulate speaking in tongues. *If anyone speaks in tongues, only two should speak, or at most three* (that is, presumably, at any one service). They should also speak *one at a time, and someone must interpret*. This directive makes most sense, if the Corinthians were in fact engaging in a riot of tongue-speaking, sometimes several at a time and without interpretation.

If there is no interpreter, then the speakers in tongues *should keep silent and speak to themselves and to God*. This shows that Paul does not conceive of speaking in tongues as an irresistible compulsion over which the speaker has no control. The Corinthians, on the other hand, probably did. The REB renderings 'ecstasy' (v. 23) and 'ecstatic utterance' (v. 26) are misleading, if they suggest such an irresistible compulsion. As in v. 2, Paul acknowledges that speaking in tongues is a genuine means of communication with God.

14.29–31 Paul now gives similar instructions for the regulation of prophecy. In view of vv. 24 and 31, the directive that only two or three prophets may speak probably means that no more than three are to hold forth before *the rest exercise their judgement on what is said*. 'The rest' is taken by some to refer to the rest of the prophets, who are thought of as forming a strictly defined group, but the context is against this view. Verse 31, for example, is most naturally taken as implying that a prophetic word may be revealed to any believer at any time, so that the group of prophets is potentially as wide as the church itself. 'The wind blows where it wills' (John 3.8). 'Prophecy' here denotes a function rather than an office.

The second half of v. 29 is particularly noteworthy. Prophets are, by definition, people who believe themselves to be the bearers of direct messages from God, but here Paul asserts the principle that, inspired though they may be, their pronouncements are not to be accepted without questioning and discussion. The actual Greek word used by Paul suggests sifting, discernment. And no more than speaking in tongues is prophecy an irresistible compulsion. *If someone also present receives a revelation, let the first speaker stop*. At both these points Paul is probably contradicting the accepted view in Corinth.

Again like the speakers in tongues, prophets are to speak one at a time, *so that all may receive instruction and encouragement*. Evidently the Corinthians were accustomed to hearing several speak at once.

14.32 This verse reads in the AV: 'And the spirits of the prophets are subject to the prophets.' The force of the verse is not immediately clear, but a good case can be made for taking it the way the REB does, as meaning that prophetic inspiration is not something over which prophets themselves have no control. Though inspired by the Holy Spirit, they still have the power to stop themselves and wait their turn.

14.33a   This clause grounds the last statement in the nature of God, who *is not a God of disorder but of peace*. If we are right in inferring that all the specific directives Paul gives in this paragraph are intended to curb the exuberance of Corinthian worship, then the Corinthians were in grave danger of conceiving of God as a God of disorder.

14.33b   The phrase, *as in all congregations of God's people*, is linked with vv. 34f. in the REB, but it is equally possible to punctuate the verse so as to link it with vv. 32 and 33a. If the latter punctuation is accepted, the point then being made is that the disorderly worship that has become prevalent in Corinth is not only out of keeping with the nature of God but with the practice of all other churches.

Paul's statement in v. 33a that *God is not a God of disorder but of peace* is likely to strike the modern, Western reader as thoroughly congenial, but it must not be forgotten that it was addressed to a community whose patterns of worship were radically different from those of most mainstream churches today. It is, in other words, directed precisely to a community whose worship had become chaotic. What would Paul have said to a community whose worship was cerebral to the point of being rigid, and totally dominated by the celebrant? We can be sure that his emphasis would have been very different from his emphasis in this chapter.

A shocking thing . . .?
14.33b–35

14.34f.   It comes as quite a surprise to find that prophets and speakers in tongues have suddenly dropped out of sight and that the sole theme is for the moment the impropriety of women talking in the meetings of the church. *It is a shocking thing for a woman to talk at the meeting.* They should therefore *keep silent*, and *keep their place* (a place of subjection) *as the law directs. If there is something they want to know, they can ask their husbands at home.*

The very abruptness of this transition is enough to justify the suspicion that these two verses are not the work of Paul but an interpolation by a later hand.

This suspicion is confirmed by a number of other considerations. Most importantly, the passage stands in clear contradiction to 11.2–16, where Paul assumes, without question, that women have the right, when suitably clothed, to pray and prophesy publicly. As Schrage observes, Paul could have spared himself the whole discussion of appropriate hairstyles for women, had he been convinced that they should not open their mouths in worship at all.[132]

Further, the appeal to 'the law' poses a real difficulty for defenders of Pauline authorship. Whenever Paul introduces a quotation from the Old Testament elsewhere, as he does some 75 times, he always cites the actual text. In this case, it would be impossible to cite an actual text, as the Old Testament law nowhere imposes silence on women.

There is also, in the Greek of vv. 33 and 34, a repetition of the phrase, 'in the churches', which reads very awkwardly.

A further reason for suspecting the authenticity of the passage is its use of words that are not typical of Paul. For example, the verb translated 'have no permission' is used in this sense only in 1 Tim. 2.12.

Again there is abundant evidence, in Romans 16 and Philippians 4 and elsewhere, that Paul worked closely with a number of women and esteemed them highly both as people and as colleagues.

Finally, there is the fact that manuscripts of the Western tradition place the verses in question after v. 40. This suggests that the verses originated in a very early marginal gloss that was subsequently inserted into the text at two different places.

If these verses are a gloss, then the likelihood is that they derive from the same circles as produced 1 Tim. 2.11f.

Among recent commentators, Barrett, Fee, Hays, Sampley, Lang, Klauck and Schrage all take the view that these verses are a gloss, as does Horrell also.[133] Collins does accept the verses in question as part of the original text but argues that they represent, not Paul's own view but rather the view of some men in Corinth who are trying to maintain their own patriarchal status. Paul rebuts their position, according to Collins, by means of the double rhetorical question in v. 36.[134] However, the linguistic signals that might be taken as supporting this view are very slight.

Thiselton, along with a number of conservative scholars, accepts the verses in question as authentic but sees them as Paul's response to a specific problem of disruptive speech, like wives interrupting their husbands with repeated questions or cross-examining them in public.[135] Against this, Paul's ruling seems to be quite general and not a response to a specific situation. Thiselton does acknowledge that 'Paul expresses no reservation at all about a woman's praying or using prophetic speech in 11.5.'[136]

If these verses are the work of Paul, then we must decide which position is truer to the gospel of Jesus Christ, the position stated here or that which is affirmed in Gal. 3.28, namely, that there is in Christ no such thing as Jew and Greek, slave and freeman, male and female. We cannot have it both ways, and neither can Paul.

I speak with authority
14.36–38

Paul now rounds off the chapter with a sharp rebuke and assertion of his own authority, before summing up the thrust of the chapter in two pithy sentences.

14.36   He begins by charging the Corinthians with acting as if they were the source of the word of God or its sole recipients. This charge takes the form of a sharp rhetorical question, which clearly indicates that the Corinthians have been questioning Paul's right to tell them what to do. Here we have corroboration of the conclusion drawn in the Introduction, and several times since, that the Corinthians in their letter to Paul had not been content to ask questions but had also taken exception to some of his pronouncements and prohibitions (see especially the Introduction, p. xvii).

14.37   Paul now claims for himself the right to speak for God. What he has written amounts to nothing less than the Lord's command (cf. 7.40b). Although there is no explicit appeal to apostolic authority here, such a claim is probably implicit (cf. 12.28). What is more, anyone who supposes that he is a prophet or spiritual person should recognize Paul's authority. Although the wording of this verse is very general, *If anyone claims . . .*, Paul surely has specific people in mind.

14.38   There follows the declaration of a conditional judgement on anyone who withholds recognition of Paul's authority. This declaration exhibits a pattern already noted at 3.17 as being a feature of a number of judgement pronouncements in other parts of the Bible. Particularly noteworthy is the correspondence between offence and penalty. As noted in connection with 3.17, Käsemann has argued that in the New Testament these pronouncements reflect the activity of Christian prophets who executed a 'holy law' by anticipating God's verdict in the last judgement. If Käsemann is right, there is an implication in this passage that the persons in question will forfeit the recognition not simply of the community but of God.

In short . . .
14.39–40

In the final two verses Paul sums up all he has said earlier in the chapter about the relative value of prophecy and speaking in tongues in public worship. As in v. 1, he urges the Corinthians to be eager to prophesy. As for speaking in tongues, all that he says is, 'Do not forbid it.' There is no evidence that anyone in Corinth was actually trying to do that. All the evidence suggests rather that they were making too much of it. The point of Paul's injunction therefore is to signal once again the markedly higher value of prophecy over tongues for the worship of the church.

14.40 Finally, Paul states a principle that has underlain all the counsel he has been giving, particularly in the specific directives of vv. 26–33: *Let all be done decently and in order*. The observance of these canons is essential, if the church is to be truly edified. There is here an echo of v. 34. By its attention to good taste and good order, the worshipping church is to reflect the nature of God.

The Resurrection of the Dead
15.1–58

Chapter 15 begins abruptly, without any introductory formula like 'Now concerning the resurrection of the dead.' Evidently therefore Paul is not responding to a question addressed to him by the Corinthian community. But neither is he introducing the subject without good reason. It becomes clear in v. 12 that the discussion is occasioned by something he has heard. There are people in the church in Corinth who are denying the resurrection of the dead.

This chapter contains the most sustained piece of theological argument in the whole letter. This is due to the specifically theological nature of the error that Paul is attacking. Yet even here he does not lose sight of the ethical implications of theology – the ethical indifference that is the implicate of an erroneous theology (v. 32) and the ethical seriousness that is the implicate of a sound theology (v. 58).

Analysis of the chapter

In vv. 1–11 Paul sets forth the basic resurrection credo, and declares it to be held in common by all who preach Christ and believe in him.

In 12–19 he invites his readers to consider what the consequences for their faith would be, if Christ had not been raised after all.

In 20–28 he argues that, since Christ has in fact been raised from the dead, the resurrection of believers inevitably follows.

In 29–34 he reflects once more on what would follow, if Christ had not been raised. Believers would be engaged in activities which were pointless.

In 35–58 he turns to the question, 'How are the dead raised?'

So we preach and so you believed
15.1–11

15.1f. In the first two verses Paul piles up a whole series of verbs to bring home to his readers the life-and-death importance of the gospel he had preached to them. Not only did I preach it to you – so he reminds them – you received it, *you have taken your stand* on it, and it *is now bringing you salvation*, provided that *you hold it fast and that your conversion was not in vain.*

Two convictions of Paul's come through here with unmistakable clarity: first, the gospel is essential for salvation; and, second, salvation is not an instantaneous process. One must build one's life upon the gospel. One must hold fast to it. Otherwise there is a real possibility that one will have believed in vain.

15.3–7 Paul now reminds his readers how he handed on to them as of first importance (*first and foremost* – REB) a specific creed. The Greek verb underlying 'handed on' together with the verb underlying 'received' (also used in v. 1) are used elsewhere of the reception and transmission of tradition (cf. 11.23).

This tradition he passed on was one he had 'received'. When? Most likely, when he first heard the call and entered the Christian community, at Damascus. This would have been, at most, four years after the crucifixion.[137]

The creed Paul then proceeds to quote speaks of Christ's death *for our sins in accordance with the scriptures,* of his burial, of his being *raised to life on the third day in accordance with the scriptures* and of his appearing to Cephas and then to the Twelve.

Where does the creed end? Probably at the end of v. 5. One of the striking formal features of the creed is the symmetry of its parallelism, and it is arguable that this symmetry would have been impaired by the inclusion of other appearances in addition to the two mentioned in v. 5.

It is natural to ask what are the specific scriptures in accordance with which Christ died for our sins and was raised to life. It is not difficult to think of Old Testament passages that might be seen as having been fulfilled in the death of Christ. Isaiah 53 is the obvious example, but not the only one. Zech. 12.10 is quoted or echoed in Matt. 24.30, John 19.37 and Rev. 1.7.

It is not so easy to think of passages that could be regarded as having been fulfilled in the *resurrection* of Christ. Hos. 6.2 springs to mind, but there could also be an allusion to other passages that speak of the vindication of a servant of God, such as Isa. 52.13; 53.10–12; possibly also to Ps. 16.10 (see Acts 2. 25–28). On the other hand, a number of texts in the Old Testament speak of salvation or vindication 'on the third day', so that the force of the phrase could be that the Old Testament as a whole bears witness to the resurrection of Christ.[138]

What is the precise force of the words, *he was buried*? Some scholars argue that this reference only makes sense if the burial, as well as the death, was reversed in the resurrection. They thus find here an implicit allusion to an empty tomb.[139] Yet this argument is not conclusive. It could be that the burial is mentioned only to underline the reality of the death.

In contrast to the verbs rendered *died* and *was buried*, the verb underlying *was raised to life* is not in the aorist tense but the perfect tense, which regularly denotes a present state resulting from a past action. The implication is therefore that Christ, having been raised, is now risen Lord.

The verb translated in the REB and most modern translations as *appeared* is, strictly speaking, a passive and therefore could be translated 'was seen', as in the AV. However, the consistent use of the dative for the human witnesses throughout vv. 5–8 suggests that the appearing one was the active party and that the usual modern rendering, 'appeared', is correct. This supposition is confirmed by the observation that the same construction is used in the LXX at Gen. 12.7 and Exod. 3.2 to refer to God coming forth out of hiddenness to address God's people.

The tradition that Peter was the first to see the risen Lord may be reflected in Luke 24.34. Two of the Gospels, however, Matthew and John, attribute the first sight of the risen one either to Mary of Magdala or to a group of women including Mary of Magdala. Her name, moreover, is the only one that is common to all the different accounts of the discovery of the empty tomb.

Why does Paul make no reference to women witnesses? A popular view is that he has chosen not to refer to women because of the minimal value attaching to the witness of a woman within the Jewish legal system.[140] Another explanation which, in my judgement, is more likely is that accounts of women discovering the empty tomb and seeing the risen Jesus were handed down, for several decades, in women's circles, before they eventually found their way into the mainstream of Christian tradition.

The occasion of the appearance to more than 500 followers at once has given rise to considerable discussion. Some have argued that it must be the same event as Luke records in Acts 2, partly on the grounds that it is unlikely that an appearance with so much evidential value would have dropped out of the tradition, leaving no trace apart from this brief reference. It is also argued that in other sources apart from Acts, notably John 20.22, the gift of the Spirit is associated much more closely with the resurrection appearances, so that an incident that in Luke's (comparatively late) second volume has the function of marking the gift of the Spirit might at some earlier stage have marked both the gift of the Spirit and an appearance of the risen Lord. However, the fact that no detailed account has been preserved elsewhere of any appearance either to Peter alone or to James alone is a reminder of how much oral tradition has been lost.

'James' here means not the son of Zebedee but the brother of Jesus (Mark 6.3), who, along with his whole family, was opposed to the mission of the earthly Jesus (see Mark 3.21) and probably only came to faith after Easter. If so, the appearance to James, like the appearance to Paul himself, had been a signal act of grace.

As for the appearance to *all the apostles*, Paul consistently uses the latter term to denote a considerably larger group than 'the Twelve', namely, a group that evidently included not only himself but James (Gal. 1.19), Andronicus and Junia (Rom. 16.7 – probably husband and wife), Silas and Timothy (1 Thess. 2.7) and Barnabas (Gal. 2.7–9; 1 Cor. 9.5f.). There is no reason to think that he is not using the term in this wide sense here also.

15.8   Paul's comparison of the appearance to himself with *a sudden abnormal birth* has occasioned a great deal of discussion. The underlying word means essentially 'untimely birth, miscarriage'. The problem is that a miscarriage is a premature birth, whereas the appearance to Paul must have been perceived as being irregular not because it came *too early* but because it came so long *after* the other appearances (cf. the phrase, *Last of all* in v. 8). Paul was a late entrant to the group of those who claimed to have seen the risen Lord.

There is some evidence that the word could be used to mean a 'monster', a 'horrible thing', and some have suggested that it was hurled at Paul in this sense by his opponents and hence picked up by Paul here.

However, it is possible to retain the meaning, 'miscarriage', 'premature birth', and still make sense of the passage. As J. I. H. McDonald puts it, Paul had been 'untimely ripped . . .' from the womb of Pharisaic Judaism into apostolic ministry . . . The other apostles, with whom there is an implied contrast, had been prepared for their encounter with the risen Christ through their previous association with Jesus. Paul, later in time, had been unceremoniously thrust into witness to the resurrection and into apostolic ministry without any positive preparation. His record was a disqualification, rather than the reverse.[141]

15.9   The interpretation just given makes good sense in the context of the present verse, in which Paul declares himself *the least of the apostles, indeed not fit to be called an apostle*, because he had *persecuted the church of God*. This statement is more than an expression of wonder that one so unworthy should be granted such a privilege. It also has some apologetic value. Given Paul's previous record, nothing less than the action of God can have made him an apostle, transforming him from a violent persecutor of the church into its most effective missionary, nothing less than the action of God in revealing his Son to him as risen. He argues along the same lines in Gal. 1.11f.

15.10   It was grace alone that had made Paul what he was, a Christian and, more than that, an apostle of Jesus Christ. But not only the fact of his apostleship but its productivity was also due entirely to the grace of God. He can fairly claim to have outdone all the other apostles in his apostolic labours, but immediately adds the qualification – *not I, indeed, but the grace of God working in me*. The word 'grace' is used three times in this verse. Indeed, the words, 'not I but the grace of God', could well stand as a summary of Paul's theology as a whole. The very essence of his gospel is that 'Salvation is of the Lord' (Jonah 2.9 – AV).

15.11   This being so, all comparisons between himself and the other apostles are invidious. *No matter whether it was I or they!* What matters is that all the apostles are united in preaching the resurrection of Christ. Indeed the very definition of an apostle is inextricably bound up with the resurrection, in so far as an apostle is one who has both seen the risen Christ and been commissioned by him (see the commentary on 1.1–9). Moreover, the message of the resurrection is the heart of the continuing apostolic proclamation, and it is what the Corinthians themselves accepted. *This is what we all proclaim, and this is what you believed.*

If Christ be not risen . . .
15.12–19

15.12 Paul has now reminded his readers that the gospel he preached to them, which they accepted, was one that centred around the death and resurrection of Christ. Such a reminder could be designed to introduce the question, 'How has it come about then that some of you are denying that Christ has risen after all?' Verse 12 makes it clear, however, that that is not the way that Paul perceives the situation: *Now if this is what we proclaim, that Christ was raised from the dead, how can some of you say there is no resurrection of the dead?*

What some are denying is the notion of a general resurrection. Paul evidently does not believe that they have drawn from this general denial the consequence, 'Therefore Christ has not risen either.'

15.13 Paul now declares that *if there is no resurrection, then Christ was not raised.* His language here suggests that he is drawing his readers' attention to a consequence that necessarily follows from their denial but which they have not yet seen. Assuming that he is correct in supposing that they have not yet drawn this consequence, the question naturally arises, Why have they not done so? That in turn raises the question of the grounds on which they were denying that there was a resurrection of the dead.

Their denial of the (general) resurrection was probably related to their dualistic understanding of human nature, according to which body and soul confront each other as opponents. We have seen evidence of this dualism in earlier chapters, both in passages revealing tendencies to libertinism (1 Cor. 5.1; 6.12–20) and in those revealing tendencies to asceticism (1 Cor. 7.1–7). It is not difficult to see how people holding such a dualistic understanding would have heard what was proclaimed to them as *good* news, namely, the resurrection of the dead, as *bad* news. Within a dualistic world-view the soul, and the soul alone, is seen as being in need of redemption, for the body, which belongs to the material world, passes away at death. Once the soul receives knowledge, its redemption is accomplished, yet it must still linger for a while in the body, which can be described as the prison of the soul. The soul's hope lies in gaining freedom from the body, in order to be able to set out on the heavenward journey.

If one brings to someone who holds this dualistic understanding of human nature a message of the *resurrection* of the *body*, such a message can only be heard as a denial of all hope. For, if it is true, it means that

160

the soul is condemned to its prison for ever. Such a message must inevitably be perceived as a message of total hopelessness. Hope, for the dualist, consists precisely in liberation from the body.

The likelihood of this reconstruction being on the right lines is strengthened by the form of the question that Paul anticipates in v. 35b: *How are the dead raised? In what kind of body?* The thought of the resurrection *of the body* was evidently the sticking point.

Probably also the problem was further complicated for the Corinthians by the assumption that the resurrection of the body was to be understood quite crudely as the reanimation of a corpse to continue bodily existence in its present form.

However, we have also seen ample evidence that the Corinthians held an over-realized eschatology, and it is likely that this had also shaped their hopes for the future. A natural inference for the Corinthians to draw, given such an eschatology, would be that the resurrection of the dead, or at least the only kind of resurrection that made any sense to them, had already taken place. Such a view seems to be echoed in 2 Tim. 2.18, where we read of Hymenaeus and Philetus, who say that *our resurrection has already taken place.* Entertaining the belief that we are suggesting would not necessarily entail the denial of any life beyond death. Indeed, it seems more likely that these Corinthians considered death to be irrelevant, since they were already living the life of the Spirit. The likelihood of this view is strengthened by v. 29, with its reference to people who are getting themselves baptized on behalf of the dead. It is unlikely that they would have done this, had they believed that there was no future for the dead.

If this is a correct reconstruction of the Corinthian position, it follows that Paul has not fully understood their position.[142]

15.14   In v. 14 Paul begins to spell out the consequences both for himself and his readers, if the resurrection of Christ is denied: *our gospel is null and void, and so too is your faith.* Underlying the rendering 'null and void' is a word that literally means 'empty', hence 'lacking substance', 'ineffective'. Paul has already used it in v. 10. At this point Barrett aptly quotes Schlatter: 'No one can give himself to a dead man; no one can expect anything, or receive anything, from a dead man.'[143]

15.15f.   Furthermore, Paul continues, *we turn out to have given false evidence about God, because we bore witness that he raised Christ to life, whereas, if the dead are not raised, he did not raise him.*

Three times over within the space of four verses – in vv. 13, 15 and

16 – Paul declares that if the dead are not raised, then Christ is not risen. There is, he is insisting, an indivisible nexus between belief in the resurrection of Christ and belief in the general resurrection. Affirm his resurrection, and you are committed to affirming the general resurrection. Deny the general resurrection, and you are committed to denying his resurrection too.

15.17   Nor is this all that follows from the explicit or implicit denial of the resurrection of Christ, for *if Christ was not raised, your faith has nothing to it and you are still in your old state of sin.*

Underlying the rendering 'has nothing to it' is a word that could be translated 'vain', futile'. So v. 17b restates what has already been said in v. 14. Verse 17c goes further, and may seem an extravagant thing to say. Could we not still believe that Christ died for our sins, even if we no longer believed that God had raised him from the dead? Paul's answer is an unequivocal 'No'. That Christ had died as a faithful witness to God's truth – that we could still believe, but not that he had died *for our sins*, not that he had died as the divinely appointed agent for the expiation of our sins (cf. Rom. 3.25). We could not believe that in this man's dying God was present, reconciling the world to Godself, making him one with human sinfulness, so that in him we might be made one with the righteousness of God (2 Cor. 5.18–21). To be sure, we do not believe all this solely because of the resurrection, but we would not dare to believe it without the resurrection. Whatever else the resurrection of Jesus means in the New Testament, it implies a vindication that is total and unqualified. This note of vindication is expressed even more emphatically in passages that speak of Christ having been not merely raised from the dead but exalted to the right hand of the Father. These affirmations of faith should not be taken to mean simply that God has honoured Jesus in the way in which God no doubt honours any righteous hero, or that God has encouraged us to believe that Jesus was right, after all. They mean rather that, in the most emphatic way we can conceive of, God has said 'Yes' to Jesus and all that he stood for. God has identified himself totally with him who during his life identified himself totally with God's cause.[144]

15.18   In v. 18 Paul spells out a further consequence that follows from the denial of the resurrection of Christ: *those who have died within Christ's fellowship are utterly lost.* This may also seem to be an extravagant statement. In Paul's day the majority of the Jews probably believed in the resurrection of the dead. Certainly the Pharisees did, of whose community Paul himself had been an ardent member. The form in which such a belief might be expressed varied considerably, but the belief that God would act creatively towards the dead is widespread in Jewish literature roughly contemporary with the New Testament.[145] How then can Paul say, 'If Christ was not raised, then those who have died within Christ's fellowship (literally 'who have died in Christ') are utterly lost (literally 'have perished')?

Here we need to ask, what were the grounds of this widespread belief in some form of resurrection? How did it arise? The first unambiguous statement of belief in the resurrection of the dead is found in Dan. 12.2. The author of Daniel, reflecting on the fate of the Maccabean martyrs, who had suffered torture and death rather than renounce their faith in the God of Israel, was driven to the conclusion that God would surely not abandon to the power of death those who had been faithful to God even unto death. If God is indeed one who keeps faith with those who keep faith, then God must restore to life and to fellowship with Godself those who have died under such circumstances. But what becomes of such a conviction, if one comes to the conclusion that Jesus, the faithful servant of God par excellence, was in reality abandoned to the power of death and not restored to life? It surely loses all its cogency. If God has not raised Jesus, what right have we to believe that God will raise anyone? Does it not rather follow that those who have died in Christ have perished?

15.19   In v. 19 Paul draws yet another consequence that follows from the denial of the fullness of the Easter faith: *If it is for this life only that Christ has given us hope, we of all people are most to be pitied.*

Here Paul is considering the possibility that we may indeed draw hope from Christ *for this life*, since Christ is risen, but for this life only. This would imply that while we may indeed share in Christ's victory over sin, we will not share in his victory over death. If that is how the verse is to be read, does it make sense to say that in that case we would be of all people most to be pitied? Would we not still be deserving of envy? Would we not still have even now peace with God (cf. Rom. 5.1)? Would we not know even now the power of the Holy Spirit and even now enjoy the freedom to walk in newness of life (Rom. 6.4)? No doubt, these things would still be true, for they are true of our life in Christ here and now. But our life in Christ here and now is characterized by 'not yet' as well as by 'now already', by hoping as well as by having, and between the two there is tension, a tension so acute that we groan. To be sure, Paul declares in Rom. 8.22, *the whole created universe in all its parts groans as if in the pangs of childbirth,* but we Christians are not exempt from that groaning. *We also to whom the Spirit is given . . . are groaning inwardly while we look forward eagerly to our adoption, our liberation from mortality* (Rom. 8.23). For it is *as the firstfruits of the harvest to come* that the Spirit has been given to us, or, as Paul puts it elsewhere, as a pledge or first instalment of the full payment yet to be made (2 Cor. 1.22; 5.5).

But what if God's final word were that resurrection in the sense of restoration to life beyond physical death is for Christ and Christ alone? What would then become of all this longing of the believer for what is yet to be? It would be doomed to disappointment. Would we not then become deserving of pity, a pity commensurate with the depth of our disappointment? Could it not be truly said then that we were of all people most to be pitied?

That to which the whole creation moves
15.20–28

Paul has now rehearsed, almost to the point of repetitiveness, the consequences that follow from the denial of the resurrection of the dead. If there is no resurrection of the dead, then Christ is not risen; and, if Christ is not risen, the bottom drops out of the Christian faith. The Corinthians are still in their sins, and without hope either for this life or for any other. They have believed in vain.

15.20   But, thanks be to God, they do not need to accept such a bleak and cheerless prospect. For *the truth is, Christ was raised to life – the firstfruits of the harvest of the dead.* Paul has repeatedly insisted that belief in the resurrection of Christ and belief in the resurrection of believers stand or fall together. Here he comprehends both beliefs in a single, triumphant affirmation.

The word 'firstfruits' denotes the first instalment of the crop, which is a sign and promise of the full crop yet to come. The same word is used at 1 Cor. 16.15 and Rom. 8.23; 11.16; and 16.5. The word implies not only temporal sequence but causal connection. The full harvest will necessarily follow.

But how can Paul affirm so confidently that Christ is 'the firstfruits of the harvest of the dead'? To understand this statement, and indeed the whole paragraph, it is important to realize that in Jewish thought the notion of resurrection is both eschatological and collective. That is to say, resurrection is something that God will do when God establishes God's glorious kingdom and fulfils God's saving purpose towards creation. It is a necessary part of the establishment of the kingdom, because death is an intruder in God's creation. The moment of resurrection is also envisaged as an act that affects all of God's people. God will raise all the faithful together.

To be sure, we read occasionally in Jewish literature contemporary with the New Testament, as well as in the Gospels themselves, of raisings from the dead (see e.g. Mark 6.14; Luke 9.7–9; John 11), but these are always resuscitations, restorations to earthly life. The central event to which the New Testament testifies at every level is no mere resuscitation but a raising to glory, an anticipation within history of the final conquest of death. To this belief, namely, the belief in the raising to glory of a single individual in the midst of history, there is no Jewish precedent whatever. As Pheme Perkins insists repeatedly in her major study of the subject, 'The resurrection is more than the vindication of an individual righteous sufferer. It is the climax of the fulfillment of the promises of salvation.' And again: 'Resurrection is not a miracle by which God merely intervenes on behalf of Jesus but is the beginning of God's renewal of all things.'[146]

In the light of this background of belief, we can understand why Paul is so adamant that the resurrection of Christ must be seen as the guarantee of our own. To deny the resurrection of believers would be to deny the ultimate triumph of God. Indeed God cannot be held to be content with anything less than the restoration of the whole creation.

15.21f. In vv. 21 and 22 Paul develops the thought of Christ as the firstfruits of the resurrected dead by means of a contrast between Christ and Adam – a contrast that is elaborated in greater detail later in the chapter (vv. 45–49), as well as in Rom. 5.12–21. Adam and Christ are alike in that each is the inaugurator of a humanity. As creatures, we are in Adam; as Christians, in Christ. But whereas Adam through his sin *brought death into the world,* so that all his descendants were inevitably mortal, Christ by his obedience has overcome death, so that all who are in him *will be brought to life.*

Paul's language about two humanities may strike us, in our obsession with individual freedom, as strange, yet it points to the profound truth of the close interlocking of human lives both with one another and with the structures of society, for evil and for good. As H. H. Farmer has written, 'You cannot hope ever to restore Jones completely without first restoring a hundred other folk besides, to say nothing of reforming social systems which are mighty with tradition and hoary with age.'[147]

But if solidarity can be effective for evil, it can also be effective for good. Our being in Adam has a saving counterpart in our being in Christ.

Paul's actual words in v. 22 are that *in Christ all will be brought to life*, yet in the chapter as a whole, as indeed elsewhere, he does not seem to contemplate the whole of humanity being resurrected but rather the resurrection of the total company of believers. In v. 23 he speaks only of the resurrection of those who belong to Christ.

15.23f. From v. 23 on, Paul outlines the principal moments in the drama of the eventual conquest of death. Everything will happen in an ordered sequence. *All will be brought to life; but each in proper order: Christ the firstfruits, and afterwards, at his coming, those who belong to Christ.* Nothing is said about those who do not belong to Christ. *Then comes the end, when he delivers up the kingdom to God the Father, after deposing every sovereignty, authority, and power.*

From here on there is an increasing emphasis on the subjection of *all* powers to God through Christ. The word 'all' occurs twelve times in the passage as a whole and no fewer than ten times in vv. 24–28.

15.25 In v. 25 we have the first of two allusions to scriptural passages that reinforce the conviction that the Messiah will triumph over all his enemies. Along with the emphasis that has already been noted on the universality of the rule of Christ, there is an equally striking emphasis on the inevitability of the final consummation. As risen and exalted, Christ is already reigning, and *he is destined to reign* (literally, 'he must reign'), until all is consummated.

The scriptural passage alluded to here is the opening of Ps. 110: *This is the Lord's oracle to my lord: 'Sit at my right hand, and I shall make your enemies your footstool.'* This psalm played a decisive role in the formulation of early Christian belief about the resurrection of Christ. It was evidently through this psalm above all that Christians were led to affirm not just that Christ had been exalted to heaven but that he had been exalted to the right hand of God. In all, this psalm is quoted or alluded to in the New Testament no fewer than 31 times. No other passage of Scripture is referred to so frequently in the christological expressions of the New Testament.[148]

15.26   This verse adds that *the last enemy to be deposed is death*. Like sin, death is an intruder into God's universe, and the fulfilment of God's purpose for creation demands its annihilation. Here again, as in v. 24, Paul uses the verb *katargeō*, which he introduced in 1.28 and used repeatedly in 13.8–11.

15.27   The second scriptural passage to which Paul appeals is Ps. 8.6, which he interprets christologically. The one under whose feet God *has put all things in subjection* is not humanity, as in the psalm, but Christ, the founder of the new humanity. There is a similar application of this psalm to Christ, seen as the representative of redeemed humanity, in Heb. 2.5–9.[149]

Something that no doubt facilitated the application of Ps. 8.6 to Christ was the use in v. 4 of the expression, 'the son of man' (translated *a human being* in the REB). Indeed, Paul's interpretation of Ps. 8.6 in a christological sense makes it likely that he was familiar with 'Son of man' as a christological title.

In v. 27b Paul adds that the subjection of all things to Christ is not to be taken as implying the subjection of the one who is in control of the whole process, namely, God the Father. Paul is here preparing for the description of the final stage. The verb, 'subject', occurs six times in vv. 27 and 28.

15.28   In the final act of the drama *the Son himself will also be made subject to God, who made all things subject to him*. This notion of the subordination of the Son to the Father is entirely consistent with the emphasis on the obedience of the Son which is found not only elsewhere in Paul but also in two other writers who, along with Paul, articulate the most exalted Christology in the New Testament, namely, John and Hebrews (see e.g. Rom. 5.18f.; John 5.19; Heb. 10.5–10).

The final goal of the whole process is that *God will be all in all*. This is a deceptively simple expression that conveys very effectively the thought of the total subjection of the universe to the will of God.

No resurrection? Then what's the point?
15.29–34

Paul has already made one attempt, in vv. 12–19, to impress upon the Corinthians the serious consequences that follow, if the resurrection of the dead is denied. He has, as it were, looked for a moment into the abyss that life would be, if there were no resurrection of the dead. The following paragraph, however, namely, vv. 20–28, has been entirely different in tone. Thanks be to God, we need not fall into that abyss of hopelessness. The truth is that God has raised Christ from the dead and, in raising Christ, has set in motion a chain of events which will lead inevitably not only to our own resurrection but to the sovereignty of God over the whole creation.

Now that Paul has 'blown the minds' of his readers with such a stunning vision, we might expect him to turn to some outstanding questions, as he does in vv. 35ff., or to bring the chapter to a conclusion. Instead he reverts to the line of argument pursued in the last paragraph but one, and seeks once again to bring home to his readers the disastrous consequences of denying the resurrection of the dead. This time, however, he is more specific in his formulation of his argument. First of all, he spells out the implications of denying the resurrection for a particular group known to himself and the Corinthians; then the implications for himself.

15.29   The particular group that he alludes to first of all consists of *those who receive baptism on behalf of the dead*. The thrust of the verse is clear: whatever these people are doing becomes pointless, *if the dead are not raised to life at all*.

Paul clearly expected his readers to understand this allusion, but we are at a loss to know exactly what it was all about. The fact that at least 40 different interpretations have been proposed is an indication of how much we are in the dark.[150]

The commonest reading of the text is that there were people in Corinth who were undergoing baptism on behalf of deceased relatives who had not been baptized, in the belief that their own faith, enacted in baptism, would be vicariously effective for the deceased and be sufficient to bring them within the community of the redeemed. According to Chrysostom (*I Cor. Hom.*, 40:2), a similar custom was practised by the followers of Marcion. It was condemned by the Council of Carthage. The Corinthians can easily be credited with such an understanding of baptism, in view of their sacramentalism, attested in 1.13–17; 10.1–23; and 11.16–33. But how could Paul have refrained from commenting on the assumption that someone could be a surrogate believer for someone else?

Some scholars, such as Fee, favour a modification of this view, namely, that those for whose benefit some were being baptized were, or were on their way to becoming, believers, when they died, but had never been baptized.[151]

Thiselton reviews 13 different solutions and expresses strong preference for a view first proposed by G. G. Findlay, and restated by Maria Raeder, that the people seeking baptism have the desire to be reunited with believing relatives who have died. The sort of scenario envisaged is that of believers inspiring their surviving relatives by the manner of their dying and awakening in them the desire to emulate their faith and be reunited with them at the resurrection. This seems the most likely solution of those proposed so far.

Whatever the practice was, Paul accepts it as something given and says, in effect, 'Does not such a practice become pointless, if the resurrection is denied?'

15.30f. Paul now appeals to his own situation. *Why do we ourselves face danger hour by hour?* To reinforce the point, Paul goes on to swear by the legitimate pride that he has in his friends that he dies every day.

Again Paul's words are tantalizingly allusive. However, this is not the only hint in his letters that his relatively long stay in Ephesus, during which he wrote this letter, was far more hazardous than Luke's account in Acts would lead us to believe, 'anything but an Aegean holiday', as Fee puts it.[152] In 2 Cor. 1.8–10 Paul speaks of deliverance, while in Asia Minor, from almost certain death. Just how incomplete Luke's account is may be gauged from reading 2 Cor. 11.22–27 and asking oneself how many of the trials listed by Paul in these verses are also recorded in Acts. The great majority are not.

15.32a This verse may seem at first sight to throw light on the nature of these trials. Are we to suppose that Paul had literally been thrown into the arena to fight with wild beasts? This possibility has been entertained from time to time in church history but is now generally discounted. For one thing, Paul's Roman citizenship should have protected him from such a punishment. For another, if Paul had been matched with wild beasts, it is very unlikely that he would have survived. It would also be remarkable that Paul should have made no mention of the incident in his catalogues of sufferings, like 2 Cor. 6.4–10 or 11.23–27. The underlying Greek word can be used metaphorically and is so used by Ignatius. Probably therefore it should be taken here too as a metaphorical allusion to savage human opponents.

The phrase translated in the REB *with no more than human hopes* should probably be taken, as in the REB, as a reference to merely human resources and human grounds for hope.

In v. 32b Paul takes a final look into the abyss that life becomes, if the resurrection of the dead is denied, and declares it to be an abyss of meaninglessness: *If the dead are never raised to life, 'Let us eat and drink, for tomorrow we die.'*

One cannot help asking, however, whether Paul is not overstating his case. If the resurrection of the dead is denied, does this really cut the nerve of all moral action, all altruism? Does it really follow that the immediate gratification of physical pleasure becomes the only way of life left that has any point to it? What about the many people known to us, and surely known to Paul, who have not been sustained by the hope of life beyond death or even, in some cases, by belief in God at all and yet have lived lives of rectitude that put many of us to shame? And what about the generations of Old Testament believers who served God faithfully without the support of any belief in a life after death that was worthy of the name?

The force of the problem is mitigated somewhat, when we note that Paul is quoting Isa. 22.13 word for word.

Perhaps we can say too in Paul's defence that for anyone who, like Paul, does believe in the resurrection of the dead and, along with that, in the final judgement of God upon the living and the dead, the loss of that belief must appear to involve such an impoverishment of the motivation for moral action as to make Paul's exclamation here entirely understandable. Christians who retain their faith in the life everlasting have ever so much more reason for seeking to live in a way that is well-pleasing to God than those who do not.

15.33f. The passage is rounded off with a stern warning against evil associations and an exhortation to be sober and not continue sinning. The warning that *bad company ruins good character* is a quotation from a lost comedy of Menander, *Thais*, which had become proverbial. The word translated 'company' can mean either 'companionship' or 'conversation'. The point in the context appears to be that the Corinthians should avoid the company of anyone whose philosophy is so nihilistic as to provide no adequate sanction for moral conduct. Paul may well have in mind the sceptical philosophical school of the Epicureans.

Paul's final word in this passage is a curt summons to *wake up, be sober, and stop sinning*. The REB has used two verbs, 'wake up' and 'be sober', to translate a single Greek verb that means to 'sober up' and hence to come to one's senses. Paul thus leaves his readers in no doubt that he considers their present state to be one of stupor, sin and ignorance, though the Greek is not quite so direct as is suggested by the rendering, *some of you have no knowledge of God*. Nevertheless, there is a strong implicit criticism of Corinthian pretensions to knowledge.

Earlier in the letter, at 4.4, Paul has disclaimed any intention to shame his readers, but here he freely acknowledges that that is his intention: *to your shame I say it* (cf. 6.5).

God, the limitless Creator
15.35–49

15.35 Paul's argument now takes a new direction, as he anticipates an objection to what he has just been saying. *But, you may ask, how are the dead raised? In what kind of body?*

This device of advancing the argument by anticipating an objection from an imaginary conversation partner is characteristic of Hellenistic philosophy and is used constantly in Romans (see e.g. Rom. 3.1, 9; 4.1; 6.1), but (again as in Romans) it is highly probable that the question which Paul anticipates here is one which he had already encountered in his own preaching. The way he rephrases the question suggests that he is aware that it is the notion of the resurrection of the *body* which is causing puzzlement and offence. If, as we have maintained both in the introduction to the letter and the introduction to this chapter, the Corinthians held a dualistic anthropology, then the very notion of the resurrection of a body would have been to them anathema. It is likely that this repugnance lay at the root of their denial of the doctrine. Unable to conceive of resurrection in any other way than as the reanimation of a corpse, they had abandoned the notion altogether.

15.36f. Paul's response, after upbraiding his imaginary partner for asking stupid questions, is to appeal to the process of growth from a seed. *The seed you sow does not come to life unless it has first died.* At first sight, this seems to be little more than an argument by analogy, thus: as God brings a new plant into being through the death of the seed, so God can give new life to the dead. But there is more to Paul's argument than this. For Paul, every growing organism is a fresh realization of the primordial, creative will of God.[153] Paul's argument at this point, therefore, is more of an illustration than an analogy.

Can anything be said about the nature of the new life? Both in v. 36 and in v. 37 the emphasis falls on the discontinuity between the new life and the old. Anyone who had never seen a field of wheat could never guess from the sight of a bare grain of wheat the nature of the plant that was capable of springing from it, and yet there is a real continuity of life. In the same way, anyone whose knowledge of human bodies is limited to this present order (and that means all of humanity) can have no conception of the nature of the bodies God has in store beyond death for those who love God. So Paul does not respond to the question he poses in v. 35 by attempting to describe in advance the nature of the resurrection body. Rather he argues in effect that the question is unanswerable, this side of the consummation.

15.38 But there is also a deeper side to Paul's argument. This verse emphasizes both the sovereign freedom of the Creator – *God gives it the body of his choice* – and the endless variety of God's creation – *each seed its own particular body.*

15.39 The mention of different seeds leads Paul on to the thought that there is more than one kind of flesh. *All flesh is not the same: there is human flesh, flesh of beasts, of birds and of fishes – all different.* We have already noted, in connection with 3.1–4, the wide range of meanings which the word 'flesh' can have in Paul. Here it denotes the substance of which the body is composed.

15.40 But now Paul's thought takes a further leap. In v. 39 he has spoken of the different kinds of flesh proper to different kinds of earthly creature. In v. 40 his thought embraces heaven as well as earth, as he distinguishes between 'heavenly bodies' and 'earthly bodies', each with their own proper 'splendour'.

15.41 Not only do the heavenly bodies differ from earthly bodies, the various heavenly bodies also differ from one another. *The sun has a splendour of its own, the moon another splendour, and the stars yet another; and one star differs from another in brightness.* Paul's starting-point in this paragraph is the objection of a sceptic, but what looks like a simple analogy has now led to a jubilant celebration of the variety and fecundity of God's creation. Herein lies Paul's real answer to the initial question, 'How are the dead raised? In what kind of body?' His ultimate appeal is not to the analogy of the germination of a seed, it is rather an appeal to the limitless creativity of God. God, who gave us a body in the first place, will also give us a new body, as God chooses, when God raises us from the dead.

There is therefore a fundamental similarity between Paul's response here to the question of his sceptical partner and the response of Jesus to the sceptical question of the Sadducees in Mark 12.18–27. Jesus too makes a simple profession of faith in the creative power of God. The One who made us for this life on earth can remake us for another life in which the changing circumstances of earth, in which one generation succeeds another, will have no place. Men and women will be as the angels, neither marrying nor being given in marriage.

15.42–44a   Paul now declares that the resurrection of the dead will mean the revelation of a further dimension of God's creative power. Just as God has called into being an endless variety of forms of bodily existence appropriate to this present order, so God will call into being new forms of bodily existence appropriate to the age to come. To be sure, there will be continuity between the old and the new, just as there is continuity in the germination of a seed into a new plant. It will be the person who has died who is raised to new life, but raised to *new* life, life that is free from all the limitations of fleshly existence. What comes into being is something new but not something completely alien. To underscore the difference between the body of the present order and the body that will be ours in the resurrection of the dead, Paul has recourse to a fourfold contrast: *what is sown as a perishable thing is raised imperishable. Sown in humiliation, it is raised in glory; sown in weakness, it is raised in power; sown a physical body, it is raised a spiritual body.*

As N. T. Wright argues at length, the translation of the two key adjectives in the final clause as 'physical' and 'spiritual', though favoured by several recent translations as well as the REB, is misleading, if it suggests that by 'spiritual' Paul means something non-physical. The same two adjectives are used in 2.14f. to differentiate believers from unbelievers. The Greek word *psychikos,* which is translated by the REB in the present passage as 'physical', is translated in 2.14f. by 'unspiritual'. In both passages the word appears to refer to ordinary human life apart from the transforming power of God. A possible, if clumsy, translation would be 'the nature-animated body'.

The 'spiritual' person of 2.14f., on the other hand, is not someone who is composed of spirit but rather someone who is animated by the Spirit. This parallel suggests that here the term 'spiritual body' means 'a body animated by, enlivened by, the Spirit of the true God'.[154] The expression would certainly have shocked the Corinthians, for whom 'body' and 'spirit' were antithetical.

15.44b   But is all such talk mere speculation? How can we be sure that it is not a mere projection of our own unfulfilled desires? Paul seems to anticipate such a question by reiterating that *if there is such a thing as a physical body, there is also a spiritual body*. Not 'will be', 'is'. 'Is'? Where? The concept of the spiritual body is not just a fanciful extrapolation from present experience. Nor does it belong entirely to the future. It already exists, it is exemplified, he goes on to argue, in the risen Christ.

15.45   Paul now follows up the contrast he has just drawn between the physical body and the spiritual body with a parallel contrast between *the first man, Adam*, and *the last Adam*, Christ, also described as 'the heavenly man'. *It is in this sense*, he continues, *that scripture says, 'The first man, Adam, became a living creature,' whereas the last Adam has become a life-giving spirit.* 'Become'? When? Paul's answer must be: not in his pre-existent state and not at the incarnation, when he came *in the likeness of our sinful nature* (Rom. 8.3), but in and through his resurrection and exaltation.

Why does Paul speak of a 'life-giving spirit' and not of a 'spiritual body'? He evidently does not wish to imply that Christ's present existence is entirely on a par with what ours will be. Of him can be said what can never be said of us, namely, that he is 'life-giving'. As 'life-giving', therefore, he is more appropriately described as 'spirit' than as 'body'. The Corinthians, however, must have been more than a little bewildered by Paul's terminology here, and not only by his switch from the concept of 'spiritual body' to that of 'life-giving Spirit'. The very notion of a spiritual body must have seemed to them a contradiction in terms.

The two words used to describe Adam and Christ, respectively, in v. 45, namely, *(living) creature* and *(life-giving) spirit* are the nouns that correspond to the adjectives 'physical' and 'spiritual' in v. 44. The implication is that Adam and Christ are the original bearers of the two kinds of bodies which have just been mentioned.

Paul is here adopting the idea, evidently widespread at the time, of a primal, archetypal or heavenly man, in contrast to earthly, physical man. Philo, for example, distinguishes between a heavenly, ideal, man, of whose creation Gen. 1.26f. speaks, and empirical man, described in Gen. 2.7 (*Op. Mund.* 134). Paul alters this scheme. For him, Adam is the primal man, whereas the ideal man is Christ. So the first contrast between two kinds of body is now amplified by a further contrast between two kinds of representative man. As we were created in the likeness of the first man, so shall we be recreated in the likeness of the second. But with one decisive difference: of him can be said what can never be said of us, namely, that he is life-giving.

15.46   Paul now makes the rather puzzling observation that *the spiritual does not come first; the physical body comes first, and then the spiritual.* Such an emphatic statement suggests that he is contradicting a view known to be held at Corinth. But what?

It seems likely that Paul's target is once more over-realized eschatology. The Corinthians, it seems, though they would have been puzzled by the expression, 'spiritual body', believe they have already entered into the fullness of spiritual existence. Against this view Paul asserts once again the 'not yet'. They must accept that their present life in the Spirit has to be lived in the physical body. The consummation of life in the Spirit is yet to come, and, when it comes, it will still be a form of bodily existence, albeit in a spiritual body.

15.47   Paul now restates the contrast between the two Adams, echoing again, in his reference to the first Adam, the language of Gen. 2.7: *The first man is from earth, made of dust: the second man is from heaven.*

The two phrases, 'from earth' and 'from heaven', are usually taken to refer to the origin of Adam and Christ. This view has generated a vast amount of discussion of Paul's possible dependence on a myth of a heavenly man. It is more likely, however, as Fee argues, that the two phrases refer not to the origin of the two Adams but to their nature.[155] In v. 48, for example, the counterpart to 'from heaven' is the adjective 'heavenly'.

15.48   In vv. 48 and 49 Paul draws out the consequence of describing Christ as the last Adam, namely, that as he is, so shall we be. Just as *the man made of dust is the pattern of all who are made of dust,* so *the heavenly man is the pattern of all the heavenly*. Neither exists simply as an individual. Each is the archetype of a humanity.

15.49   Changing the metaphor, Paul continues: *As we have worn the likeness of the man made of dust, so we shall wear the likeness of the heavenly man.*

Here, as in v. 22, the future tense, 'shall', appears to be used in deliberate contrast to the Corinthian position. A strong case can be made, however, for an alternative reading at this point, not 'we shall bear' but 'let us bear'. If the latter reading is preferred, Paul is to be understood as urging his readers to look to Christ as the source and hope of their transformation.

The Triumph of God
15.50–58

15.50 Having affirmed the reality of the spiritual body, Paul now declares that a body different from our present physical body is necessary for the resurrection status, *for flesh and blood can never possess the kingdom of God*. The transition from the old body to the new will be part of something bigger, the consummation of God's purposes for the creation. That consummation is regularly described in apocalyptic literature and in the Synoptic Gospels as the kingdom of God. In place of the earlier expression, the 'physical body', Paul here uses a common biblical phrase for the creature as against the Creator, namely, *flesh and blood*.

15.51 Paul now embarks upon a detailed description of the moment of transition to the consummation. He prefixes his description with the solemn announcement, *Listen! I will unfold a mystery*. This is the sixth occurrence of the word 'mystery' in this epistle since its first occurrence at 2.7. Its use here implies a claim on Paul's part to have received a prophetic revelation, direct divine illumination. The main thrust of this 'revelation' is that all believers, whether they die before the Lord comes or whether they are still alive, will be transformed. Paul himself apparently still expects to be among the living (see v. 52), but at the end any distinction between the deceased and the surviving will be irrelevant, for *we shall all be changed*. The living will lose their earthly bodies and receive a spiritual body without having to pass through physical death, but their transformation too will be the work of the creative, miraculous power of God.

15.52 This transformation will happen *in a flash, in the twinkling of an eye, at the last trumpet-call*. Paul's language here is reminiscent of 1 Thess. 4.16 but has its roots in Jewish apocalyptic. Paul, however, makes very sparing use of apocalyptic furniture.

15.53 For those who die before the consummation this will mean resurrection from the dead. As for those who are still alive, *this perishable body must be clothed with the imperishable, and what is mortal with immortality*. In the previous two paragraphs Paul has been stressing the discontinuity between present existence and the future state, while maintaining at the same time that there will be continuity. The use of the metaphor of clothing enables him to make both emphases at once. The new person will not be a totally new creation but rather the same person finding expression through a new body, imperishable and immortal.

15.54 Such a consummation will mark the fulfilment of prophecies from the Old Testament of the destruction of death. In its context, the first quotation, from Isa. 25.8, *Death is swallowed up; victory is won!* forms part of a prophetic description of the coming kingdom. The second quotation, from Hos. 13.14, is linked with the first by the catch-word 'victory'. We have already noted, in connection with 15.27 (see note 149), Paul's use of the rabbinic exegetical device of *gēzerāh shāwāh*, that is, the association of two passages of Scripture that have a term in common and the interpretation of each in the light of the other. Verse 54 is another example. The verse from Hosea is not in its context predictive but readily lends itself to a predictive interpretation, when read out of its context.

15.55 The double question posed in v. 55, *O Death, where is your victory? O Death, where is your sting?* is to be taken as rhetorical. Death has been denied the victory and robbed of its sting.

15.56 Picking up the last word of the previous quotation, Paul now declares that *the sting of death is sin*. This is usually taken to mean that it is our sinful condition that makes death a bitter experience, but Rom. 5.12 suggests another interpretation, namely, that it is by means of sin that death gains entry into the world. 'Were it not for sin, death could not reach us.'[156]

The polemical edge to Paul's further comment that *sin gains its power from the law* should not be missed. For the rabbis the law was the strength of Yahweh. Paul declares it to be just the opposite. Once again, this line of thought is expounded in much more detail in Romans, especially Rom. 7.7–25.

15.57 Here Paul returns to the theme of God's victory over death, introduced in vv. 54f. In v. 54 victory over death was held out as a hope for the future. Now Paul breaks into a doxology: *Thanks be to God! He gives us victory through our Lord Jesus Christ.* This victory mentioned without further definition must be not only victory over death but over all the powers opposed to God's will. Into that victory we may already begin to enter. The resurrection of the saints still lies in the future, but Christ has risen and we may live in the power of his resurrection even now.

15.58　Paul has worked up to an impressive climax. It is striking, however, that, having concluded his vindication of the certainty of resurrection and his exposition of the manner of it, he ends on the note of exhortation. That he should conclude the theological argument not only of this chapter but of the whole letter on such a sober note provides striking evidence of the centrality of ethics in his thought as a whole. As Barrett observes, 'he is not the kind of preacher to finish his discourse with a purple patch that evaporates in pure rhetoric'.[157] The grand indicative of the resurrection hope also leads to a corresponding imperative.

At the same time there is a subtle echoing of the opening verses of the chapter. In v. 2 Paul expressed the fear that their coming to faith, and therefore his own labours to bring them to faith, might be rendered futile by their abandonment of the belief in the resurrection of the dead (cf. v. 14). Now, having summoned all the powers of his intellect and imagination to vindicate the resurrection hope, he points to that hope as the ground of their confidence that in the Lord their labour cannot be lost, cannot be futile. For the resurrection hope means that life, not death, is the destiny of all those for whom Paul or any other Christian worker has ever laboured. Inspired by such a hope and confidence, they surely cannot do other than *work for the Lord always, work without limit*, standing firm and immovable.

It is especially noteworthy that in this closing verse Paul greets his readers as *my dear friends*. He is painfully aware of the deficiencies in their theology and their behaviour. He has also caught wind of criticisms of his own style of leadership. Yet they are still his *dear friends*.

Plans and Greetings
16.1–24

The collection for Jerusalem
16.1–4

Paul concludes the letter with some practical matters, beginning with the organization of a collection described as being *in aid of God's people*. However, v. 3 implies that it is for the church in Jerusalem, and other references to this collection make it clear that it was intended for the poorer members of that church. The initiative for this collection came from the conference described in Gal. 2.1–10, at which Paul undertook to continue to remember the poor. Paul solicits the support of the Corinthians, at considerably greater length, in 2 Corinthians 8 and 9.

In Acts there is only one brief and misleading reference to the collection (at 24.17), but it is quite clear from Paul's own letters, particularly 1 and 2 Corinthians and Romans, that he prosecuted it with great vigour over several years throughout the whole of his missionary territory. At the time of writing this letter, he is still undecided whether or not to accompany the bearers of the gift in person. By the time he writes to the Romans, however, he has become convinced that this is something he must do, even though he is acutely aware that it is dangerous for him to visit Jerusalem. Why this sense of inescapable obligation, in spite of his presentiments of danger in store? The answer must be that for him the offering held considerable symbolic significance. It was an expression of gratitude for the indispensable role played by the Jerusalem church in the transmission of the gospel. It was also a sign of the unity of Jewish and Gentile Christians within the one church. Paul fervently hoped that it would be accepted by the Jerusalem church as having that significance. The strange silence of Acts on this matter may be an indication that Paul's worst fears were realized and that the collection was spurned by the Jerusalem church.[158]

16.1 This is the fifth time since 7.1 that Paul has begun a paragraph with the phrase, 'Now about . . .' Here, as before, the use of this phrase suggests that he is responding to a question that the Corinthians had raised in their letter to him. This view gains support from the brevity of his reference to the collection at this point, with no indication of its purpose or theological significance. However that may be, they are to follow the instructions he has already given to the churches in Galatia.

16.2 Every Sunday, each of them is to set aside and store up *whatever he can afford, so that there need be no collecting,* when Paul arrives.

16.3 They are also to appoint people whom they consider suitable to carry their gift to Jerusalem. The motive for this directive is, no doubt, partly prudential, in that Paul is anxious to avoid any suspicion of using the gift to enrich himself. But it is probably also pastoral, in so far as the Christians of Jerusalem will have an opportunity to meet living representatives of the Gentile churches in the persons of the delegates. Paul for his part will send them on their way furnished with letters of introduction from himself to the Jerusalem church.

16.4 If it seems advisable that Paul should go as well, then the delegates will accompany him. There is in these verses an interesting blend of authority and restraint. The Corinthians are left in no doubt by Paul about what they are to do, and yet they are to appoint as bearers of the gift the people they think fit.

One is also struck by the matter-of-fact way in which Paul takes up the issue. A comment of Fee's is apposite: 'No pressure, no gimmicks, no emotion. A need had to be met, and the Corinthians were capable of playing a role in it.'[159]

Keeping in touch
16.5–12

Having just alluded to his proposed visit to Corinth, Paul now proceeds to give the Corinthians more information about his travel plans, as well as about the possibility of visits from his associates.

16.5–9 He begins by telling them when they can expect to see him, how long he hopes to stay and why he is not planning to come immediately. An early visit would be necessarily brief, and he is anxious that his next visit should be more than a flying visit. He may even spend the whole winter with them. As we noted in the Introduction, there was in the Hellenistic world a considerable amount of theoretical reflection on letter writing as a means of overcoming the pain of physical separation. The Corinthians should not suppose, however, that Paul is content to deal with them at a distance, relying on letters alone.

What is more, Ephesus, where he is at present residing, offers great opportunities for effective evangelism, in spite of the presence of many opponents.

This reference to the scope for work in Ephesus should serve to remind them that their community is but one of a number whose welfare lies very close to Paul's heart. When, in a later letter, he speaks of his daily burden of anxiety about all the churches (2 Cor. 11.28), he will not be making an idle boast.

When his visit does take place, he is counting on them to help him on his way, wherever he goes next. The Greek verb underlying the rendering 'help . . . on my way' in v. 6 is used in the New Testament virtually as a technical term for providing a person with the food, money and companions needed to ensure their safe arrival at their next destination.[160] It is clear from chapter 9 that by refusing to accept material support from the Corinthian congregation Paul had laid himself open to the criticism of not being a true apostle. By giving them this opportunity to equip him for a further journey, he may well be seeking to meet such criticisms and soothe the feelings of potential patrons who had felt slighted.

16.10f.   Paul now mentions a forthcoming visit from Timothy and urges them to give him a good reception. The REB rendering, *If Timothy comes*, is true to the usual meaning of the Greek words, but, in view of 4.17, where Paul states explicitly that he has sent Timothy to them, he probably means, 'Whenever Timothy comes.'

The REB rendering, *See that you put him at his ease*, obscures the hint that one can detect in the Greek that Paul envisages the possibility of a real rebuff to Timothy. The more literal rendering of the AV runs, 'See that he may be with you without fear.'

Why should Paul find it necessary to say this? Why should he need to remind them that Timothy, like himself, is engaged in the Lord's work and then add that he is not to be slighted by anyone? It seems that, as has been suggested in the Introduction, Paul senses that a conflict is developing between himself and the church in Corinth. Timothy has been despatched, charged with reminding them of Paul's way of life in Christ. There is therefore a very real possibility that the animus and contempt that some of them already feel towards Paul, and that may have been exacerbated by some of the things he has said in the letter, will spill over on to Timothy.

16.12   Finally, Paul tells them that it is unlikely that Apollos will visit them in the near future. The use for the last time of the phrase, 'Now concerning . . .' suggests that this was another matter that the Corinthians had raised in their letter to him. Perhaps they had requested him to ask Apollos to pay them another visit.

As to why Apollos was so determined not to go to Corinth at this time, we can only guess. One thing is clear: Paul has full confidence in him as a colleague (literally, 'the brother'). In no way does he regard him as a competitor or a rival. When, in an earlier chapter, Paul described the church as God's garden, God's building, and himself and Apollos as fellow-workers in the service of God, to whom alone they must one day give account (3.5–9), he meant what he said.

Recognition to whom recognition is due
16.13–18

16.13f.   Although the conclusions of Paul's letters do not conform to a pattern as strictly as the openings, they generally contain hortatory remarks. There are parallels to the first two of these exhortations in similar contexts in other epistles, but Paul seems to have selected these imperatives with the Corinthian situation in mind.

The Corinthians are to *be on the alert*. This word is often used in the New Testament to urge watchfulness in view of the Lord's return, but in this context it is more likely to be a call to be on guard against error, as in Acts 20.30f.

They are also to *stand firm in the faith*, the faith first proclaimed to them, and now more fully expounded, by Paul, and to reject those misapprehensions of the gospel that he has been at pains to draw to their attention. They are to resist the enticements of those who are seeking to improve on the word of the cross with a more sophisticated theology, and they are to resist with courage and strength.

Above all, they are to see to it that everything they do is *done in love*. Over and over again we have found evidence of a signal lack of any real sense of mutual responsibility in the church in Corinth. If they would but make love their ruling principle, all the problems of their life together – the factions, the lawsuits, the heartburning over meat offered to idols, the tensions in worship and all the rest – would disappear.

16.15–18 These verses combine exhortation and information. We have noted already that in this community, in which everyone 'does their own thing', there seems to be no recognized leader to whom Paul can turn with the request to put things right. He does not want to stop everyone 'doing their own thing', although he does insist, as we have seen in chapter 12, that, if they rightly discern 'their thing', they will understand it as some form of service that they are called to perform for the good of the community.

What is more, some people's 'thing', their *charisma*, in other words, consists precisely of the gift of leadership. Here we see Paul urging the Corinthians to recognize that gift in some of their own members, to accept the leadership of (literally, 'to submit themselves to') people like the family of Stephanas, along with *anyone who labours hard at our common task*. There is a sense in which that might be said of every active member of the congregation, but Paul must have in mind people who have devoted themselves to the service of God's people in a very deliberate way, as the family of Stephanas has done.

It should be noted that it is *the Stephanas family* and others like them whose leadership the Corinthians are urged to accept, not just that of Stephanas alone.

Paul certainly does not envisage anything like the church order of later denominations, with their canon laws, their constitutions and regulations, yet he does seem to be giving the Corinthian congregation something of a push towards a firmer structure.

It would also be very much in Paul's own interests, if the Stephanas family were accorded greater recognition, since not only is there a special bond between them and Paul, they being his first converts in Corinth and almost the only converts whom he had baptized there (see 1.14–16), but they have evidently remained loyal to him in the present difficulties.

That close relationship has now been enhanced by the visit of Stephanas, along with Fortunatus and Achaicus. In all probability, these three were the bearers of the letter to Paul from the Corinthian church. It is equally likely that they will carry Paul's letter back with them. They must also have brought Paul first-hand information about the situation in Corinth, much of it unwelcome. And yet they have succeeded in raising Paul's spirits. They have been a living link with that group of Christians, who, for all their folly and waywardness, are still, and will remain, Paul's dear children (cf. 4.14). By so doing, the delegates have made up for the absence of the rest of the congregation and done what the others had no chance to do. And surely it will be a lift to the spirits of the other members to hear of the service that their delegates have been able to render to Paul. *Such people deserve recognition.*

Greetings and farewell
16.19–24

Paul now transmits various greetings, as is his custom towards the end of a letter.

16.19   There is first a greeting from *the churches of Asia,* 'Asia' denoting the westernmost province of Asia Minor. We cannot tell how many churches Paul has in mind. We do know from the opening chapters of Revelation that, by the 90s, churches had been established in all the major cities of this area. The transmission of greetings like these was one of the methods that Paul used to foster relationships between different churches and heighten their awareness of being part of a far-flung family of believing communities.

Aquila and Prisca (elsewhere called Priscilla) were a couple with whom Paul had worked closely in Corinth and elsewhere (see Acts 18.2, 18, 26; Rom. 16.3). He had made his home with them, on his first arrival in Corinth. Indeed, they may already have been Christians, when they themselves arrived in Corinth from Rome. After moving to Ephesus, they remedied deficiencies in Apollos's understanding of baptism, according to Acts 18.24–26. *The church that meets in their house,* which here joins with Aquila and Prisca in sending greetings, was probably the house church in Ephesus to which Paul himself was attached.

16.20   *The whole brotherhood* probably refers to all the other Christians with whom Paul is in contact in Ephesus, including other house churches and Paul's travelling companions.

The recipients of the letter are to *greet one another with the kiss of peace* (literally 'with a holy kiss'). This is more than just a warm gesture of greeting; rather, it is a sign that this community has been brought into being by the Spirit (cf. Rom. 16.16; 2 Cor. 13.12; 1 Thess. 5.26; 1 Peter 5.14). The 'kiss of peace' later became a formal part of the eucharistic liturgy.

16.21   Paul now adds his own greeting in his own hand. It seems that this was his regular practice (cf. Gal. 6.11; Col. 4.18; 2 Thess. 3.17).

16.22   By now the reader is expecting the final benediction, but without warning Paul interposes an anathema on anyone who *does not love the Lord*. This is his parting shot at what we have identified as the deepest root of the Corinthian malaise, their false security. Christians have not arrived, they are still on the way and remain to the end answerable to God. The ultimate test, 'the bottom line', is whether they love the Lord.

Paul is probably using traditional material here, possibly a sentence of holy law similar to the pronouncements in 3.17 and 14.38.

Verse 22 concludes in the Greek with two Aramaic words that are unquestionably of traditional origin. These two words can be read as meaning, 'Our Lord has come,' but most scholars favour the interpretation given in the REB, *Come, Lord!* Here we have a clear echo of the worship of the Aramaic-speaking church, which has passed into the vocabulary of the Greek-speaking churches. It serves as a further reminder to the Corinthians that the End has not yet arrived. In Rev. 22.20 the same prayer is expressed in Greek.

16.23f.   Lastly, we have a blessing in the usual form plus the assurance of Paul's love for them all. In spite of all their shortcomings, they are still his beloved children. But love in the deepest sense cannot be summoned up by an effort of the will. It is the fruit of the work of the Spirit in the lives of those who are *in Christ Jesus*.

NOTES

1 For excellent accounts of the city of Corinth in classical and biblical times see Victor Paul Furnish, *II Corinthians*, pp. 4–26; also the same author's lavishly illustrated article, 'Corinth in Paul's Time: What can Archaeology tell us?' *Biblical Archaeology Review*, 15(3), 1988, pp. 14–27. For a comprehensive and judicious survey of attempts to delineate the Christian community at Corinth, see Adams and Horrell (eds), *Christianity at Corinth: The Quest for the Pauline Church*.

2 Sherman E. Johnson, *Paul the Apostle and His Cities*, p. 98.

3 There is a valuable discussion of the social setting of first-century Corinth in Timothy B. Savage, *Power through Weakness: Paul's Understanding of Christian Ministry in 2 Corinthians*, pp. 16–53.

4 Cf. Jerome Murphy-O'Connor, O.P., *St. Paul's Corinth*, pp. 55f.

5 See Furnish, *II Cor.*, p. 383.

6 Gordon D. Fee, *The First Epistle to the Corinthians*, pp. 5f.; p. 8, note 22.

7 See 3.16; 5.6; 6.2, 3, 9, 15, 16, 19; 9.13, 24.

8 See especially Abraham J. Malherbe, *Ancient Epistolary Theorists*, *passim*.

9 For a fuller discussion see Raymond F. Collins, *First Corinthians*, pp. 1–10.

10 Much recent scholarship is concerned with the degree to which Paul adapts the rhetorical conventions of his day. See particularly Margaret Mitchell, *Paul and the Rhetoric of Reconciliation*. For a fuller discussion see the larger commentaries, especially that of Thiselton.

11 Wolfgang Schrage, *Der erste Brief an die Korinther*, Vol. I, pp. 38–41. Cf. also the thorough and lucid discussion of the problems and possibilities of mirror-reading by John Barclay in his article, 'Mirror-Reading a Polemical Letter: Galatians as a Test Case', *Journal for the study of the New Testament*, 31, 1987, pp. 73–93.

12 Richard B. Hays, *First Corinthians*, p. 8.

13 Eduard Schweizer, *Spirit of God*, p. 55. Fee prefers to speak of a 'spiritualized eschatology', on the grounds that the Corinthians

'were not so concerned about the *future* having become present as with a new spiritual mode of existence that had now become available to them and was already being realized', *I Cor.* p. 12; cf. pp. 339f.

14 Elsewhere I have argued that warnings of coming judgement are more prominent in 1 Corinthians than in any other letter of Paul's and are directed consistently at a state of presumption, the state of being 'puffed up'. See Nigel M. Watson, 'Justified by Faith; Judged by Works – an Antinomy?' *NTS*, 29, 1983, pp. 209–21.

15 As Ernst Käsemann puts it, 'The point is that the resurrection is one aspect of the message of the cross, not that the cross is simply one chapter in a book of resurrection dogmatics' (*Jesus Means Freedom* p. 68; cf. pp. 67, 69, 82f.). Philip Leon has observed, in a penetrating critique of the Moral Rearmament Movement, that 'if medieval Christianity was morbidly fond of displaying predominantly the agony of the Cross, M.R.A., in its propaganda of the telephonic conception [of guidance], is sanitarily careful to spotlight chiefly the Resurrection' ('M.R.A., a Contemporary Crux in the Philosophy and Application of Religion', *The Hibbert Journal*, 54, 1956, p. 149). His comment is equally applicable to Corinthian Christianity.

16 Cf. Ernst Käsemann, 'The Pauline Doctrine of the Lord's Supper', *Essays on New Testament Themes*, pp. 113, 116–19.

17 Cf. Fee, *I Cor.*, pp.10, 49.

18 See Furnish, II Cor., p. 107.

19 For a careful analysis of Paul's use of the word 'wisdom' in 1 Corinthians, see C. K. Barrett, 'Christianity at Corinth', *Bulletin of the John Rylands Library*, 46, 1964, pp. 275–84.

20 In a review of A. M. Ramsey's *God, Christ and the World, Frontier* (May, 1969), p. 148.

21 Iris Murdoch, *The Good Apprentice*, p. 147.

22 Frederick Buechner, *The Life of Jesus*, pp. 189–93.

23 Quoted by Terence Cave in *The Cornucopian Text*, pp. 24f.

24 For valuable discussions of rhetoric in Paul's day, see Ruth Majercik, 'Rhetoric and Oratory in the Greco-Roman World', in *The Anchor Bible Dictionary*, vol. 5, pp. 710–12; Witherington, *Conflict and Community*, pp. 39–48, 55–61.

25 For a valuable exposition of 'wisdom' in this letter see C. K. Barrett, *1 Corinthians*, pp. 67f.

26 See Fee, *I Cor.*, p. 84, for a useful discussion of this word group.

27 See R. H. Barrow, 'Slaves', in *The Oxford Classical Dictionary*, pp. 843–5.

28 G. Theissen, *The Social Setting of Pauline Christianity*, pp. 94f.
29 For a full discussion of recent studies of this question see David G. Horrell, *The Social Ethos of the Corinthian Correspondence*, pp. 91–101.
30 C. F. D. Moule, *The Birth of the New Testament*, p. 159.
31 For a fuller discussion see my article, 'The Philosopher Should Bathe and Brush His Teeth', *Australian Biblical Review*, 42, 1994, pp. 1–16.
32 This is the closing line of the hymn of Isaac Watts, 'God is a name my soul adores'.
33 Cf. W. Eichrodt, *Theology of the Old Testament* II, p. 60.
34 Schrage, *Der erste Brief an die Korinther*, I, p. 239.
35 For Paul's use of words of the *sarx* family, see John M. G. Barclay, *Obeying the Truth*, ch. 6.
36 Antoinette Wire is correct to point out that 34 negative particles appear in 30 verses between 1.14 and 3.4, but I consider that she is overstating her case when she writes that 'the cumulative impact is shattering, leaving a great abyss between human reality and divine reality'. See Antoinette Clark Wire, *The Corinthian Women Prophets*, p. 54.
37 Barrett, *I Cor.*, p. 84.
38 Jay Shanor, 'Paul as Master Builder: Construction Terms in First Corinthians', *NTS*, 34, 1988, pp. 461–71.
39 For a careful comparison between Paul's use of these images and the use made of them in the Testament of Abraham, see C. W. Fishburne, 'I Cor. III.10–15 and the Testament of Abraham', *NTS*, 17, 1970, pp. 109–15.
40 For the possibility that such pronouncements reflect the activity of Christian prophets who executed a 'holy law' by anticipating God's verdict in the last judgement, see Käsemann, 'Sentences of Holy Law in the New Testament', *New Testament Questions for Today*, pp. 66–81.
41 Cf. Watson, 'Justified by Faith; Judged by Works – an Antinomy?', *NTS*, 29, 1983, pp. 213–15.
42 See e.g. H. H. Farmer, *The Servant of the Word*, pp. 67–72.
43 For some penetrating comments on the spiritual danger of misusing the word 'my', to the point of saying 'my God' in a sense not really very different from 'my boots', see C. S. Lewis, *The Screwtape Letters*, pp. 108–10.
44 Barrett, *I Cor.*, p. 101.
45 Gerd Theissen, *Psychological Aspects of Pauline Theology*, p. 63.

46 For a detailed advocacy of this view see John T. Fitzgerald, *Cracks in an Earthen Vessel*, pp. 123–7.

47 Wire suggests the rendering 'bloated' (*The Corinthian Women Prophets*, p. 44).

48 Fitzgerald, *Cracks in an Earthen Vessel*, p. 138.

49 Fitzgerald suggests the rendering, 'everyone's gunk' (*Cracks in an Earthen Vessel*, p. 142); Wire: 'the garbage peelings of the world' (*The Corinthian Women Prophets*, p. 44).

50 Nigel Watson, *The Second Epistle to the Corinthians*, p. 49.

51 On this verse see John Ziesler, *The Epistle to the Galatians*, p. 49.

52 For an illuminating discussion of the phrase 'kingdom of God', see James D. G. Dunn, *Jesus Remembered*, pp. 387–488.

53 For references to the relevant texts, see Fee, *I Cor.*, pp. 200f., n. 24.

54 See Käsemann, 'Sentences of Holy Law in the New Testament', *New Testament Questions of Today*, pp. 66–81, esp. pp. 70–72.

55 For a fuller discussion see the comments below on 1 Cor. 15.12–19.

56 Schrage, *Der erste Brief*, 1:377.

57 For a fuller discussion, see the Introduction, p. xvi.

58 See Dietrich Bonhoeffer, *The Cost of Discipleship*, pp. 35–47.

59 For a fuller discussion see Alan C. Mitchell, 'Rich and Poor in the Courts of Corinth', *NTS*, 39, 1993, pp. 562–86.

60 Eduard Schweizer, *The Church as the Body of Christ*, pp. 39f.

61 Käsemann, *Essays on New Testament Themes*, p. 133.

62 See E.-B. Allo, *Premiere Épître aux Corinthiens*, p. 148.

63 Brendan Byrne, S.J., 'Sinning against One's Own Body', *CBQ*, 45, 1983, p. 613.

64 This view is at least as old as Origen. See Fee, *I Cor.*, p. 273, n. 25, for a fuller discussion.

65 See Fee, *I Cor.*, p. 272, n. 15.

66 Fee, *I Cor.*, p. 280.

67 Cf. Brendan Byrne, S.J., *Paul and the Christian Woman*, p. 19; also p. 28, n.11.

68 For fuller discussions of divorce in Judaism and Graeco-Roman society, see Fee, *I Cor.*, pp. 293f.

69 For a discussion of the difficulties Paul unwittingly created for women by discouraging Christians married to non-Christians from initiating divorce, see Elisabeth Schüssler Fiorenza, *In Memory of Her*, p. 223.

70 Schrage, *Der erste Brief*, 3:104.

71 See Fee, *I Cor.*, p. 309, for a full discussion of Paul's use of 'call', 'calling', etc.

72 See Fee, *I Cor.*, pp. 316f. He lists three arguments for the view that Paul is saying, 'Stay a slave,' and eight for the view that he is saying, 'Accept freedom.'

73 See B. W. Winter, 'Secular and Christian Responses to Corinthian Famines', *Tyndale Bulletin*, 40, pp. 86–106; also Thiselton, *I Cor.*, p. 573, for a full discussion.

74 Cf. Fiorenza, *In Memory of Her*, p. 226, for a similar criticism.

75 For a description of the traces of three dining rooms attached to the temple of Asclepius in Corinth, see Murphy-O'Connor, *St. Paul's Corinth*, pp. 161–5. For a full survey of the scholarly literature on the subject, as well as a detailed examination of the archaeological and literary evidence, see John Fotopoulos, *Food Offered to Idols*.

76 For a fuller discussion, see Gerd Theissen, *The Social Setting of Pauline Christianity*, pp. 41–8.

77 Philo, *De Specialibus Legibus* 1.260.

78 John K. Chow, *Patronage and Power*, p. 69.

79 Chow, *Patronage and Power*, p. 41.

80 For an attempt to enter into the constraint felt by a typical client, see Hans Froer's imaginative reconstruction of the Corinthian side of the correspondence with Paul, *You Wretched Corinthians!* pp. 26f.

81 Chow's book is an excellent introduction to the social institution of patronage. For a discussion of the related social institution of friendship in the Graeco-Roman world, see Peter Marshall, *Enmity in Corinth: Social Conventions in Paul's Relations with the Corinthians*, chs. 1, 5 and 6.

82 Fee, *I Cor.*, p. 411.

83 Fee, *I Cor.*, p. 421.

84 G. K. Chesterton, *St. Francis of Assisi*, pp. 90f.

85 Cf. my article, 'Justified by Faith: Judged by Works – an Antinomy?', *NTS*, 29, 1983, pp. 209–21.

86 Philo, *Allegories of the Laws*, II.86.

87 For a valuable discussion of *koinōnia* as mutual participation in Christ see N. T. Wright, *The Climax of the Covenant*, pp. 51–5. *Koinōnia* was the theme of the Fifth World Conference on Faith and Order of the World Council of Churches held at Santiago in August, 1993. For an examination of the significance of *Koinōnia* for contemporary ecumenical theology, see Nicholas Sagovsky, *Ecumenism, Christian Origins and the Practice of Communion*, esp. pp. 128–35 (on the Corinthian letters).

88 Rudolf-P. Borawski, *'Frei werden von Zwängen'*, in Walter Kasper

and others (eds), *Mit der Bibel durch das Jahr 1993* (Stuttgart: Kreuz Verlag, 1992) p. 36.

89 Thiselton, *The First Epistle*, p. 773.

90 For discussions of the historical problems raised by the Apostolic Decree, see C. K. Barrett, *The Acts of the Apostles*, vol. II, pp. 709–12, 730–6; James D. G. Dunn, *The Acts of the Apostles*, pp. 195–8; Joseph Fitzmyer, *The Acts of the Apostles*, pp. 551–4.

91 Thiselton, *The First Epistle*, pp. 788–92.

92 Hays, *I Cor.*, pp. 182f.

93 Fee, *I Cor.*, p. 503, n. 44.

94 Schrage, *Der erste Brief*, 2:503.

95 Thiselton, *I Cor.*, p. 800.

96 For fuller discussions see the larger commentaries, such as those by Fee or Thiselton.

97 Fee, *I Cor.*, p. 515.

98 Wire, *The Corinthian Women Prophets*, pp. 116–34, 185f. For a critique of Wire's book see my review article in the *Australian Biblical Review*, 40, 1992, pp. 58–63.

99 For a valuable theological critique of Paul's argument at this point, see Hays, *I Cor.*, pp. 190–2.

100 See Morna Hooker, 'Authority on her Head', *NTS*, 10, 1963–4, pp. 410–16.

101 Schrage, *Der erste Brief*, 3:14f.

102 Mitchell, *Paul and the Rhetoric of Reconciliation*, p. 153.

103 Hans Froer offers a persuasive reconstruction of the feelings of one of the disadvantaged latecomers in his imaginative reconstruction of the Corinthian side of the correspondence with Paul, *You Wretched Corinthians!* p. 59.

104 See Murphy-O'Connor, *St. Paul's Corinth*, pp. 153–61; David G. Horrell, 'Domestic Space and Christian Meetings at Corinth: Imagining New Contexts and the Buildings East of the Theatre', *NTS*, 50, 2004, pp. 349–69.

105 See the texts from Juvenal, Martial and Pliny cited in Fee, *I Cor.*, p. 542, n. 55; also in Murphy-O'Connor, *St. Paul's Corinth*, pp. 159–61.

106 Thiselton, *I Cor.*, p. 862.

107 For a detailed comparison of the various traditions, see Fee, *I Cor.*, pp. 546f.

108 For a fuller discussion, see Eduard Schweizer, *The Lord's Supper according to the New Testament*, pp. 14, 17.

109 Cf. Schweizer, *The Lord's Supper*, pp. 14f.

110 See especially Fee, *I Cor.*, pp. 560, 566.

111 Thiselton, *I Cor.*, p. 918–24.

112 Ernst Käsemann, 'Ministry and Community in the New Testament', *Essays on New Testament Themes*, p. 65.

113 Arndt and Gingrich, *A Greek-English Lexicon of the New Testament*, article on *charisma*.

114 Eduard Schweizer, *Church Order in the New Testament*, p. 101.

115 J.-J. Suurmond, 'A Fresh Look at Spirit-Baptism and the Charisms', *Expository Times*, 109, 1988, p. 105.

116 For a recent discussion of Paul's understanding of *charismata*, see James R. Harrison, *Paul's Language of Grace in its Graeco-Roman Context*, esp. pp. 279–88. For a possible homiletical application of Paul's understanding of the Spirit as reflected in this chapter, see H. Wheeler Robinson, *The Christian Experience of the Holy Spirit*, p. 4.

117 Fee, *I Cor.*, p. 583.

118 For fuller discussions see M. Mitchell, *Paul and the Rhetoric of Reconciliation*, pp. 68–83, 157–64; D. B. Martin, *The Corinthian Body*, pp. 38–68, 87–103.

119 To describe Paul's language at this point as metaphorical rather than literal is not to belittle its importance. Recent studies on the nature of metaphor have made it abundantly clear that no living metaphor can appropriately be described as a 'mere metaphor'. I quote two statements by Sallie McFague: 'Poetic metaphor is used not as an embellishment of what can be said in some other way but precisely because what is being said is new and cannot be said any other way' (*Speaking in Parables*, p. 49); and again: 'Good metaphors shock, they bring unlikes together, they upset conventions, and they are implicitly revolutionary' (*Metaphorical Theology*, p. 17).

120 Wire finds here evidence of an opposition party to Paul in Corinth consisting of women prophets. See *The Corinthian Women Prophets*, p. 137.

121 Käsemann, 'Ministry and Community in the New Testament', *Essays on New Testament Themes*, pp. 76f.

122 John V. Taylor, *The Primal Vision*, p. 123.

123 See Murphy-O'Connor, *St Paul's Corinth*, pp. 75–7.

124 See Fee, *I Cor.*, p. 648, n. 45.

125 Barrett, *I Cor.*, p. 311. For a fine homiletical application of this chapter, see Walter J. Burghardt, *Grace on Crutches*, pp. 175–8.

126 Tom Wright, *Paul for Everyone: 1 Corinthians*, pp. 181f.

127 Theissen, *Psychological Aspects of Pauline Theology*, p. 79; see also pp. 276–341.

128 A. M. Ramsey, *Introducing the Christian Faith*, p. 66.

129 Fee (*I Cor.*, p. 664, n. 28) suggests that 'in modern culture the appropriate analogy would be the cacophony of the symphony orchestra tuning instruments and warming up just before the conductor raises the baton'.

130 C. H. Dodd, *The Interpretation of the Fourth Gospel*, p. 263.

131 Cf. Schweizer, *Church Order in the New Testament*, p. 101.

132 Schrage, *Der erste Brief*, 3:484.

133 Horrell, *The Social Ethos*, pp. 184–95.

134 *First Corinthians*, pp. 513–21.

135 Collins, *I Cor.*, p. 1156.

136 Thiselton, *I Cor.*, pp. 1155f.

137 Thiselton, See Calvin Roetzel, *Paul, The Man and the Myth*, pp. 178–83. Roetzel sets out four different Pauline chronologies. Ruth Schaefer offers another, which posits a gap of only about 18 months between the death of Jesus and the revelation to Paul. See Ruth Schaefer, *Paulus bis zum Apostelkonzil*, pp. 490–4.

138 See Edward Schillebeeckx, *Jesus*, pp. 526–32, for a valuable discussion of 'the third day' in the Old Testament.

139 See e.g. Fee, *I Cor.*, pp. 725f.

140 According to Jeremias, 'Her witness was acceptable only in a very few exceptional cases, and that of a Gentile slave was also acceptable in the same cases, . . . for example, on the remarriage of a widow, the witness of a woman as to the death of her husband was accepted'. See Joachim Jeremias, *Jerusalem in the Time of Jesus*, pp. 374f.

141 J. I. H. McDonald, *The Resurrection: Narrative and Belief*, p. 26.

142 This reconstruction of the Corinthian position on resurrection is in close accord with that of Schrage, who writes that both the futurity and the bodily nature of the resurrection appear to have been contested in Corinth. See Schrage, *Der erste Brief*, 1:59; cf. 4:113f. Schrage also quotes the Gospel of Thomas, 51: '"When will the resurrection of the dead occur and when will the new world come?" He said to them, "That which you await has come, but you do not recognize it."'

143 Barrett, *I Cor.*, p. 348.

144 Cf. my *Easter Faith and Witness*, pp. 17f.

145 *Easter Faith and Witness*, p. 16.

146 Pheme Perkins, *Resurrection: New Testament Witness and*

    Contemporary Reflection, pp. 125, 318; cf. my *Easter Faith and Witness*, p. 68.

147 H. H. Farmer, 'Christ and the Sickness of Humanity', in *Best Sermons of 1925*, p. 237.

148 See David M. Hay, *Glory at the Right Hand: Psalm 110 in Early Christianity*, p. 15; cf. also my *Easter Faith and Witness*, p. 17. Fee, *I Cor.*, pp. 754f., n. 43, observes that 'Ps. 110.1 is the most cited passage in the NT'.

149 Paul is here using the rabbinic exegetical device known as *gĕzerāh shāwāh*, which can be defined as the association of two passages of Scripture which have a term in common, and the interpretation of each in the light of the other. Another passage in which he appears to be using the same device is Rom. 4.6–8.

150 See Thiselton, *I Cor.*, pp. 1240–9 for an overview of the literature.

151 Fee, *I Cor.*, pp. 764–8.

152 Fee, *I Cor.*, p. 769.

153 Cf. Joachim Jeremias, *The Parables of Jesus*, p. 91.

154 N. T. Wright, *The Resurrection of the Son of God*, p. 354.

155 Fee, *I Cor.*, pp. 792f.

156 James Moffatt, *I Cor.*, p. 265.

157 Barrett, *I Cor.*, p. 384.

158 Cf. A. J. M. Wedderburn, *The Reasons for Romans*, pp. 40f.; John Knox, *Chapters in a Life of Paul*, pp. 53–8, 69–72. For the theological significance of the collection see Dunn, *The Theology of Paul the Apostle*, pp. 706–11.

159 Fee, *I Cor.*, p. 817.

160 See Fee, *I Cor.*, p. 819.